Y0-BVN-147

THE OTHER SIDE
OF THE TABLE

`*A15042 600926`

THE OTHER SIDE OF THE TABLE

The Soviet Approach to Arms Control

Edited by
Michael Mandelbaum

JX
1974.7
.O78
1990
West

Council on Foreign Relations Press
New York • London

COUNCIL ON FOREIGN RELATIONS BOOKS

The Council on Foreign Relations, Inc., is a nonprofit and nonpartisan organization devoted to promoting improved understanding of international affairs through the free exchange of ideas. The Council does not take any position on questions of foreign policy and has no affiliation with, and receives no funding from, the United States government.

From time to time, books and monographs written by members of the Council's research staff or visiting fellows, or commissioned by the Council, or written by an independent author with critical review contributed by a Council study or working group are published with the designation "Council on Foreign Relations Book." Any book or monograph bearing that designation is, in the judgement of the Committee on Studies of the Council's board of directors, a responsible treatment of a significant international topic worthy of presentation to the public. All statements of fact and expressions of opinion contained in Council books are, however, the sole responsibility of the author.

Copyright © 1990 by the Council on Foreign Relations, Inc.
All rights reserved.
Printed in the United States of America

This book may not be reproduced, in whole or in part, in any form (beyond that copying permitted by Sections 107 and 108 of the U.S. Copyright Law and excerpts by reviewers for the public press), without written permission from the publishers. For information, write Publications Office, Council on Foreign Relations, 58 East 68th Street, New York, NY 10021.

Library of Congress Cataloguing-in-Publication Data

The Other side of the table : the Soviet approach to arms control / edited by Michael Mandelbaum.
    p. cm.
   ISBN 0-87609-071-4
   1. Nuclear arms control—Soviet Union. 2. Soviet Union—Military policy. 3. Soviet Union—Foreign relations—United States.
   4. United States—Foreign relations—Soviet Union. I. Mandelbaum, Michael.
JX1974.7.O78 1989
327.47073—dc20
                                     89-22239
                                       CIP

---

90 91 92 93 94 95 96 PB 10 9 8 7 6 5 4 3 2 1

CONTENTS

ACKNOWLEDGEMENTS

This volume is part of the Council on Foreign Relations Project on East-West Relations, which is supported by the Carnegie Corporation.

The editor is grateful to Professor Ernest May for his counsel as well as for chairing the meetings at which the case studies were discussed, and to Cynthia Paddock and Theresa Weber for organizing the meetings and helping to edit the book.

INTRODUCTION

Michael Mandelbaum

The general's business in war, the Duke of Wellington once said, is to know what is happening "at the other side of the hill." The task of the military historian is to reconstruct, after the fact and at greater leisure than a general can afford, what has happened on *both* sides of the lines of battle, using official records, memoirs, and eyewitness accounts.

Nuclear weapons have not been used in warfare since 1945. The chief nuclear powers, the United States and the Soviet Union, have, however, engaged each other in negotiations about these weapons; negotiations that have simultaneously continued their rivalry and sought to moderate it. In this limited sense arms control has been the equivalent, in the nuclear age, of combat.

In this sense, as well, the chroniclers of the postwar Soviet-American negotiations are the military historians of superpower relations. The growing body of literature on the various arms talks since 1945 has a pronounced emphasis. It tells much more about what happened on one side of the negotiating table than on the other. The historians of arms control have had a good deal to say about how and why the United States government has conducted itself as it has, but very little about the Americans' Soviet counterparts.

The reason for this imbalance is obvious. The Soviet political system has been, for more than fifty years, a closed one. The kind of information about the system's inner workings that Western governments routinely furnish—sometimes, it is true, decades after the fact, when official archives are opened—is simply not available for Soviet policy. In the historical reconstructions of the Soviet-American arms negotiations there is a large gap on the

1

Soviet side of the table. The purpose of this book is to help to fill that gap.

The book includes three case studies. Rebecca Strode writes about the negotiations for the cessation of nuclear tests between 1957 and the signing of the Limited Test Ban Treaty in 1963. Coit Blacker analyzes the Strategic Arms Limitation Talks (SALT) from the signing of the first SALT accords in 1972 to the provisional agreement signed at Vladivostok in December 1974. Andrew Goldberg's subject is the negotiations on intermediate-range nuclear forces (INF) in Europe. The talks began in 1979 and concluded with a treaty signed by the leaders of the two countries in Washington in December 1987, but the issues at the heart of the negotiations had their origins in the 1960s, which is where the chapter begins. A fourth essay, by Cynthia Roberts, traces the postwar evolution of the Soviet definition of strategic interests, on which Soviet positions in the arms control negotiations with the United States were based in each instance, and speculates about the impact of the policies that have been introduced since 1985.

Together the cases cover a span of three decades and three distinct eras in postwar Soviet politics. Each involves one of the three principal post-Stalin leaders: Nikita Khrushchev signed the Test Ban Treaty, Leonid Brezhnev was in power during the SALT negotiations, and Mikhail Gorbachev completed the INF accord.

Although all three negotiations involved nuclear weapons in one way or another, the main focus of each was different. Nuclear testing, the subject of the first, was of marginal military significance. The 1963 treaty was more an environmental protection measure than a set of constraints on the two nuclear arsenals. But it was the first treaty affecting nuclear weapons in any way, and the negotiations for it touched on technical and political issues that have remained important ever since.

SALT, by contrast, involved matters of considerable military significance. A mark of the importance of the armaments that were the subject of those talks is the term used to refer to them— "central strategic systems." These weapons form the backbone of each side's nuclear arsenal. In the three decades of discussions between the United States and the Soviet Union, strategic arms have been the focus of the most intense attention, and thus of most of the literature on arms control.

Like SALT, the INF negotiations affected the actual deployment of weapons on both sides. Like the Test Ban Treaty, the INF accord had very little effect on the military balance, and none on the arms the two sides have considered most important. At the heart of these negotiations was an issue with which the United States has struggled for the three decades during which serious arms talks have taken place: how to provide for the nuclear defense of Europe.

The procedure by which the first three essays in this volume were written is an unusual one. For each case study, the Council on Foreign Relations organized a one-day conference, chaired by Professor Ernest May of Harvard University, which brought together not only academic specialists on the period in question but also people who had been active in the American government at the time and who had had some responsibility for the American side of the negotiation. (A list of those who attended these sessions is in the appendix.) For each meeting, the author prepared and circulated a chronology of the principal events and a list of the most important questions about Soviet policy, which served as the basis for discussion.

The meetings were designed to provoke the recollections of those who had taken part in the events, and thus to produce a kind of oral history of the historical episode—albeit an oral history at one remove, because the recollections were those of American, not Soviet, officials. Each author drafted an analytical essay on the basis of the conference proceedings, and Cynthia Roberts drew on them in writing her chapter. The four essays were then reviewed at another one-day meeting at the Council in New York.

The Other Side of the Table is not a history of Soviet arms control policy. The chapters that follow consider specific cases, not the entire record of thirty years. Nor do they examine what seem, in retrospect, the most important negotiations, those that yielded the SALT I and SALT II agreements in 1972 and 1979, respectively. These were omitted because a proper account would have exceeded the boundaries of a book chapter.

Nor can any of the case studies be regarded as the last word on its subject. Despite the contributions of American participants in these events, each chapter had to be written without the documentary records that are normally available in writing about the contemporary foreign policies of Western countries.

Thus, each of the three chapters is an exercise in inference as much as in observation and interpretation, as is the case with many studies of Soviet affairs. As Coit Blacker writes in his essay, "Analysts are left to draw conclusions from data that are often fragmentary, inconsistent, and less than completely reliable." The Duke of Wellington said, in an observation partly cited above that can stand as the epigraph not only for these essays but for much of the rest of the Sovietological literature as well: "All the business of war, and indeed all the business of life, is to endeavor to find out what you don't know by what you do; that's what I called 'guessing what was at the other side of the hill.'"

Once the Soviet archives are opened, students of Soviet arms control policy will be able to approach their subject less as generals in the midst of battle and more as conventional scholars. These essays represent an effort, in the absence of much crucial information but on the basis of the best information that is currently available, to shed light on the hopes, the fears, the strategies, and the tactics of the men on the Soviet side of the table in three important negotiations concerning nuclear weapons in the postwar period.

1

SOVIET POLICY TOWARD A NUCLEAR TEST BAN: 1958–1963

Rebecca Strode

Soviet policy in the nuclear test ban negotiations of 1958–1963 was formed at a time of great change in the Soviet Union's domestic and international environment. Internally, the country was struggling to overcome the debilitating trauma of a quarter century of Stalinist rule. Externally, the USSR faced a complex and changing world that no longer seemed to fit the bipolar model of international relations that had guided Stalin's foreign policy since 1945. Schisms in the socialist movement presented new opportunities. Meanwhile, the military situation in Europe was becoming increasingly dangerous from the Soviet perspective, as the North Atlantic Treaty Organization (NATO) armed itself with more and more nuclear weapons.

The task of adapting to the nuclear age was forcing the Soviet Union to make major changes in its military strategy during this period, too—changes that Communist Party First Secretary Nikita Khrushchev himself was pushing hard to implement, sometimes against the advice of his military commanders. At the Twentieth Party Congress, in 1956, Khrushchev declared that a nuclear war was no longer "fatalistically inevitable," eliminating an ideological barrier in Moscow to the search for a less confrontational approach to East-West relations. Meanwhile, Khrushchev pushed hard to develop Soviet nuclear forces, often at the expense of the more traditional weapons that the Soviet

Note: This material has been reviewed by the CIA to assist the author in removing classified information, if any. However, the review neither constitutes CIA authentication of material as factual nor implies CIA endorsement of the author's views.

THE OTHER SIDE OF THE TABLE

armed services preferred. As nuclear missiles were developed and deployed, political and military leaders sought to adjust to what they viewed as "the revolution in military affairs." The Strategic Rocket Forces were created in December 1959. The following month, in a landmark speech before the Supreme Soviet, Khrushchev summarized his view that a future war would be short, with nuclear missiles playing the decisive role. Asserting that the strength of the country no longer depended on the size of the army, but on its total firepower, he announced his intention to demobilize 1.2 million men. He then announced the Soviet government's new strategic priorities:

> Almost the entire air force is being replaced by rockets. We have now cut sharply, and will continue to cut sharply, even perhaps discontinue, production of bombers and other obsolete equipment. In the navy, the submarine fleet assumes great importance, while surface ships can no longer play the part they once did. In our country, the armed forces have to a considerable extent been transformed into rocket forces.[1]

Against this political and strategic backdrop, the Soviet Union called for an end to all nuclear testing and, during the period 1958–1963, engaged in a series of test ban negotiations. During the course of the negotiations, however, Khrushchev's testing policy shifted significantly and sometimes dramatically. The Soviet Union joined the United States in a three-year test moratorium, only to end it with a series of enormous nuclear explosions while still calling publicly for a test ban. Moreover, while the Soviets originally rejected the idea of a limited test ban on the grounds that it would not prevent continued development of more powerful nuclear weapons, in the end they signed the Limited Test Ban Treaty (LTBT) rather than accept the verification measures the United States considered necessary for a comprehensive ban.

Military and, to a lesser extent, environmental concerns appear to have played a role in the evolution of Soviet test ban policy during the Khrushchev period, but for Khrushchev the most important motives were political. He saw the test ban negotiations as a symbol of his desire to restructure East-West relations. Accordingly, he tried to use the testing issue to project an image of the Soviet Union as both powerful and responsible in its approach to international security. When the Cuban missile crisis shook the image both in the West and in China, Khrushchev's efforts to reach agreement became more urgent.

BACKGROUND TO THE TEST BAN NEGOTIATIONS

U.S. and Soviet efforts to achieve agreement on the control and limitation of atomic weapons in the early postwar years rapidly reached an impasse. In 1946, in an initiative known as the Baruch Plan, the United States proposed the establishment of the International Atomic Development Authority, which would be empowered to own and operate all materials and facilities involved in the production of atomic energy. The United States insisted that the establishment of effective safeguards, "including international inspections and punishments" for violations of international agreements, was essential to any international commitment to abolish, regulate, or reduce armaments.[2]

The Soviet Union rejected the Baruch Plan on the grounds that what purported to be a blueprint for international control of atomic energy was in fact a scheme designed to preserve the American monopoly of nuclear weapons. The Soviets countered the American proposal with a call for a halt to the production of nuclear weapons and the destruction of atomic stockpiles.[3] The United States found this proposal unacceptable, first, because it lacked the compliance safeguards the United States considered essential, and, second, because it would have required the United States—at the time the sole possessor of atomic weapons—to dismantle its nuclear forces without reciprocal reductions by the Soviet Union of its conventional forces.

The impasse in negotiations over the control of nuclear weapons continued throughout the early 1950s. Stalin's death in 1953, however, brought to power leaders who were willing to show greater flexibility in foreign policy. On May 10, 1955, the Soviet Union introduced at the United Nations a comprehensive plan to reduce conventional forces and to eliminate nuclear weapons. The Soviets included in this plan the first proposal to ban nuclear tests. While they tied the test ban proposal to a proposal for general disarmament, for the first time they showed interest in pursuing comprehensive disarmament through a series of intermediate, partial steps. This shift toward a more realistic approach to arms control suggested that the Soviet leadership might seriously consider mutual constraints on nuclear weapons. On July 12, 1956, the Soviets showed additional flexibility by proposing a ban on all nuclear tests, separate from progress toward general disarmament.[4]

Differences between the United States and the Soviet Union over the issue of verification of a test ban arose very quickly. On September 11, 1956, Soviet Premier Nikolai Bulganin explained the Soviet position on verification in a letter to President Dwight Eisenhower. Modern technology, Bulganin contended, made it possible to sidestep the difficult political problem of international control: "Stopping atomic and hydrogen weapon tests does not require any international agreements on control, because today's science and technology makes it possible to detect any explosion of an atomic or hydrogen bomb, no matter where it occurs."[5] The United States insisted, however, that a test ban agreement would require cooperative verification.

In a proposal they introduced to the UN Disarmament Subcommittee on June 14, 1957, the Soviets for the first time accepted the principle of international control of a test ban. The proposal called for a 2–3-year test ban, to be monitored by an international commission with instrumented stations on the territories of the nuclear powers to detect nuclear explosions. While the Soviets produced few details about the verification system they had in mind, their recognition of the need for verification procedures was an important step toward the U.S. position, and, according to former Atomic Energy Commission (AEC) Chairman Glenn Seaborg, President Eisenhower was at first favorably disposed to the idea. He was dissuaded, however, by AEC Chairman Lewis Strauss and scientists from the national laboratories, who contended that the Soviets could conduct clandestine tests that would be undetected by the monitoring system.[6]

On March 31, 1958, while the U.S. Senate Disarmament Subcommittee, chaired by Hubert Humphrey, was holding hearings on the impact and verifiability of a test ban, Khrushchev, who three days earlier had also become chairman of the Council of Ministers, increased political pressure on the Eisenhower administration to move forward on the test ban issue. When the Soviet Union had just completed a test series, Khrushchev announced that it would stop testing nuclear weapons, provided other countries did not test. Khrushchev sent letters to Eisenhower and British Prime Minister Harold Macmillan urging them to follow suit.[7]

Eisenhower responded in April by proposing that the United States, Britain, and the Soviet Union jointly examine the technical requirements for verifying a test ban. This U.S. proposal made no mention of halting production of fissionable material for military uses, thus dropping a linkage that had been unacceptable to the Soviet Union. In May, the Soviets accepted the proposal for technical discussions, "in spite of the serious doubts on our part" as to the need for such discussions rather than an immediate cessation of nuclear tests.[8]

THE GENEVA CONFERENCE OF EXPERTS

The Geneva Conference of Experts, including physicists, seismologists, and nuclear weapons specialists from the United States, Britain, and the Soviet Union, convened on July 1, 1958, for technical discussions on verification of a test ban. The group's analyses of the requirements for detecting and identifying nuclear underground explosions were based mainly on the U.S. Rainier test of September 1957, the only fully contained underground nuclear test that had been conducted at that time.[9] The conference adjourned on August 21, 1958, and released a report that presented a fairly optimistic assessment of the prospects for verification.

The U.S., British, and Soviet experts concluded that the probability of detecting atmospheric explosions with yields as low as one kiloton if detonated at altitudes below 50 kilometers was

9

good. They also concluded that a new seismographic network could be constructed that would enable the sides to detect underground explosions with yields as low as five kilotons. The experts expected some 20–100 earthquakes per year that would not be distinguishable from nuclear tests without on-site inspection. The proposed Geneva System for monitoring a test ban envisioned 160–170 (later increased to 180) control stations, each equipped with detection apparatus and manned by 30–40 people, including scientists. Twenty-four of these control posts were to be located in North America and Greenland, six in Europe, thirty-four in Asia, twenty on large ocean islands, forty on small ocean islands, and ten on instrumented ships. The conference report did not specify how many were to be located on Soviet territory. It provided little advice on how to detect high-altitude explosions, except to suggest the use of satellites, nor did it address in much detail the possibility of concealed testing.[10]

THE GENEVA CONFERENCE ON THE DISCONTINUANCE OF NUCLEAR WEAPONS TESTS

Throughout the Eisenhower and into the Kennedy administration, efforts to reach a test ban agreement were centered in the Geneva Conference on the Discontinuance of Nuclear Weapons Tests. These talks, in which the United States, the Soviet Union, and United Kingdom participated, elevated discussion of the test ban issue from the technical to the political level.

Negotiating with the Eisenhower Administration

Two days after the Conference of Experts presented its report, President Eisenhower proposed that the three nuclear powers negotiate a permanent end to nuclear tests. He pledged that, to create a favorable atmosphere, the United States would abstain from tests for a year from the date negotiations began. The Soviet Union agreed to negotiate, but did not indicate whether it would suspend tests during the negotiations. The Geneva Conference on the Discontinuance of Nuclear Weapons Tests, as the political negotiations were called, was scheduled to convene in late October, and as the date drew near all three nuclear powers conducted intensive series of nuclear tests.[11]

For the United States, these included the Hardtack Phase II series of eighteen tests in Nevada, four of them underground.[12] The Hardtack II underground tests raised questions in the minds of U.S. scientists as to whether the recently concluded Geneva Conference of Experts had been too optimistic about the scientific community's ability to distinguish between earthquakes and underground nuclear explosions.[13] Thus, even before the political negotiations were under way, new technical questions on verifiability began to emerge. The Soviet Union also concluded a series of tests from late September to early November, the last two shots of which took place during the first week of the Geneva test ban negotiations.[14]

The Geneva Conference on the Discontinuance of Nuclear Weapons Tests convened on October 31, 1958. The United States and Britain instituted a moratorium on nuclear tests, which the Soviet Union joined one week later, after concluding its ongoing test series.[15] The Soviet Union tabled a simple draft text early in the negotiations, calling on the three nuclear powers to stop testing, to set up a control system based on the Geneva System, and to dissuade other countries from testing nuclear weapons.[16]

As the negotiations were beginning, however, U.S. experts were beginning to doubt the effectiveness of the Geneva System, on the basis of new evidence from the Hardtack II test series. In December 1958, President Eisenhower's special assistant for science and technology, James Killian, established the Panel of Seismic Improvement, which came to be known as the Berkner Panel, after its chairman, Lloyd Berkner. This panel of scientists was charged with reviewing the feasibility of detection and identification of underground explosions in light of the Hardtack II findings.[17] In January, the head of the U.S. delegation to the Geneva talks, Ambassador James Wadsworth, informed the Soviet delegation's leader, Semen Tsarapkin, that, according to the Hardtack data, the minimum yield of underground tests that could be reliably detected and distinguished from earthquakes

11

was twenty kilotons, not five kilotons as the Geneva Conference of Experts had concluded. Consequently, the United States now thought that many more control systems than were contemplated by the Geneva System would be necessary to achieve the same level of confidence in verification, and many of these would have to be on Soviet soil.[18] An additional complication was introduced in early 1959, when U.S. scientist Albert Latter presented his "decoupling" theory, which predicted that seismic signals from nuclear explosions could be muffled if the devices were fired under certain conditions in large underground cavities.[19]

By March 1959, when the second session of the Geneva Conference ended, the two sides remained far apart on the verification of a test ban. The Soviet Union wanted to adopt the Geneva System; the United States and Britain wanted a larger, more complex control system, including provision for on-site challenge inspections to resolve ambiguous events. The United States held that the number of such inspections should depend on the number of ambiguous seismic events that occurred. During a visit to Moscow in February 1959, however, British Prime Minister Macmillan told Khrushchev that a fixed quota of on-site inspections might be acceptable and, moreover, that the quota need not be large. The Soviet Union proposed that whatever control posts were established be staffed by nationals of the country in which the control posts were located; the United States and Britain called for 50 percent staffing by nationals of the other nuclear powers and 50 percent by scientists from neutral countries. The sides agreed on the establishment of the seven-member International Control Commission to supervise the test ban, but they disagreed about its authority. The USSR wanted each of the "original parties" to the agreement (the United States, Britain, and the Soviet Union) to have a veto in the commission; the Western parties opposed the veto, fearing that the Soviet Union would use it to prevent on-site inspections. The sides also disagreed over the national composition of the commission. The USSR wanted it to comprise three Western, three Eastern, and one neutral-country member; the United States and Britain wanted three Westerners, two Easterners, and one or two neutrals.[20]

In an attempt to break the deadlock that had developed over the verification issue, Eisenhower wrote to Khrushchev on April 13, 1959, proposing an agreement to end nuclear weapons tests in phases, deferring the most difficult issue—the banning, and hence also the verification, of underground and very high altitude nuclear tests—until a later date. Tests conducted in the atmosphere at altitudes up to fifty kilometers could be banned immediately, Eisenhower proposed, without the requirement for automatic on-site inspections, "which has created the major stumbling block in the negotiations so far."[21] Khrushchev responded ten days later. He rejected Eisenhower's proposals on the grounds that anything less than a comprehensive ban would still enable the United States to modernize its nuclear forces. As an alternative to a partial test ban, however, Khrushchev suggested for the first time that the Soviets would be willing to consider Macmillan's idea of a fixed quota of on-site inspections on the territory of each nuclear power.[22]

On May 5, Eisenhower and Macmillan both sent letters to Khrushchev agreeing to explore the inspection quota idea. Eisenhower added in his letter, however, that for negotiations on a comprehensive ban to continue, the Soviet Union would have to drop its demand for a veto in the International Control Commission and agree to an early discussion of techniques for detecting high-altitude nuclear tests.[23] The Soviets contended that the United States wanted to use secondary technical issues to delay a fundamental political agreement.[24] Nevertheless, Khrushchev responded on May 14 to the Western leaders' letters by agreeing to technical discussions. He made no commitment, however, on the veto issue.[25]

The Technical Working Group (later called Technical Working Group I) of the Geneva Conference convened on June 22, 1959, to consider problems of detecting high-altitude explosions. The group made rapid progress and released a report on July 10. The proposed system would have comprised 5–6 satellites to detect radiation from nuclear explosions in outer space, plus equipment to be installed in the 170–180 manned control posts called for in the Geneva System. Both the Western and the Eastern delegations recognized that such a monitoring system would be expensive and difficult to maintain. Moreover, even if an explosion were detected, it might not be possible to identify the country that conducted it.[26]

Still, the progress made by the Technical Working Group encouraged all three nuclear powers. On August 26, Eisenhower announced that the United States would extend its test moratorium, which was due to expire in October, until the end of the year. Britain followed the next day, pledging not to resume testing as long as the Geneva negotiations showed prospect for success. The USSR announced a day later that it would not test as long as the Western powers continued their moratorium.[27]

Difficult issues remained to be resolved, however, on the problem of verifying a ban on underground nuclear tests. In June 1959 the Berkner Panel released its report, concluding that the Geneva System would be less capable than originally expected: it would be capable of detecting with confidence only explosions of greater than twenty kilotons yield. The report recommended several means of improving detection, however, and estimated that a well-funded program to upgrade seismic monitoring capabilities could enable the United States to achieve the verification capability envisioned by the Geneva System within three years.[28] Meanwhile, although Moscow had indicated that it might accept some on-site inspections, the sides remained far apart on the number that would be required.

To move the negotiations forward in light of the increased U.S. concern about the detection of underground tests, the Soviet delegation at Geneva proposed the establishment of Technical Working Group II to consider new seismic data and criteria for dispatching on-site inspection teams.[29] The Western powers agreed, and the group convened in November 1959. Soviet scientists acknowledged the theoretical possibility of decoupling, but contended it would not work in practice. They also proposed conditions for on-site inspections that the Western side considered too restrictive. The Soviets agreed to increase the number of seismometers at control posts from ten to one hundred, as suggested by the Berkner Panel, but disagreed with the U.S. position that more on-site inspections were required. The United States, they contended, had not used procedures and seismic instruments recommended by the Geneva Experts' report to collect data on the Hardtack II tests. They therefore rejected the implication that the number of earthquakes in the USSR that could be confused with explosions was greater than had been estimated by the Geneva Conference of Experts. Unlike Technical Group I, the scientists in Technical Group II could not resolve their differences. In December they concluded their efforts without reaching agreement. E. K. Fedorov, chief of the Soviet technical group, delivered an angry, public denunciation of the American technical group, especially its leader, James Fisk, as unscientific and subservient to politicians.[30]

Having failed to overcome differences with the Soviets on verification, the Eisenhower administration shifted direction. On December 29, Eisenhower announced that although the U.S. moratorium was to expire at the end of the year, the United States would "not resume nuclear weapons tests without announcing our intention in advance." With this reminder that the United States was not committed indefinitely to a moratorium, the administration did in fact continue to refrain from testing after the announced expiration date had passed. At the same time, it shifted its policy in the Geneva negotiations. Convinced that the Soviet Union would not accept any major changes in the Geneva System, the United States in February 1960 tabled a proposal that would prohibit only those tests that, in the West's judgment, could be verified by that system. Initially, these would include all atmospheric and underground tests, tests in outer space to an altitude (unspecified) at which detection would be feasible, and underground tests producing seismic signals greater than 4.75 on the Richter scale. Prohibitions were to be expanded as verification capabilities improved. A joint East-West seismic research program, to include nuclear detonations, was proposed to make it possible to lower the seismic threshold on underground tests. The West offered to accept any of three formulas for determining the number of on-site inspections, all of which worked out to be about twenty per year on the territory of each side.[31]

Only a few weeks later, on March 19, the Soviets agreed to the West's new proposals, with three changes. First, they proposed banning all nuclear tests in outer space. Second, they insisted that the sides agree to a 4–5-year moratorium on all underground nuclear tests below the treaty threshold, after which the parties would confer on whether to extend it. Finally, the Soviets rejected all U.S. formulas for determining the number of on-site inspections. The formulas related the number of inspections to the number of seismic events that would occur in a given year. The Soviets argued that the number of on-site inspections was a political issue, not a technical one, and should be fixed at a specific number. "We cannot agree about the inspection quota on any other basis," the Soviet delegation insisted.[32] The United States responded to the Soviet counteroffer by stating its preference for a moratorium on all underground nuclear tests lasting only one year. In the meantime, however, both sides agreed to pursue the possibility of a joint seismic research program to help drive the threshold down.[33]

Throughout the spring of 1960, U.S.–Soviet relations appeared to be progressing on a broad front. Willingness by both sides to consider intermediate steps had broken the deadlock at the test ban negotiations, and plans were laid for a major East-West summit in mid-May. Progress came to a sudden halt during the first week of May, however, when the Soviet Union shot down an American U-2 aircraft flying over Soviet territory and captured its pilot, Francis Gary Powers. The Paris summit collapsed, and against the backdrop of a subsequent chill in U.S.–Soviet relations, the Soviet delegation at the Geneva test ban negotiations backed away from the flexibility it had shown a few weeks earlier on the verification issue. On May 27, Tsarapkin stated that the Soviet Union would not engage in joint seismic research, because it had "no doubts" regarding the validity of the 1958 Geneva System.[34] Once again the negotiations had reached a deadlock, and on December 5, 1960, they adjourned to give the incoming Kennedy administration time to develop its policy toward the test ban issue.

By the end of the Eisenhower administration, verification had emerged as a difficult, but not necessarily intractable, obstacle to achieving a test ban. The overall East-West political climate, however, had proven to be a wild card that could either foster or inhibit progress on substantive test ban issues.

Negotiating with the Kennedy Administration

President John Kennedy tried to move the test ban negotiations forward quickly. When the negotiations resumed in Geneva in March 1961, the U.S. delegation presented its new position, which sought to meet Soviet concerns on several issues. The United States was willing to increase the length of the moratorium on underground tests below the 4.75 seismic magnitude threshold from one year to 2–3 years. The West agreed to a total ban on tests in outer space under the verification procedures recommended by Technical Working Group I, despite the limited effectiveness of those procedures for detecting very high altitude explosions. In addition, the West accepted the Soviet proposal that each originating party be assigned an equal quota of on-site inspections. The United States proposed twenty per year in each country.[35]

Meanwhile, Kennedy and Khrushchev prepared to meet in Vienna in June. As plans for the summit progressed, the United States offered to replace its proposed quota of twenty on-site inspections per year in each country with a new formula that would lead to between 12–20 on-site inspections per year in each country, depending on the number of ambiguous seismic events that occurred. The Soviet delegation replied that these numbers were still too high and reiterated its position that the number of inspections was a political issue, not a scientific one.[36]

On June 3–4, 1961, Kennedy and Khrushchev met in Vienna for what Kennedy described upon his return to the United States as "a very sober two days."[37] The summit came only weeks after the Bay of Pigs invasion, and in the soured political atmosphere, Khrushchev adopted a hard line on the Berlin issue, calling for the conversion of West Berlin into a "free city" with the termination of Western occupation and access rights. Shortly after the Vienna summit, Khrushchev declared in a televised address that the Soviet Union would sign a separate treaty with East Germany by the end of the year if the West would not accept an all-German treaty.[38] A separate Soviet–East German treaty would have ended the Four Powers' responsibility for Berlin, put all of Berlin under Warsaw Pact control, and undermined the West's approach to security in Central Europe.

Tension over the Berlin issue mounted quickly. On July 25, Kennedy delivered a speech on U.S. policy toward Berlin in which he announced a series of steps to strengthen American military forces. On August 13, the Soviets and East Germans closed the border between East and West Berlin and began construction of the Berlin Wall.[39] On August 29, Radio Moscow announced that the release of Soviet servicemen into the reserves was temporarily suspended "until conclusion of a treaty with Germany."[40]

The following day Tass, the official Soviet news agency, announced that the USSR would resume nuclear weapons tests. Speaking to two British Labour members of Parliament, Khrushchev said this decision "was intended to shock the Western powers into negotiations over Germany and disarmament."[41] From September through November 1961, the Soviets conducted a series of nuclear tests, bringing to an end three years of adherence to the test moratorium the United States, Britain, and the Soviet Union had observed since the fall of 1958. All but one of the thirty-one announced tests in the series were atmospheric, including a twenty-five-megaton detonation on October 23 and a fifty-eight-megaton detonation—still the largest single detonation by any country—on October 30.[42]

Two days after the Soviet Union resumed testing, the United States and Britain tried to salvage progress that had been made in negotiations by proposing that the sides agree to ban nuclear tests in the atmosphere without requiring any international inspection.[43] The Soviets continued to test, however, and in response, the United States resumed nuclear testing on September 15.[44]

On November 28, the Geneva test ban negotiations reconvened for the first session since the sides had resumed nuclear testing. The Soviet side called for a ban on tests in the atmosphere, outer space, and underwater, using only national means to verify compliance. In addition, the Soviets called for a moratorium on all underground tests while a verification system was negotiated. The United States, noting that the Soviets had just broken the existing moratorium, criticized the Soviet position as one of "colossal hypocrisy." Ambassador Arthur Dean, the chief U.S. negotiator, stated that as a result of the recent Soviet tests, "there is naturally no chance whatsoever—and I want to make this very clear—of any pre-treaty commitment by the United States not to conduct any nuclear tests of any character in any environment which it deems essential for the national security of itself and its associates."[45] In January 1962, the United States formally rejected the Soviet draft text and recommended that the Geneva negotiations be suspended. When the Soviet Union opposed suspending the talks, the United States and Britain refused to schedule additional meetings. The Geneva Conference on the Discontinuance of Nuclear Weapons Tests thus came to a halt, after 353 sessions.[46]

THE EIGHTEEN-NATION DISARMAMENT CONFERENCE

Both the United States and the Soviet Union conducted numerous nuclear tests during 1962. About half the U.S. tests were carried out underground. The Soviets' first underground nuclear test took place in February 1962, but the rest were in the atmosphere or at high altitude.[47] Although the Geneva Conference had collapsed, test ban negotiations during this period did not cease, but rather were shifted in March 1962 to the United Nations Eighteen-Nation Disarmament Conference. Here, too, the Soviets contended that international control measures—such as internationally staffed control posts on the nuclear powers' territory and on-site inspections—were not necessary to verify compliance with a comprehensive test ban; the United States disagreed.[48]

The United States and Britain presented two draft treaties at the Eighteen-Nation forum, one for a comprehensive test ban, the other for a ban only on tests in the atmosphere, underwater, and in outer space. The comprehensive proposal called for an on-site inspection; the limited test ban draft did not. The Soviet Union rejected both proposals, the comprehensive ban because it required on-site inspections and the limited ban because it would allow continued testing.[49]

The negotiations were approaching a deadlock when two events—the Cuban missile crisis and the deterioration of Sino-Soviet relations that followed it—appear to have significantly altered Soviet perspectives on the test ban negotiations. The Cuban missile crisis unfolded from October 15 to 28, ending with Khrushchev's agreement to remove Soviet nuclear missiles from Cuba. The Chinese leadership later criticized this decision as "capitulationist."[50] Meanwhile, on October 20, China attacked Indian military forces in a disputed border area. The Soviets took a mildly pro-Chinese position on the conflict, thus, according to Sino-Soviet specialist William Griffith, offending both China and India. After the Cuban missile crisis, Soviet statements on the Sino-Indian dispute became still more noncommittal, reflecting rising Sino-Soviet tension.[51]

On December 19, 1962, in the aftermath of these events, Khrushchev sent President Kennedy a letter devoted exclusively to the test ban. The main obstacle to agreement, he wrote, was the U.S. insistence on international control and inspection. Khrushchev stated that Ambassador Dean had told Soviet First Deputy Foreign Minister V. V. Kuznetsov that the United States would accept 2–4 on-site inspections per year on Soviet territory. "With a view to overcoming the deadlock," Khrushchev offered to accept a quota of 2–3 on-site inspections per year on the territory of each nuclear power.[52] Kennedy replied to Khrushchev's letter two weeks later, stating that he found it encouraging because the Soviet Union was once again accepting the principle of on-site inspections. He added, however, that there had been a misunderstanding concerning the number of inspections the United States considered necessary. According to Kennedy, Ambassador Dean had discussed an annual quota of 8–10 inspections with Kuznetsov. The president noted that this higher number was still a substantial reduction from the previous U.S. requirement for 12–20.[53] During early 1963 the two sides continued to differ over the number of on-site inspections to be allowed, with the United States eventually insisting on an annual quota of at least seven, and the Soviet Union refusing to allow more than three. Then, on April 20, Khrushchev—perhaps believing the United States had reneged on what he had understood to be a commitment from Ambassador Dean—withdrew the Soviet proposal to accept even three such inspections in its territory.[54]

In an effort to regain momentum in the talks, the United States and Britain proposed in a joint letter from Kennedy and Macmillan to send high-level representatives to the Soviet Union to discuss the test ban. Khrushchev agreed. President Kennedy, in a June speech delivered at American University, stressed the need to avoid being "caught up in a vicious and dangerous cycle in which suspicion on one side breeds suspicion on the other, and new weapons beget counter-weapons." He also announced that the United States would not be the first to resume nuclear tests in the atmosphere.[55] The Soviets appear to have welcomed the president's initiative, and the stage was set for new negotiations.[56] In July 1963, Ambassador Averell Harriman and Lord Hailsham (Quinton Hogg) led U.S. and British delegations, respectively, to Moscow. The Soviet delegation was headed by Soviet Foreign Minister Andrei Gromyko, and Khrushchev attended the first day's discussions.[57]

The Soviet Union tabled a draft of a limited test ban agreement prohibiting nuclear tests anywhere except underground, to enter into force upon signature by the United States, Soviet Union, Britain, and France. Harriman insisted that mention of France be deleted from the text. As for on-site inspections, Khrushchev made it clear on the first day of the talks that the

Soviet Union would not accept any on-site inspections. Harriman concluded that the differences on the issue of verification precluded achievement of a comprehensive ban, and the rest of the talks therefore focused on achieving a limited ban. With an unlimited number of underground nuclear detonations now allowed, and with only underground detonations permitted, the problems of distinguishing between earthquakes and nuclear tests on the one hand, and between peaceful nuclear explosions and weapons tests on the other, could be set aside. All the parties agreed that national means of control would be adequate to verify the ban on all nuclear detonations in the atmosphere, outer space, or underwater.[58] The key obstacles to verification having thus been removed by limiting the scope of the proposed ban, the United States, Britain, and the Soviet Union signed the Limited Test Ban Treaty on August 5, 1963.

EXAMINING SOVIET POLICY OBJECTIVES

When the Soviets proposed a nuclear test ban in the Memorandum on Partial Measures toward Disarmament, which they tabled at the UN in September 1956, they specified several rationales for halting tests: "The need for such an agreement is dictated not only by the fact that continued tests of atomic and hydrogen bombs pose a great danger for human health and that such tests permit the production of still more threatening and destructive types of atomic and hydrogen bombs, but also by the fact that positive resolution of this question would greatly increase the possibility of achieving agreement on other questions of disarmament and stopping the continuation of the arms race."[59] This statement identified four specific objectives of a test ban: reduction of the health hazard posed by nuclear radiation, constraint on the modernization of nuclear weapons, improvement of the international political environment, and facilitation of broader disarmament agreements. In 1987, a retrospective Soviet commentary attributed the same basic benefits to the Limited Test Ban Treaty:

This treaty signified a major step in the struggle to restrict the nuclear arms race, even though it did not encompass all nuclear explosions. It signified an important victory of the policy of peaceful coexistence over the policy of cold war, of the diplomacy of negotiations over the policy of banking on strength in international relations, of concern for the health and welfare of people over disregard for the demands, interests and the very destiny of mankind.

It was also important that this treaty ensured the elimination of one of the key sources of our planet's radioactive contamination. . . . A symbolic "first step," a harbinger of further agreements—this is how the treaty was regarded on both sides of the Atlantic.[60]

The remainder of this chapter will examine the extent to which political, military, and environmental objectives shaped Soviet policy toward a nuclear test ban.

General Political Climate

The East-West political climate repeatedly complicated the course of the negotiations. After the 1962 Paris summit collapsed, the Soviets toughened their position on the adequacy of the Geneva monitoring system, and no further progress in the talks was made during the remainder of the Eisenhower administration. The Soviet Union ended its test moratorium in the midst of the 1961 Berlin crisis.

Yet if the Soviet Union viewed the test ban issue primarily from a political, rather than a technical, point of view, then political considerations might not only raise obstacles, but also provide the impetus for agreement. Moscow's decision to accept a limited test ban, after years of insisting on a comprehensive ban, can most readily be explained by political considerations. The United States had proposed a limited test ban as early as 1959, but the Soviet Union had rejected it, apparently calculating that the military and political advantages of a comprehensive treaty merited continued effort toward that goal. By 1963, the Soviets evidently concluded that the advantages of a limited treaty, which could be achieved quickly, justified a narrowing of Soviet objectives in the test ban talks.

The event that seems to have been primarily responsible for the Soviets' reassessment of their test ban objectives was the

23

Cuban missile crisis of October 1962. In an interview with essayist Norman Cousins, Khrushchev recounted his desire to achieve concrete measures that would improve U.S.–Soviet relations in the wake of the crisis: "After Cuba, there was a real chance for both the Soviet Union and the United States to take measures together that would advance the peace by easing tensions. The one area on which I thought we were closest to agreement was nuclear testing."[61] Following the crisis, Khrushchev appeared to soften Soviet objections to on-site inspections by offering to allow 2–3 such inspections per year on Soviet territory. While the misunderstanding between the two sides over the minimum number of inspections the United States would require prevented immediate agreement, the flexibility both sides showed reflected their desire to improve relations in the aftermath of the crisis. When prospects for a quick conclusion of a comprehensive test ban again floundered on the verification issue, both sides settled on a limited test ban accord as the next best thing. At the Moscow talks of July 15–26, 1963, the Soviet Union tabled a draft text that would allow only underground nuclear tests, and in a matter of days, the two sides reached an agreement.[62]

The question still remains why, when Soviet and U.S. positions on the number of on-site inspections appeared to have come so close, Moscow opted for only a limited ban rather than accept on-site inspections. Throughout the negotiations, Soviet officials insisted that a test ban and the verification measures associated with it were essentially political problems, not technical ones, and hence required political solutions. These solutions, the Soviets insisted, had to reflect the nature of relations between the parties to any agreement. Soviet scientist E.K. Fedorov described the USSR's position in a 1959 article in the *Bulletin of the Atomic Scientists:*

> The complete absurdity of putting the control organization in the position of a super-government, acting on the territories of sovereign states irrespective of their will and desire, is obvious. It is hardly necessary to mention the obvious fact that any control organization on the territory of any country may be conducted only so far as the governments of these countries agree to it, and more than that, actively support it.[63]

By 1963, however, the United States had agreed to accept a relatively low limit on such inspections and had accepted the Soviet position that the quota of inspections should be fixed, not the result of a formula involving the number of seismic events. The Soviet Union's political concerns thus appear to have been largely met. At the same time, Khrushchev's offer to accept a small number of on-site inspections seemed to indicate that despite Soviet concern with military secrecy, Moscow might show flexibility on the verification issue to achieve a comprehensive ban. Just when the two sides appeared to be drawing close to agreement, however, Khrushchev reversed his position and rejected on-site inspections altogether. It remains unclear whether, in the leadership's perception, the requirements of military secrecy outweighed whatever political and military advantages Moscow expected from a comprehensive ban or whether the Soviets never really wanted a comprehensive ban at all.

Constraints on Weapon Modernization

If the USSR's proposals for a comprehensive test ban during the period 1956–1963 reflected a genuine policy preference and were not just propaganda ploys, they imply that the Soviet government thought that the benefits gained through a test ban would outweigh the constraints it would impose on Soviet nuclear weapon programs. The threat the Soviets faced from U.S. strategic forces in the late 1950s and early 1960s was formidable, including a large inventory of strategic nuclear bomber weapons and a smaller number of cruise missiles and ballistic missiles.[64] The Soviet Union's intercontinental strategic nuclear forces during this period were much smaller, although its intermediate-range missile forces were significant.[65] The United States, meanwhile, had placed considerable emphasis on tactical nuclear weapons for the European theater during the middle to late 1950s.[66] A nuclear test ban, however, could not be counted on to redress quantitative imbalances between the U.S. and Soviet nuclear forces. Weapons that had already been tested could have continued to be produced and deployed.

25

In considering the impact that a comprehensive test ban would have on the qualitative balance, the Soviet policymakers probably attempted to estimate the balance of technical knowledge of nuclear physics in the United States and Soviet Union. How they viewed this balance is unknown. During Senate hearings in 1963, Admiral George Anderson, chief of naval operations, said that the Soviet Union probably had more knowledge of high-yield nuclear technology than did the United States and less knowledge about low-yield and tactical nuclear warheads.[67] General Curtis LeMay was unsure, however, whether the evidence was sufficient to conclude that the United States was ahead in low-yield nuclear technology.[68]

However the Soviets evaluated their relative knowledge of tactical nuclear weapons, they may have thought constraints on further U.S. progress in this area to be especially useful, given their publicly expressed doctrinal views on limited nuclear war. Soviet military writers during the 1950s and early 1960s denied that tactical nuclear weapons could be employed to destroy military targets while avoiding massive collateral casualties to noncombatants, because even tactical nuclear weapons still had large destructive radii and because many military targets were located in or near populated areas. Soviet spokesmen therefore claimed that the use of tactical nuclear weapons would almost certainly lead to the massive use of atomic and hydrogen bombs. While publicly rejecting the possibility of keeping a nuclear war limited, the Soviets may have believed that further improvements in U.S. tactical nuclear weaponry would increase American interest in tactical nuclear options and could reduce the effectiveness of the Soviet Union's strategic deterrent.[69]

Soviet assessments of the military advantages and disadvantages of a comprehensive test ban were probably complicated by uncertainty over the extent to which qualitative improvements in nuclear forces could be expected even under such a ban. The nuclear powers could pursue continued modernization through several avenues. First, they could incorporate the knowledge gained from previous tests into new weapon systems. For example, the Soviet Union tested vigorously in the weeks prior to the institution of the test moratorium. According to a Soviet historian, these tests

> showed the great effectiveness of certain new principles developed by Soviet scientists and engineers. As a result, the Soviet armed forces received still more powerful, more perfected, more reliable, more compact, and cheaper atomic and hydrogen weapons.[70]

Information acquired from these tests could have been incorporated into new weapons even if a test ban had been achieved.[71]

New nuclear delivery vehicles could still have been tested, and resulting improvements in propulsion and guidance systems would presumably have improved the operational effectiveness of the weapon systems even if no changes were made in the nuclear devices themselves. Furthermore, some qualitative improvements in the nuclear weapons might have been possible even without nuclear tests, although untested design changes would have been subject to considerable uncertainty. Khrushchev reported in his memoirs that during mid-1958, when the Soviets were not conducting nuclear tests, Soviet scientists "considerably reduced the cost and increased the power of a single explosion. But that was only on paper."[72]

Uncertainty about the effectiveness and reliability of nuclear weapon concepts that had been developed but never tested was of major concern to Soviet military planners, according to Khrushchev: "There was no way our scientific and military experts could see if the new improved designs really worked."[73] Khrushchev, however, may have been willing to accept such uncertainty. First, it would have applied to both sides. Second, Khrushchev's use of nuclear "rocket rattling" in his conduct of foreign policy (for example, during the Berlin crisis) suggests that he considered the psychological and political impact of the possession of nuclear weapons to be perhaps as important as their actual military capabilities.[74]

Eventual Soviet acceptance of a limited, rather than comprehensive, test ban may indicate that Soviet military concerns about the impact of a comprehensive test ban on modernization outweighed whatever advantages a comprehensive ban promised. Some American specialists voiced concern that allowing only underground nuclear tests would give the USSR advantages in high-yield weapons, on which the Soviets had focused much attention in their atmospheric tests.[75] Kennedy administration officials argued, however, that the LTBT would not enable the Soviets to gain strategic advantages. Harold Brown, then director of defense research and engineering, stated during the treaty hearings that

> the main question in my mind is, Does it inhibit us from getting knowledge but allow the Soviets to get knowledge that will have an important effect in a decisive area? And there my answer is that it will not.[76]

It was even possible that the Soviets' limited experience with underground testing in 1963 would put them at a temporary disadvantage. Secretary of Defense Robert McNamara believed that the LTBT would at least delay Soviet achievement of technical parity.[77] President Kennedy stated that "the United States has more experience in underground testing than any other nation; and we intend to use this capacity to maintain the adequacy of our arsenal."[78]

Given these considerations, it is possible that the Soviets agreed to accept a limited test ban not because they believed it would contribute more to Soviet security than a comprehensive ban would but because they believed resolution of the verification issues involved in a comprehensive ban was unlikely—at least in the near term—and that, in the wake of the Cuban missile crisis, a limited ban was better than no ban at all.

Nuclear Proliferation

The possibility of nuclear proliferation loomed large in the years leading up to the LTBT. Britain, an atomic power since 1952, tested a thermonuclear device in 1957.[79] A Soviet historian has noted that Soviet concern about the French nuclear program dates at least as far back as 1956, when France's first plutonium production reactor began operation.[80] France first detonated an atomic device in February 1960.

Soviet concern about the nuclear proliferation was compounded by the emerging discussion among the NATO allies of the desirability of creating a multilateral nuclear force. Early proposals for some form of shared NATO nuclear force appeared as early as 1960, and the idea continued to be discussed throughout the early 1960s.[81] The Soviet Union viewed any form of shared decision making in NATO on the use of nuclear weapons as bringing Germany one step closer to possession of such weapons.[82]

The late 1950s also saw increased Soviet concern about China's nuclear ambitions. In October 1957, the Soviet Union and China signed a defense technology agreement that, according to the Chinese, included a Soviet pledge to provide China technology needed to develop an atomic bomb.[83] Less than two years later, however, in June 1959, the USSR withdrew this offer,[84] and in July 1960 it withdrew technicians from China and terminated its foreign aid there.[85]

The timing of Soviet test ban initiatives, statements made by Soviet officials, and statements made by the Chinese Communist Party in its polemics with the Communist Party of the Soviet Union suggest that Soviet test ban policy was intended in part to arrest the growth of independent nuclear weapon programs. The USSR's first proposal to ban nuclear tests was made in May 1955, the same month that West Germany joined NATO. The Soviet proposal to pursue a test ban separately from negotiations on general disarmament came in mid-1956, shortly after France began to produce plutonium. Former AEC Chairman Glenn Seaborg has written that Soviet Ambassador Menshikov asked Washington whether the United States could "deliver the French" on a test ban agreement.[86] The Soviet test ban proposal at the Geneva talks called for French participation in a test ban, even though France was not involved in the negotiations.[87] Similarly, the Soviet draft text for a comprehensive test ban tabled in Moscow during the 1963 high-level negotiations between the United States, Britain, and the USSR, which eventually produced agreement on the LTBT, was to come into force only after those three parties signed—again despite France's refusal to participate in the UN Eighteen-Nation Disarmament Talks.[88]

The Chinese government, meanwhile, accused the Soviet Union of colluding with the United States to prevent China from acquiring nuclear technology. China claimed to have sent the Soviet Union a message in September 1962 expressing opposition to a nonproliferation treaty and noting that while it was up to the Soviet Union to decide whether to transfer nuclear weapons and technical information about them to China, it was China's sovereign right to decide whether to manufacture nuclear weapons. China again informed the Soviets in October 1962 that it would not be bound by any U.S.–Soviet agreement on nuclear weapons to which it was not a party.[89]

French and Chinese refusal to participate in a test ban meant that while the Soviets may have hoped a test ban treaty would convince other states that they did not need to pursue independent nuclear weapon programs, they had little basis for expecting these hopes to be realized. The Soviet Union's decision in 1963 to accept a limited rather than a comprehensive ban probably reflected in part its recognition of this fact. Nevertheless, the LTBT was the most important arms control agreement the major nuclear powers had achieved at that time, and Khrushchev may have hoped it would send a signal to other states considering whether to develop nuclear weapons. In any event, Khrushchev's appreciation of the quantitative nuclear advantage that the Soviet Union would have over China even after the latter developed an atomic bomb may have allayed immediate Soviet concern, especially if, at the same time, relations were improving with the United States—the country that, by virtue of the size and sophistication of its nuclear weapons, the Soviets surely viewed as the greatest nuclear threat.[90]

Environmental Concerns

Concern about the dangers of radiation grew among the Western scientific and political communities in the late 1950s as the United States and the Soviet Union began testing thermonuclear devices. In March 1954, in the Bravo test at Bikini atoll, the United States exploded what remains the largest thermonuclear device it ever detonated. The fifteen-megaton yield of the shot was almost twice what had been expected.[91] Radioactive debris spread over an unexpectedly large area of Micronesia, exposing Marshall Island residents to high levels of radiation. The inhabitants of Rongelap atoll, located about 100 miles downwind from Bikini, received radiation doses of up to 175 rem before they were evacuated.[92] A few days later, the crew of a Japanese fishing trawler, the *Lucky Dragon,* also received severe radiation doses from the fallout from the Bravo test.[93] Following the *Lucky Dragon* incident, fifty-two Nobel laureates, led by Albert Einstein and Linus Pauling, and some 9,000 other scientists from around the world signed a petition urging an end to nuclear testing.

Measurements of the growing concentration of the radioactive strontium-90 (Sr 90) in the bones of children during the late 1950s and early 1960s also underscored the health hazards involved in atmospheric testing.[94] Glenn Seaborg has noted that President Kennedy was particularly concerned about the dangers of radioactive fallout.[95] Environmental problems associated with nuclear tests in outer space were also demonstrated dramatically in 1962 when a U.S. high-altitude test added significantly to the radiation in the Van Allen belts and altered their shape.[96] To establish the distribution of radioactive debris injected into the stratosphere by nuclear explosions, U-2 aircraft collected over 4,000 samples of the atmosphere at altitudes of about 70,000 feet from the Arctic to Antarctica during 1957–1959.[97]

Soviet researchers began to take occasional measurements of the deposition and accumulation of radioactive products from nuclear explosions during the early 1950s, and they appear to have performed tests more systematically beginning in 1956. Between 1954 and 1957, for example, Soviet scientists made daily and monthly measurements of radioactive products deposited in the vicinity of Leningrad. In the autumn of 1956, they began to perform systematic analyses of dust samples collected daily by aircraft flying at 5,000 meters' altitude in the vicinity of Moscow and Odessa. The first radiochemical analyses of the soil in the USSR for Sr 90 were made in the summer of 1956.[98] Data published from this research indicate that accumulation of Sr 90 in the western Soviet Union was approximately the same as that in the eastern United States. Accumulation of Sr 90 in milk samples taken in Moscow in 1957 averaged 7.85 picocuries per gram of calcium (pCi/gCa).[99] Western scientists' analysis of milk in New York City in 1957 indicated a concentration of 5 pCi/gCa.[100] Soviet analyses in 1957 of the bones of six children aged four years and younger indicated an average Sr 90 concentration of 2.3 pCi/gCa.[101] The figure for the bones of children analyzed in New York in 1958 was 2.1 pCi/gCa.[102]

The potential hazards of the Soviet nuclear weapons program—though not of nuclear testing—were dramatically demonstrated to the Soviet leadership in September 1957, when an explosion of radioactive waste at an atomic weapons plant in the Ural Mountains forced the evacuation of more than 10,000 people, according to a recent statement by Tass. More than thirty years later, large areas north of the city of Cheliabinsk are still contaminated and water reserves undrinkable, Tass said. Soviet officials did not reveal the accident until 1989.[103]

Environmental concerns were important to some Soviet specialists involved in nuclear testing, particularly Soviet scientists. In all, 216 full and corresponding members of the Soviet Academy of Sciences signed Linus Pauling's petition for an international ban on nuclear weapons testing.[104] Physicist Andrei Sakharov has written of his misgivings about continued testing:

> Beginning in 1957 (not without the influence of statements on this subject made throughout the world by such people as Albert Schweitzer, Linus Pauling, and others), I felt myself responsible for the problem of radioactive contamination from nuclear explosions. . . . When the radioactive products of an explosion get into the atmosphere, each megaton of the nuclear explosions means thousands of unknown victims.[105]

Sakharov has also reported that Igor Kurchatov, scientific director of both the atomic and the hydrogen bomb research projects in the Soviet Union, appealed personally to Khrushchev to cancel a test series scheduled for late 1958. His effort failed, however, and the tests were performed as planned. Sakharov, too, found the Soviet political leadership unreceptive to his concerns about the environmental impact of nuclear testing. "In my attempts to explain this problem," he wrote, "I encountered great difficulties—and a reluctance to understand."[106]

Despite the concerns of prominent Soviet scientists, however, environmental issues seem to have played little part in shaping Soviet policy on nuclear testing. Certainly Soviet leaders and military planners did not have to contend with the pressure of public opinion that Western officials faced, pressures that were strong enough to lead Arthur Dean to conclude that in the absence of an agreement, the United States would be forced by public opinion to halt atmospheric testing in 2–4 years.[107] Commentator Ralph Lapp, for example, concluded in the *Bulletin of the Atomic Scientists*, "I gather from the technical data presented that although the Soviets have a great interest in the biological effects of atomic radiation, they have no research project on a scale comparable to that of the AEC for measuring strontium-90 in the biosphere."[108]

The Soviet Union's testing patterns in the late 1950s and early 1960s also suggest that its authorities made little effort to reduce the environmental impact of nuclear tests prior to the signing of the Limited Test Ban Treaty. While the United States conducted numerous underground nuclear tests even before the LTBT was signed, the USSR conducted only one underground explosion prior to the signing of the treaty.[109] Moreover, the Soviet atmospheric tests frequently involved very high yields, with many in the megaton range, several equaling or exceeding twenty megatons (larger than any U.S. test), and one reaching a staggering yield of fifty-eight megatons.[110] The Soviet leadership may have hoped its calls for an end to nuclear testing would improve the Soviet Union's image abroad among groups concerned about the health hazards associated with nuclear testing, but such high-yield testing tended to undercut Soviet professions of concern about the environmental impact of nuclear tests. Nevertheless, the existence of a group of scientists in the Soviet nuclear program who had access to high-level policymakers and who were concerned about the health hazards associated with atmospheric nuclear tests ensured that there were experts eager to support a limited test ban once the political leadership became interested in the idea for its own, and perhaps quite different, reasons.

CONCLUSION

The LTBT promised to reduce the health hazards associated with nuclear testing and to contribute indirectly to Soviet non-proliferation goals. Its greatest benefit from the Soviet stand-point, however, was in the political realm, where it provided a concrete symbol of the willingness of the superpowers to search for cooperative measures to manage their relations in the nuclear era. The speed with which the United States and the Soviet Union proceeded to conclude the LTBT following the Cuban missile crisis demonstrated the importance of political will in the arms control process, while the limited nature of the test ban agreement—which prohibited nuclear tests only in environments that could be monitored confidently without on-site inspection or internationally manned seismic monitoring posts—underscored the importance of technology in establishing what is politically feasible.

NOTES

1. *Pravda,* January 15, 1960. Quoted in Carl Linden, *Khrushchev and the Soviet Leadership, 1957–1964* (Baltimore: Johns Hopkins Press, 1966), pp. 92–93n. See also Thomas Wolfe, *Soviet Strategy at the Crossroads* (Cambridge, Mass.: Harvard University Press, 1964), pp. 30–32.
2. JCS 1731/22, *Guidance for Discussions on the Military Aspects of Regulation of Armaments,* June 5, 1947, in *Foreign Relations of the United States, 1947,* vol. 1, pp. 485–486. Reprinted in Thomas H. Etzold and John Lewis Gaddis, eds., *Containment: Documents on American Policy and Strategy, 1945–1950* (New York: Columbia University Press, 1978), p. 280.
3. U.S. Department of State, *Documents on Disarmament, 1945–1959,* vol. 1 and 2 (Washington, D.C.: U.S. Government Printing Office, 1960), pp. 17–24 and 66 in vol. 1.
4. Ibid., pp. 461–462 and 682; Glenn T. Seaborg, with the assistance of Benjamin Loeb, *Kennedy, Khrushchev, and the Test Ban* (Berkeley: University of California Press, 1981), p. 7; and A. N. Kaliadin, *Problemy zapreshcheniia ispytanii i rasprostraneniia adernogo oruzhiia* (Moscow: Nauka, 1976), p. 36.

5. *Pravda,* September 15, 1956. Cited in Kaliadin, *Problemy zapreshcheniia ispytanii,* p. 37.
6. U.S. Department of State, *Documents on Disarmament,* vol. 2, p. 791; and Seaborg, *Kennedy, Khrushchev, and the Test Ban,* pp. 8–9.
7. Seaborg, *Kennedy, Khrushchev, and the Test Ban,* p. 11.
8. U.S. Department of State, *Documents on Disarmament,* vol. 2, pp. 1006–1007 and 1036–1038.
9. Joint Committee on Atomic Energy, Special Subcommittee on Radiation and Subcommittee on Research and Development, *Technical Aspects of Detection and Inspection Controls of a Nuclear Weapons Test Ban: Hearings,* 86th Cong., 2d sess., pt. 1, April 19–22, 1960, pp. 31–35.
10. Joint Committee on Atomic Energy, Subcommittee on Research, Development, and Radiation, *Status of Current Technology to Identify Seismic Events as Natural or Man Made: Hearings,* 92nd Cong., 1st sess., October 27–28, 1971, p. 17; Seaborg, *Kennedy, Khrushchev, and the Test Ban,* p. 13; and Bruce A. Bolt, *Nuclear Explosions and Earthquakes: Parting the Veil* (San Francisco: W.H. Freeman, 1976).
11. Seaborg, *Kennedy, Khrushchev, and the Test Ban,* p. 14; and Samuel Glasstone, ed., *The Effects of Nuclear Weapons* (Washington, D.C.: U.S. Department of Defense and U.S. Atomic Energy Commission, 1964), app. B.
12. Glasstone, *Effects,* p. 45 and app. B. Throughout this study, when a number of nuclear tests is given, it is the number of announced tests.
13. George Kistiakowsky, *A Scientist at the White House: The Private Diary of President Eisenhower's Special Assistant for Science and Technology,* intro. by Charles S. Maier (Cambridge, Mass.: Harvard University Press, 1976), pp. xlvii and 6–7.
14. Glasstone, *Effects,* app. B.
15. U.S. Arms Control and Disarmament Agency, *Arms Control and Disarmament Agreements* (Washington, D.C.: U.S. Government Printing Office, 1980), p. 39.
16. Seaborg, *Kennedy, Khrushchev, and the Test Ban,* p. 15.
17. Bolt, *Nuclear Explosions and Earthquakes,* p. 108; and Seaborg, *Kennedy, Khrushchev, and the Test Ban,* p. 18.
18. Seaborg, *Kennedy, Khrushchev, and the Test Ban,* pp. 16–17.
19. Bolt, *Nuclear Explosions and Earthquakes,* p. xvii.
20. Seaborg, *Kennedy, Khrushchev, and the Test Ban,* pp. 16–17, 47, and 56.
21. U.S. Department of State, *Documents on Disarmament,* vol. 2, pp. 1392–1393.
22. Ibid., pp. 1396–1398; and E. K. Fedorov, "The Agreement on the Cessation of Nuclear Tests Must Be Concluded without Delay!" *Bulletin of the Atomic Scientists* 15, no. 8 (1959), p. 332.
23. U.S. Department of State, *Documents on Disarmament,* vol. 2, pp. 1403–1405; and Seaborg, *Kennedy, Khrushchev, and the Test Ban,* pp. 17–18.
24. Fedorov, "Agreement," p. 331.
25. U.S. Department of State, *Documents on Disarmament,* vol. 2, pp. 1409–1412.

26. Joint Committee on Atomic Energy, *Technical Aspects*, pt. 2, pp. 589–598; "News Roundup," *Bulletin of the Atomic Scientists* 15, no. 7 (1959), p. 317; and Seaborg, *Kennedy, Khrushchev, and the Test Ban*, p. 19.
27. "News Roundup," *Bulletin of the Atomic Scientists* 15, no. 8 (1959), p. 351.
28. Bolt, *Nuclear Explosions and Earthquakes*, p. 109; Kistiakowsky, *A Scientist at the White House*, pp. 18–19; Seaborg, *Kennedy, Khrushchev, and the Test Ban*, p. 18; and Joint Committee on Atomic Energy, *Status of Current Technology*, pp. 17–19.
29. Bolt, *Nuclear Explosions and Earthquakes*, p. 104; and Seaborg, *Kennedy, Khrushchev, and the Test Ban*, p. 20.
30. Joint Committee on Atomic Energy, *Technical Aspects*, pp. 605–617; and Kistiakowsky, *A Scientist at the White House*, p. 212.
31. Seaborg, *Kennedy, Khrushchev, and the Test Ban*, pp. 21–22; and Kistiakowsky, *A Scientist at the White House*, p. 222.
32. Seaborg, *Kennedy, Khrushchev, and the Test Ban*, pp. 22–23. See also E. K. Fedorov, "Controlled Cessation of Atomic Weapons Tests," *Bulletin of the Atomic Scientists* 15, no. 1 (1959), pp. 8–11.
33. Seaborg, *Kennedy, Khrushchev, and the Test Ban*, p. 23.
34. Ibid., pp. 24 and 39; and Kistiakowsky, *A Scientist at the White House*, pp. 311–312.
35. Ibid., pp. 46–47; and U.S. Arms Control and Disarmament Agency, *Arms Control and Disarmament Agreements*, p. 38.
36. Seaborg, *Kennedy, Khrushchev, and the Test Ban*, pp. 41 and 59.
37. Walter LaFever, *America, Russia, and the Cold War, 1945–1975*, 3rd ed. (New York: John Wiley & Sons, 1976), p. 219.
38. Ibid., and Thomas Wolfe, *Soviet Power and Europe, 1945–1970* (Baltimore: Johns Hopkins Press, 1970), pp. 93–94.
39. Wolfe, *Soviet Power and Europe*, pp. 93–94.
40. Hannes Adomeit, *Soviet Risk-taking and Crisis Behavior* (London: George Allen & Unwin, 1982), p. 212.
41. Ibid., p. 212.
42. Glasstone, *Effects*, app. B.
43. U.S. Arms Control and Disarmament Agency, *Documents on Disarmament, 1961* (Washington, D.C.: U.S. Government Printing Office, 1962), p. 351.
44. Glasstone, *Effects*, app. B.
45. U.S. Arms Control and Disarmament Agency, *Documents on Disarmament, 1961*, pp. 664, 666, and 669.
46. Seaborg, *Kennedy, Khrushchev, and the Test Ban*, pp. 121–122.
47. Glasstone, *Effects*, app. B.
48. Seaborg, *Kennedy, Khrushchev, and the Test Ban*, pp. 146–147.
49. Ibid., p. 170.
50. William Griffith, *The Sino-Soviet Rift* (Cambridge, Mass.: MIT Press, 1964), pp. 60–63; and Adam Ulam, *Expansion and Coexistence*, 2nd ed. (New York: Praeger, 1974), pp. 661–676.
51. Griffith, *The Sino-Soviet Rift*, pp. 58–59.
52. U.S. Arms Control and Disarmament Agency, *Documents on Disarmament, 1962*, vol. 2 (Washington, D.C.: U.S. Government Printing Office, 1963) p. 1241.

53. Ibid., p. 1278.
54. Seaborg, *Kennedy, Khrushchev, and the Test Ban*, p. 209.
55. See U.S. Arms Control and Disarmament Agency, *Arms Control and Disarmament Agreements*, p. 39; and Lawrence Freedman, *The Evolution of Nuclear Strategy* (New York: St. Martin's Press, 1983), p. 244.
56. Kaliadin, *Problemy zapreshcheniia ispytanii*, p. 101; and Arkady Shevchenko, *Breaking with Moscow* (New York: Alfred A. Knopf, 1985), p. 123.
57. Ibid., pp. 209–210 and 238–240.
58. Ibid., pp. 238–257.
59. Cited in Kaliadin, *Problemy zapreshcheniia ispytanii*, p. 37.
60. "Chernyshev Marks Test Ban Treaty Anniversary," Foreign Broadcast Information Service, August 6, 1987, p. AA5.
61. Norman Cousins, "Notes on a 1963 Visit with Khrushchev," *Saturday Review*, November 7, 1964, p. 21. Quoted in Seaborg, *Kennedy, Khrushchev, and the Test Ban*, p. 180.
62. Seaborg, *Kennedy, Khrushchev, and the Test Ban*, pp. 238–247.
63. E. K. Fedorov, "Agreement," p. 332.
64. See Scott D. Sagan, "SIOP-62: The Nuclear War Plan Briefing to President Kennedy," *International Security* 12, no. 1 (1987), pp. 24–25.
65. Ibid., pp. 26–28; John Prados, *The Soviet Estimate* (New York: Dial Press, 1982), p. 89; Robert P. Berman and John C. Baker, *Soviet Strategic Forces: Requirements and Responses* (Washington, D.C.: Brookings Institution, 1982), pp. 102–107 and 138; and Raymond Garthoff, "The Meaning of the Missiles," *Washington Quarterly* 5, no. 4 (1982), pp. 77–79.
66. For a discussion of U.S. army tactical nuclear doctrine during this period, see John J. Midgley, Jr., *Deadly Illusions: Army Policy for the Nuclear Battlefield* (Boulder: Westview Press, 1986), pp. 31–85.
67. U.S. Senate Committee on Armed Services, Preparedness Investigating Subcommittee, *Military Aspects and Implications of Nuclear Test Ban Proposals and Related Matters: Hearings*, 88th Cong., 1st sess., pt. 1, May–August 1963, pp. 247 and 307.
68. Ibid., p. 356.
69. See Raymond Garthoff, *Soviet Strategy in the Nuclear Age* (New York: Praeger, 1962), pp. 107–112; and Wolfe, *Soviet Strategy at the Crossroads*, pp. 119–124.
70. P. Astashenkov, *Kurchatov* (Moscow: Molodaia gvardiia, 1967), p. 186.
71. Dr. John Foster, director of Lawrence Livermore National Laboratory in 1963, testified that during the U.S. test moratorium, many laboratory scientists worked on devices that had already been tested, modifying them to permit their mass production and to satisfy the military requirements for the particular weapon systems to which they were to be adapted. See U.S. Senate Committee on Armed Services, *Military Aspects*, pt. 1, p. 395.
72. Nikita Khrushchev, *Khrushchev Remembers: The Last Testament*, trans. and ed. by Strobe Talbott (Boston: Little, Brown & Co., 1979), p. 68.
73. Ibid. Some U.S. scientists were similarly concerned about the impact of a comprehensive test ban on the confidence that could be placed in U.S. nuclear forces. "Each nuclear explosion," Edward Teller wrote in 1960,

"is, in fact, an experiment whose outcome is very much in doubt." See his "The Feasibility of Arms Control and the Principle of Openness," *Daedalus*, Special Issue: Arms Control (1960), p. 791. John Foster told the Senate Armed Services Committee that when the United States resumed nuclear tests after the moratorium, "surprises came with almost every test." See U.S. Senate Committee on Armed Services, *Military Aspects*, pt. 1, p. 396.

74. See Wolfe, *Soviet Power and Europe*, p. 93, for an example of Khrushchev's nuclear threats against Berlin.

75. U.S. Senate Committee on Armed Services, *Military Aspects*, pt. 1, pp. 293 and 431.

76. U.S. Senate Committee on Foreign Relations, *The Nuclear Test Ban Treaty: Hearings*, 88th Cong., 1st sess., p. 543.

77. Ibid., pp. 104–105.

78. U.S. Arms Control and Disarmament Agency, *Documents on Disarmament, 1963* (Washington, D.C.: U.S. Government Printing Office, 1964), p. 300.

79. Glasstone, *Effects*, app. B.

80. Kaliadin, *Problemy zapreshcheniia ispytanii*, p. 54.

81. Wolfe, *Soviet Power and Europe*, p. 114.

82. Ibid., pp. 114–115.

83. *Peking Review* 6, no. 33 (1963), pp. 7–15. Reprinted in Griffith, *The Sino-Soviet Rift*, p. 351.

84. Griffith, *The Sino-Soviet Rift*, p. 361.

85. Lucian Pye, *China: An Introduction* (Boston: Little, Brown & Co., 1972), p. 204.

86. Seaborg, *Kennedy, Khrushchev, and the Test Ban*, p. 47.

87. U.S. Arms Control and Disarmament Agency, *Documents on Disarmament, 1961*, p. 664.

88. Ibid., pp. 238–239.

89. Griffith, *The Sino-Soviet Rift*, p. 351.

90. On Khrushchev's possible view of China's nuclear capabilities, see Seaborg, *Kennedy, Khrushchev, and the Test Ban*, pp. 238–239.

91. Glasstone, *Effects*, app. B; and U.S. Arms Control and Disarmament Agency, *Arms Control and Disarmament Agreements*, p. 34.

92. Samuel Glasstone and Philip Dolon, eds., *The Effects of Nuclear Weapons*, 3rd ed. (Washington, D.C.: U.S. Department of Defense and U.S. Energy Research and Development Administration, 1977), pp. 437–438. See also William Ellis, "Bikini: A Way of Life Lost," *National Geographic* 169, no. 6 (1986), pp. 813–834. A rem is a unit of biological dose of radiation. According to the U.S. Congressional Office of Technology Assessment (OTA), a dose of 450 rem in a short period of time creates a fatal illness in about half the people exposed to it; a dose of 50–200 rem will cause nausea and lower resistance to other diseases. See OTA, *The Effects of Nuclear War* (Washington, D.C.: U.S. Government Printing Office, 1981), pp. 109–110.

93. Bolt, *Nuclear Explosions and Earthquakes*, p. 91; and U.S. Arms Control and Disarmament Agency, *Arms Control and Disarmament Agreements*, p. 34.

94. Sr 90 is a radioactive fission product with a half-life of 27.7 years that is deposited onto the earth's surface through fallout from nuclear tests. It can enter the human body through ingestion of food, especially milk, that contains it. The long-term effects of Sr 90 on the body are not fully understood, but experiments on animals indicate that large doses may cause bone cancer. The International Commission on Radiological Protection has suggested that the concentration of Sr 90 averaged over the whole population should not exceed 67 picocuries per gram of calcium. See Glasstone and Dolon, *Effects,* pp. 443–450 and 605–608.

95. Seaborg, *Kennedy, Khrushchev, and the Test Ban,* p. 32.

96. U.S. Committee on Armed Services, *Military Aspects,* pt. 1, p. 179; and Curtis Cochran, Dennis Gorman, and Joseph Domoulin, eds., *Space Handbook* (Maxwell Air Force Base, Ala.: Air University Press, 1985), pp. 1–10.

97. U.S. Department of Defense, *Annual Report of the Secretary of Defense, July 1, 1959, to June 30, 1960* (Washington, D.C.: U.S. Government Printing Press, 1960), p. 21.

98. For the results of these measurements, see the following chapters in A. V. Lebedinsky, ed., *What Russian Scientists Say about Fallout* (New York: Collier Books, 1962): V.P. Shvedov and L. I. Geneonov, "Contamination of the Biosphere in the Environs of Leningrad by Nuclear Explosions," pp. 55–59; and B.V. Kurchatov et al., "A Study of the Content of Radioactive Strontium in the Atmosphere, Soil, Foodstuffs and Human Bone," pp. 76–91.

99. Kurchatov et al., "A Study of the Content," p. 86.

100. United Nations Scientific Committee on the Effects of Atomic Radiation, *Sources and Effects of Ionizing Radiation,* report to the General Assembly (New York: United Nations, 1977), p. 124.

101. Kurchatov et al., "A Study of the Content," p. 89.

102. Bolt, *Nuclear Explosions and Earthquakes,* pp. 85–86.

103. The Tass report and additional information provided by Soviet officials to visiting foreigners are summarized and discussed in *The New York Times,* June 17, 1989; and *The New York Times,* July 10, 1989. See also Zhores Medvedev, *Nuclear Disaster in the Urals* (New York: Vintage Books, 1979).

104. Kaliadin, *Problemy zapreshcheniia ispytanii,* p. 45.

105. Harrison E. Salisbury, ed., *Sakharov Speaks* (New York: Alfred. A. Knopf, 1974), p. 32.

106. Ibid. For an early indication of Sakharov's concern about the genetic damage caused by atmospheric nuclear explosions, see Andrei D. Sakharov, "Radioactive Carbon of Nuclear Explosions and Nonthreshold Biological Effects," in Lebedinsky, *What Russian Scientists Say.*

107. U.S. Senate Committee on Foreign Relations, *The Nuclear Test Ban Treaty: Hearings,* 88th Cong., 1st sess. p. 818.

108. Ralph Lapp, "Soviet Scientists on Bomb Tests," *Bulletin of the Atomic Scientists* 15, no. 8 (1959), p. 349.

109. Glasstone, *Effects,* app. B.

110. Ibid.

2

THE SOVIETS AND ARMS CONTROL: THE SALT II NEGOTIATIONS, NOVEMBER 1972–MARCH 1976

Coit D. Blacker

On May 26, 1972, in an elaborate ceremony staged in the Kremlin's St. Vladimir Hall, President Richard Nixon and Leonid Brezhnev, general secretary of the Communist Party of the Soviet Union, affixed their signatures to two agreements limiting U.S. and Soviet strategic military forces, the first such accords between Washington and Moscow in the nuclear era. One was a treaty of unlimited duration severely restricting the advanced development and deployment of anti-ballistic missile systems (ABMs). The other, the Interim Agreement on Offensive Weapons, placed important though more porous constraints on the deployment of U.S. and Soviet long-range ballistic missile systems; it was to last for five years, during which time the two countries would seek to negotiate permanent and more comprehensive limitations on their central strategic forces. With the signing of these agreements, Nixon and Brezhnev successfully concluded the first phase of the Strategic Arms Limitation Talks (SALT I), initiated in November 1969.

Six months after the Moscow summit, the talks resumed. U.S. and Soviet negotiators met in Geneva amid optimistic reports that a new accord to limit the two sides' strategic offensive forces might be concluded within the year, perhaps even in time for the second Nixon-Brezhnev summit, tentatively scheduled for the late spring or early summer of 1973. By late 1975, however, a treaty had not materialized and the negotiations were at a virtual impasse, despite Secretary of State Henry Kissinger's assurance that a new agreement was "90 percent complete."[1]

With the inability of the two sides to compose their remaining differences in the period immediately following Kissinger's January 1976 mission to Moscow, the negotiations entered a political form of suspended animation. Among other factors, SALT had fallen victim to a number of relatively minor though difficult-to-resolve problems of a largely technical nature, to the disarray in American foreign policy attributable to the Watergate scandal, and to a manifest deterioration in superpower relations. It would take three more years, a new administration, and a bewildering series of negotiating starts and stops before the second SALT Treaty would be ready for signing in June 1979.

The story of SALT II from the resumption of the negotiations in late 1972 to the final year of the Ford presidency has been told before. Raymond Garthoff, William Hyland, Strobe Talbott, and Thomas Wolfe, among others, have provided important and insightful treatments of this complex period in U.S.–Soviet relations.[2] Henry Kissinger, in the second volume of his memoirs, devotes considerable attention to the subject.[3] Most of these analyses focus more on the American than on the Soviet perspective—though Garthoff and Wolfe, in particular, do an estimable job of tracking Soviet negotiating proposals during these years and of noting shifts in Moscow's positions. It is the purpose of this chapter, by focusing more narrowly and systematically on the Soviet side of the equation, to investigate how Kremlin leaders perceived, understood, and negotiated during the first phase of the second round of SALT.

The analysis will address five questions:

- How did Soviet leaders conceive of the association between strategic arms control and the broader fabric of U.S.–Soviet relations during these years? In their calculation, what was the proper relationship between "political" and "military" détente? Did the Soviets' thinking on this issue change over time; if so, how, when, and why?

- In the negotiations, what were Soviet objectives? What did the Kremlin's SALT proposals suggest about the leadership's preferences for the development of strategic military relations between the superpowers during the remainder of the 1970s and beyond?

- From Moscow's vantage point, what were the principal substantive issues separating the two sides, and how were they to be overcome? What price were the Soviets prepared to pay in the hard currency of military power to secure a new SALT agreement with Washington?

- In light of the foregoing, what does Soviet conduct during this period suggest about the development in bureaucratic terms of an arms control "process" within the Soviet system? Is there evidence to indicate, for example, that the negotiations precipitated the creation of a new and distinct "cluster" of Soviet decision makers, led by Leonid Brezhnev, vested with particular responsibilities in the areas of arms control and national security policy?

- Finally, how did Soviet leaders assess the impact of the Watergate scandal, and the processes of American domestic politics more generally, on the SALT negotiations?

To set the context for the discussion that follows, the chapter begins with a review of the negotiations from the period immediately preceding the resumption of the talks in November 1972 to the suspension of the process in early 1976. It concludes by extracting from the analysis those "lessons" that might contribute to our understanding of how the Soviets negotiated in this first phase of SALT II, which can also shed light on the extent to which Soviet goals and conduct in strategic arms control have— or have not—changed over the course of the succeeding years.

THE NEGOTIATIONS

During the nearly six months that separated the May 1972 Moscow summit from the formal reconvening of the SALT negotiations the following November, relations between Washington and Moscow, on an upswing for the better part of two years, continued to develop in a positive and "constructive" way. On

August 3 the Senate voted 88 to 2 to ratify the ABM Treaty. Two weeks later the House of Representatives endorsed the Interim Agreement by an equally lopsided majority; Senate concurrence followed on September 14. The mood was no less upbeat concerning trade and economic relations. In July the two countries concluded an accord by which the United States agreed to underwrite the sale to the Soviet Union of 17 million tons of American grain over a three-year period, a transaction valued at some $750 million. Though it was soon to become controversial, the grain sale was welcomed initially in all quarters. In mid-October the Soviets consented to pay $722 million toward their World War II lend-lease debts, thus clearing the way for the completion of a draft U.S.–Soviet trade agreement by which the USSR would be awarded most-favored-nation (MFN) status and be invited to apply for hundreds of millions of dollars in credits.[4]

Not all the news was favorable, of course. That September the Senate, distressed by the numerical advantage in missile launchers granted the Soviet Union in the Interim Agreement—totaling some 640 land- and sea-based systems—passed Senator Henry Jackson's amendment strongly urging the administration to accept nothing less than equal force levels in the negotiation of any subsequent constraints on U.S. and Soviet strategic weapon systems. The following month Jackson also introduced legislation (subsequently known as the Jackson-Vanik amendment) linking both the extension of credits and the Soviet Union's prospective MFN status to a liberalization of its policies regarding emigration. Despite the administration's clear if quiet opposition to the measure, seventy-two senators signed on as cosponsors.[5]

Off to a Slow Start

It was, therefore, with considerable anticipation—and with only the vaguest sense of foreboding—that U.S. and Soviet observers welcomed the resumption of the SALT negotiations in Geneva. Their optimism was misplaced. By the time the initial round adjourned in mid-December, there was little doubt that SALT II would be a difficult and time-consuming negotiation. The first sessions were given over largely to posturing. The United States, in fact, offered no formal proposals whatsoever. The White House had instructed the U.S. negotiating team to treat the meetings as exploratory and conversational in nature. "We need to feel our way with the Russians," remarked one American official at the time.[6] In actuality, according to Kissinger, U.S. negotiators could do little else, given that the administration—preoccupied with both the presidential election and the negotiations to conclude the Vietnam War—had yet to develop its SALT position.[7] Apparently the U.S. side did communicate Washington's determination to equalize strategic force levels in any new agreement, a position that could hardly have taken Moscow by surprise, in view of the attention devoted in the American press to the Senate debate that accompanied adoption of the Jackson amendment.

For their part, the Soviets proposed that the two sides exercise "restraint" in the development and deployment of new strategic weapon systems, without specifying precisely what such restraint might entail. They also called on the United States to dismantle its ballistic missile submarine installations in Spain and Scotland.[8] More ominously, Soviet negotiators expressed satisfaction with the terms of the Interim Agreement, suggesting that the accord provided a perfectly acceptable basis for the conclusion of a permanent treaty to limit strategic offensive forces. At the same time, they insisted, as they had throughout the SALT I negotiations, that all U.S. forward-based systems (FBS) capable of delivering nuclear weapons, including tactical aircraft based in Europe and those deployed with aircraft carriers, be counted against U.S. strategic weapons totals.[9]

Notwithstanding the exploratory nature of these early discussions, both sides recognized that differences over aggregate force levels and U.S. forward-based systems would constitute important and divisive issues in the negotiations. When the talks resumed in March, U.S. negotiators also learned that devising a mutually acceptable formula for limiting multiple warheads—multiple independently targetable reentry vehicles (MIRVs)—would be no less contentious.

The U.S. proposals of March 1973 called for a new accord to supersede the Interim Agreement, providing—as urged by Congress—for strict numerical equality in intercontinental and submarine-launched ballistic missile (ICBM and SLBM) launchers and heavy bombers. In addition, the United States proposed that the two sides be permitted to deploy *equal* numbers of ICBMs of *equal* throwweight. If implemented, such an agreement would have allowed the United States to add up to 400 large ICBMs to its existing land-based missile arsenal; alternatively, it would have required the Soviet Union to dismantle all of its "heavy" ICBMs—some 300 SS-9s—which accounted for much of the Kremlin's marked advantage in land-based missile throwweight. One purpose of the U.S. proposal was to limit indirectly the anticipated deployment of Soviet MIRVed missiles by mandating deep reductions in ICBM throwweight—given that Moscow was, in the opinion of U.S. officials, unlikely to accept a nearly 40 percent increment to the U.S. land-based missile forces. Predictably, Soviet negotiators turned aside the American initiative and urged reconsideration of their November 1972 proposals, now sharpened to include a prohibition on the deployment of any new strategic weapon systems. The ban on new weapons was not to be a complete one, however, as the United States was to learn over the course of the next several months.[10]

In late April Kissinger met with Soviet Ambassador Anatoly Dobrynin, at which time the Soviet envoy presented the U.S. national security adviser with a condensed draft of a Soviet SALT proposal advanced earlier in the month at Geneva. In his memoirs Kissinger reports that the initiative was little more than a rehash of existing Soviet positions, offering no real basis for negotiation.[11] In preparation for a May trip to Moscow—itself preparatory to Brezhnev's June visit to the United States—Kissinger and other senior members of the administration met shortly after the former's session with Dobrynin to reformulate the U.S. SALT position. In the course of that meeting it was decided that the United States would propose equal aggregate ceilings of 2,350 for strategic launchers (ICBMs, SLBMs, and heavy bombers) and, effective July 1, 1973, a freeze on land-based MIRVed missile deployments and on the further testing of MIRVed warheads. The proposal was patently one-sided, in that the United States had already deployed 300 Minutemen III missiles armed with three warheads each, while Moscow had yet to begin its MIRV testing program. At the time, however, a more "negotiable" proposal was beyond the administration's reach, according to Kissinger, because of sharp differences between the State and Defense departments over how to proceed in SALT; President Nixon, increasingly preoccupied with Watergate, proved either unwilling or unable to adjudicate the dispute.[12]

Kissinger got nowhere in Moscow with the new American scheme. Brezhnev, who advanced few ideas of his own, declined to consider such prejudicial constraints on MIRVs and MIRVed systems. With the failure of his mission, Kissinger knew by the time of his departure from the Soviet capital on May 9 that Nixon and Brezhnev would have no new SALT agreement to sign during the Washington summit.[13] At the end of their meetings in June, the two leaders did approve the Basic Principles of Negotiations on the Further Limitation of Strategic Offensive Weapons, by which the U.S. and Soviet governments committed themselves to the conclusion during 1974 of a permanent treaty to replace the Interim Agreement. The declaration also reaffirmed the hallowed principles of "equality" and "equal security," and called for the inclusion in any new agreement of qualitative as well as quantitative constraints.[14] The failure to produce a new SALT accord overshadowed the release on June 21 of the Agreement on the Prevention of Nuclear War, an accord to which the American side seemed to attach scant importance but that the Soviets heralded as a significant milestone in superpower relations.

There the negotiations languished throughout the summer and fall of 1973. At the American end, the corrosive effects of Watergate—as manifested in the erosion of presidential authority and the persistence of bureaucratic wrangling over arms control and defense policy—took their toll. The paralysis eased only slightly with Kissinger's elevation to the position of secretary of state in August, and then set in again as a consequence of three profound though unrelated crises in October: the "Saturday Night Massacre" at the Justice Department, Spiro Agnew's abrupt resignation as vice president, and the Arab-Israeli war in the Middle East. Late in 1973 Ambassador U. Alexis Johnson, the head of the U.S. SALT delegation, was still negotiating on the basis of instructions issued to him the previous May.[15]

Immobility also characterized the Soviet position during the latter half of 1973, though the exact cause was, and remains, more difficult to pinpoint.[16] Twice during the summer, first in July and again in August, Kissinger met with Dobrynin to discuss ways around the SALT impasse. In the first of these encounters, the Soviet ambassador proposed, among other things, limits on MIRVed ICBMs and SLBMs on the basis of equal security. No numbers were discussed. Dobrynin insisted, as had other Soviet officials, that the Soviet Union was entitled to some degree of permanent numerical superiority in strategic nuclear delivery vehicles because of its "unique" security needs—primarily the fact that Moscow confronted not one nuclear-armed adversary, like the United States, but four.[17] At the second meeting, Dobrynin returned to the earlier Soviet theme of barring the deployment of "new" strategic weapon systems, proposing that the two sides sign a ten-year agreement to that effect. Conveniently enough, according to Kissinger, the Soviet plan would have permitted the Kremlin to deploy its fourth-generation ICBMs—the SS-17, SS-18, and SS-19 missiles—as "modernized" versions of existing types, while preventing the deployment of the U.S. Trident SLBM. A successor to the Minuteman ICBM might or might not be permitted under terms of the Soviet proposal, depending on the missile's dimensions and performance characteristics.[18] The administration deemed neither Soviet plan a breakthrough, and the negotiations continued to drift without a visible sense of purpose or direction.

One Step Forward, Two Steps Back

Early in 1974 SALT's tempo quickened. The catalyst was again a summit meeting between Nixon and Brezhnev, set for midyear. In February, over Kissinger's objections, the administration sanctioned a new proposal calling for a ceiling of 2,350 on missile launchers and heavy bombers, as well as equality in MIRVed ICBM throwweight.[19] The American negotiating team was advised that the United States was unlikely to approve a limit for throwweight that exceeded the lift potential of the 1,000 deployed Minuteman missiles. Under the terms of the proposal, the Soviet Union could have deployed multiple warheads on only a fraction of its land-based missile force, given its 2−1 advantage in ICBM throwweight (which was expected to increase to 3−1 by 1978).[20] That the U.S. proposal was unlikely to precipitate a major advance in the negotiations was self-evident, at least to Kissinger. "Quick deadlock was inevitable," he wrote in 1982, "when American and Soviet delegations resumed their deliberations in Geneva on February 19, 1974."[21]

Three days before his scheduled departure for Moscow in late March, Kissinger was authorized to explore with the Soviets a rather different proposal. In exchange for a three-year extension of the Interim Agreement, the Soviets would undertake to limit their MIRVed ICBM deployments to 270—or 280 missiles below the expected number of U.S. multiple-warhead systems. Kissinger rationalized the proposal by arguing that this figure corresponded almost exactly to the Kremlin's overall numerical advantage in deployed land-based missiles under the terms of the 1972 agreement on offensive weapons. In Moscow Brezhnev had other ideas. The general secretary suggested a six-year extension of the Interim Agreement and a limitation of 1,000 MIRVed missiles for each side. He dismissed Kissinger's offering in a sentence: "If I agree to this, this will be my last meeting with Dr. Kissinger, because I will be destroyed."[22] In what Kissinger took as a hopeful sign for the future, Brezhnev did accept the *principle* of asymmetrical ceilings on MIRVed weapons when he announced toward the end of their meetings that the Soviet Union could live with a force balance of 1,100 multiple-warhead missiles for the United States and 1,000 for the Kremlin. When Kissinger pressed further for a sublimit on MIRVed ICBMs, however, Brezhnev demurred.[23]

The following month Kissinger met with Andrei Gromyko, Soviet foreign minister, in Geneva for a review of bilateral relations, including SALT, and to set the agenda for the summit. On this occasion the secretary of state proposed limits of 1,000 MIRVed systems—ICBMs and SLBMs—for the United States and 850 for the Soviet Union, as well as an extension of the Interim Agreement to 1980. As the administration had calculated that Moscow was likely to deploy 250 SLBMs with multiple warheads over the next six years, the proposal would have limited Soviet land-based MIRVed missiles to approximately 600— or 50 more than the United States was deploying. Gromyko was unmoved.[24]

At this point the negotiations stalled again. According to Kissinger, the Soviets evidenced no further interest in exploring possible limitations built around the notion of counterbalancing asymmetries and advanced no new proposals of their own. The uneasy consensus within the U.S. administration that had permitted Kissinger to explore various schemes first in Moscow and later with Gromyko in Geneva collapsed, its end hastened, it seems, by Nixon's deepening preoccupation with the Watergate scandal. As the country's domestic crisis intensified, the thinly disguised differences within the government over U.S. SALT policy erupted publicly. On June 14, Paul Nitze, the Defense Department's principal representative in Geneva, resigned, citing the "depressing reality of the traumatic events now unfolding in our nation's capital."[25] A week later, at the final National Security Council meeting before the president's departure for Moscow, Secretary of Defense James Schlesinger presented the department's SALT recommendations: equal launcher aggregates of 2,500; limits of 660 and 360 MIRVed ICBMs for the United States and the Soviet Union, respectively; and no constraints on MIRVed SLBMs. In his memoirs, Nixon characterizes the Schlesinger proposal as "an unyielding hardline . . . It was a proposal the Soviets were sure to reject out of hand."[26] Nixon clearly implies, as does Kissinger, that it was the former's greatly reduced stature that emboldened the defense secretary to put forth such a nonnegotiable position. It was, Nixon alleges, "an insult to everyone's intelligence and particularly mine."[27]

The 1974 summit produced no measurable progress on SALT. In the end, the two sides chose to finesse the issue; they agreed, in essence, to set aside their substantive differences and to concentrate instead on procedural matters. A communiqué released on July 3 announced that the United States and the Soviet Union had reached agreement on a new negotiating "framework"—a ten-year treaty, to run from 1975 to 1985, to regulate aspects of both the quantitative and the qualitative strategic military competition.[28] The two leaders also agreed to meet again later in the year to review the status of the negotiations. Despite the disappointing results in SALT, the summit was not without its successes. Among the results were the Threshold Test Ban Treaty and a protocol to the 1972 ABM Treaty limiting each country to one operational anti-ballistic missile installation (as signed, the treaty had permitted the sides to deploy two such facilities).[29]

The Vladivostok Agreement

Barely a month after his return from the Soviet Union, Richard Nixon resigned from office. The following September, his successor, Gerald Ford, met with Gromyko in the Oval Office. Among the issues discussed were U.S.–Soviet trade relations and SALT. On the strength of Gromyko's assurance that the Kremlin was prepared to conclude a new accord on strategic arms consistent with the framework developed during the last Nixon-Brezhnev summit, Ford authorized Kissinger to travel to Moscow—his fourth such trip in a little over two years—to explore with Soviet leaders the terms of a possible agreement. The negotiations went well. By the time Kissinger departed Moscow on October 27, it had already been announced that Ford would meet with Brezhnev in the Soviet city of Vladivostok in late November.[30]

Raymond Garthoff reports that Kissinger and Brezhnev discussed two approaches to a new SALT treaty during the secretary of state's October trip. The first would provide for equal launcher aggregates and equal ceilings on MIRVed missiles. The second would permit the Soviet Union a modest lead in the total number of launchers, to be counterbalanced by an American advantage in MIRVed missile systems.[31] Brezhnev indicated his willingness to consider either option. In the course of these discussions the general secretary also stated that the Soviet Union, in the interests of invigorating the talks, might be prepared to drop its demand that U.S. forward-based systems—nuclear-capable fighter and fighter-bomber aircraft deployed around the periphery of the Soviet Union and at sea—be included in the American launcher totals, the first hint that Moscow might be willing to defer consideration of the FBS issue since an oblique reference to this effect in the Geneva negotiations six months before.[32]

The summit in Vladivostok on November 23 and 24 was almost an anticlimax, given the success of Kissinger's October mission. By the end of the first day of deliberations, Ford and Brezhnev had reached substantive agreement on most issues of consequence. As revealed in an aide-mémoire released on December 10, each country would be permitted 2,400 land- and sea-based ballistic missile launchers and heavy bombers—some 100 below existing Soviet deployments and 200 above the U.S. totals. A sublimit of 1,320 would be applied to MIRVed ICBMs and SLBMs. As Brezhnev had indicated they might, the Soviets agreed to set aside the FBS issue, neither insisting that these aircraft be included in U.S. weapons aggregates nor requesting explicit compensation. The agreement would run for eight years, from October 1977, when the 1972 Interim Agreement was to lapse, to December 1985. Officials from both governments said they expected a formal treaty to be concluded and ready for signature in 1975.[33]

The fact that the aide-mémoire, which set out the actual terms of the accord, took over two weeks to complete was significant and symptomatic of the troubled times that lay ahead. In setting the weapons totals, the two sides had agreed that each long-range air-launched missile deployed with heavy bombers would count against the aggregate ceiling of 2,400. The Soviets argued that this provision covered not just air-to-surface ballistic missiles, but air-launched *cruise* missiles, as well. The Americans rejected this interpretation, alleging that constraints on cruise missiles should be considered as a separate issue. In the end, the language of the aide-mémoire reflected more the Soviet than the U.S. position, though the administration was quick to state for the record that it did not regard the document's treatment of the subject as binding.[34]

A second ambiguity emerged within days of the Vladivostok meeting. In 1974 the Soviets had begun to deploy a new medium-range bomber, code-named Backfire in the West, at a rate of approximately three aircraft per month. Despite assertions by both the Defense Department and the Joint Chiefs of Staff that the Backfire had at least a residual capability for intercontinental bombing missions and should, therefore, be considered a strategic weapons platform, no mention was made of the aircraft in either the Vladivostok communiqué or the December 10 aide-mémoire. From the Soviet perspective, in other words, Backfire was not a heavy bomber, subject to limitation. At Vladivostok, Ford and Kissinger appear to have accepted the Soviet position. In early 1975, however, the United States shifted its view—under Defense Department prodding—and a second contentious issue emerged to plague the negotiators.[35] A third problem area, how to monitor which missile systems had been deployed with multiple warheads, took some time to resolve, but in the end constituted a less difficult issue than how to count air-launched cruise missiles (ALCMs) and how to dispose of the Backfire.[36]

In January and February 1974 the Senate and House of Representatives passed resolutions endorsing the Vladivostok accord, despite criticisms from both ends of the American political spectrum that the agreement, with its high weapons ceilings, did little more than legitimate a new round of the arms competition. Singled out for special censure were the MIRVed missile limits, which were correctly seen as a retreat from the proposals previously advanced by the two sides. Given that only the number of MIRVed launchers was to be limited, and not, at least directly, the number of MIRVed warheads, U.S. critics dismissed the constraints as more cosmetic than real. Whatever else administration spokesmen might say in defense of the agreement, they could not claim that Vladivostok would help to ease the emerging problem of vulnerability of U.S. ICBMs to Soviet missile attack.[37]

Aftermath

In any event, the Vladivostok "boost" to SALT proved to be short-lived. By mid-1975 the negotiations were once again deadlocked. A spate of meetings took place during the year, involving Kissinger and Gromyko (in July and September); Ford, Kissinger, and Gromyko (in September); and Ford, Brezhnev, and Kissinger (in Helsinki in July and August). These failed to produce the required consensus.[38] In addition to the problems of ALCMs and the Backfire, the two sides found themselves at loggerheads over both ground- and sea-launched cruise missiles, as well as a host of issues having to do with large ICBMs, ranging from sublimits and permissible silo modifications to the very definition of what constituted a heavy missile. The Soviets in October rejected a revised set of U.S. proposals, hammered out between Kissinger and Defense Secretary Schlesinger that fall.[39]

In January 1976 Kissinger traveled to Moscow in what was to be his last visit to the Soviet Union as secretary of state in an effort to negotiate a compromise. He took with him two proposals. The first was a complex package containing a bewildering array of range and deployment limitations on all three cruise missile variants (ground-, sea-, and air-launched), only some of which were likely to appeal to Moscow, as well as a rather contrived solution to the Backfire problem (only those Backfires produced after October 1977, the proposal stipulated, would be counted as heavy bombers and thus subject to aggregate ceilings negotiated at Vladivostok). The second proposal, simple only in comparison to the first, offered to place more constraints on cruise missiles and to exclude the Backfire from the Vladivostok ceilings (though limiting their production to 275 for five years), in exchange for Soviet agreement to reduce the strategic weapons aggregates from 2,400 to 2,300. Brezhnev showed interest in the second proposal, and Kissinger returned to Washington confident that the long-sought breakthrough in the negotiations was finally at hand.[40]

It was not to be. Upon his return to the United States, Ford shifted ground again. He instructed Kissinger to try out yet another approach with the Kremlin, whereby the two sides would agree to ratify the Vladivostok ceilings in a treaty and, in a separate understanding to last three years, to regulate cruise missile testing and deployment in a manner largely consistent with previous U.S. proposals—permitting the deployment of long-range ALCMs on heavy bombers and counting the bombers so equipped as MIRVed delivery vehicles while restricting the deployment of sea- and ground-launched cruise missiles to those with a 600-kilometer range. Resolution of the Backfire problem also would be postponed to the period after January 1979. Ford conveyed the offer to Brezhnev in writing in February, following discussions between Kissinger and Dobrynin. In March Brezhnev responded. As Garthoff notes, "He flatly rejected the attempt to defer the remaining issues in this way and angrily described the proposals as a 'step back' from the second January proposal."[41]

With the receipt of Brezhnev's March letter, the first phase of the SALT II negotiations, begun just over three years before, effectively came to a halt. Ford, in the midst of a bruising fight with former California Governor Ronald Reagan for the Republican presidential nomination, had recently come under withering fire from conservatives for his continuing support of détente and arms control; he was therefore loath after the February–March exchange of letters with Brezhnev to expend the precious political capital necessary to secure a new SALT agreement, the projected terms of which were already controversial. The Soviets, no strangers to the vagaries of American politics, proved only slightly more willing to press for an agreement than the administration was, preferring to wait, it seems, for the outcome of the November election.

And wait they did. Serious negotiations on strategic arms were not to resume for twelve months, until Kissinger's successor at the State Department, Cyrus Vance, arrived in Moscow in March 1977 to begin the second phase of SALT II.

THE VIEW FROM MOSCOW

Reconstructing the first phase of the SALT II negotiations provides, at best, a context for understanding the evolution of Soviet strategic arms control policy during these important years. The remainder of the chapter focuses in detail on Soviet attitudes toward a number of discrete issues—from the link between SALT and the development of superpower relations to the impact of U.S. domestic politics on the character and conduct of American foreign policy—that, taken together, significantly enrich our understanding of this unique and under-studied episode in the history of postwar U.S.–Soviet security relations.

SALT and U.S.–Soviet Relations

In reviewing the history of SALT between 1972 and 1976, a number of interesting themes emerge regarding the Soviet conception of and approach to strategic arms control. One is the extent to which Soviet leaders appear to have been first surprised by and then frustrated at the actual course of negotiations—especially the increasing complexity of the discussions and, toward the end of the period, the persistent inability of the two sides to achieve closure on the terms of a new agreement. Why this should have been the case, when American policymakers appear to have had fewer illusions on this score, is not immediately apparent. To get at this issue in a satisfying way requires some understanding of how Soviet decision makers thought of the SALT process during these years and, in particular, the connection in Soviet thinking between what might be considered the political dimension of superpower relations, on the one hand, and the negotiated limitation of U.S. and Soviet strategic nuclear forces, on the other.

We know from many sources, some Soviet, that devising a mutually acceptable way to delimit the U.S.–Soviet strategic military competition was only one of the Kremlin's several goals in détente; it may not even have been the most important. Putting an end to the country's relative diplomatic isolation, improving ties with the United States in order to counterbalance the steady deterioration in relations with China, securing Western trade and credits to bolster its own sagging economic performance, and obtaining formal American recognition of the Soviet Union's status as a military and political superpower were all, it seems, at least as important to the Soviet leadership as was the conclusion of agreements to regulate superpower military relations.

During the early 1970s, Soviet political figures, foreign policy analysts, and academics spoke and wrote of a "world-wide shift in the correlation of forces" to Moscow's advantage, made possible by a general increase in the "material and human resources" available to the socialist camp over the course of the previous decade. In this ongoing process of evaluation, particular attention was devoted to the dramatic growth in the Soviet Union's strategic military capabilities since the mid-1960s.[42]

The advent of parity, the Soviets argued, was an altogether positive development, in that it served to restrain the worst military and political excesses of the United States and its imperialist allies. In the Soviet view, the Kremlin's growing military power left Washington no real option but to adopt a more conciliatory line toward the USSR and to engage Moscow, for the first time, as a political and military equal. From the Kremlin's perspective, therefore, it was the development of the Soviet Union's military capabilities that made possible in a direct, almost linear way the relaxation of international tensions that characterized world politics during the first half of the 1970s. With an optimism that seems curiously out of place with the benefit of hindsight, Soviet officials routinely spoke of new and exciting opportunities to "restructure" bilateral relations with leading Western countries, according to the principles of peaceful coexistence and mutual advantage, as a consequence of the perceived ongoing shift in "the correlation of forces." By 1973, high-ranking Soviet decision makers, typically not the most expansive of orators, were so encouraged by the trends under way, especially in U.S.–Soviet relations, that they were moved to proclaim détente's pending "irreversibility."[43]

In short, many senior Soviet leaders seemed to conceive of their country's newfound military potential in largely political terms, as a vehicle to assist in the realization of certain key foreign policy objectives, including confirmation of the Soviet Union's status as the "other" superpower, manifest improvement in relations with the United States, lessening of tensions in Europe, and enhanced capacity to influence developments in such proximate regional environments as the Middle East and northeast Asia. This is not to suggest that the leadership was altogether insensitive to the possible military advantages that might accrue to the Kremlin as a result of the steady growth in Soviet strategic nuclear capabilities; the military, for example, appears to have been quite dazzled, at least for a time, by the prospect of attaining some meaningful degree of military superiority over the United States.[44] It is to suggest, however, that for senior political leaders, including Brezhnev, such considerations may have been secondary to an explicit set of political objectives.

Viewed in such terms, Soviet goals in SALT, especially during the period 1972–1976, look rather different than they might otherwise. It is notable, for example, that in the weeks and months following the first Moscow summit in 1972, the Soviet press devoted at least as much attention to the twelve-point Basic Principles of Relations agreement, signed by Nixon and Brezhnev on May 29, as it did to the ABM Treaty and the Interim Agreement on Offensive Weapons, signed three days before. Moreover, in reviewing the various documents concluded at the summit, Soviet sources generally discussed the Basic Principles agreement first. By contrast, neither official Washington nor the American media said much about the agreement one way or the other.[45] The Soviets treated the accord as a fundamental breakthrough in superpower relations, opening up new and important opportunities for cooperation between Moscow and Washington. The Americans demonstrated no such enthusiasm—Nixon called it a road map for the possible future developments of relations—and, in general, were much more restrained in their characterization of the agreement.[46]

Even in describing the ABM Treaty and the Interim Agreement, Soviet spokesmen tended to emphasize their political and symbolic importance more than their military significance—nearly the reverse of the way in which the accords were assessed in the United States. Doubtless the leadership both understood and appreciated the value of the ABM Treaty, in particular, in closing off one potentially disturbing avenue of the strategic military competition. At the same time, the impression is inescapable that to Brezhnev and his Politburo colleagues, the simple existence of the SALT I agreements mattered no less than the actual content of the accords. For the Soviet Union, in other words, SALT I symbolized U.S. recognition of Moscow's fundamental military and political equality.

Having disposed of the central military issues in a satisfactory manner, Soviet leaders seemed to anticipate the further positive development of political and economic relations with the United States. As the leadership never tired of explaining to Western audiences, the relaxation of political tensions was a precondition for arms control, which, in turn, made possible additional progress at the political level.[47] According to the Kremlin's notion of sequencing, then, the period after May 1972 in U.S.–Soviet relations should have been devoted to the extension and refinement of the nascent political structure of the relationship—to détente—and not, as the Americans seemed to believe, to the conclusion of yet another series of agreements to regulate military forces. After all, the Soviets may have reasoned, the Interim Agreement was not due to expire until mid-1977—leaving more than enough time to "concretize" the improvement in political relations (and to develop more extensive economic ties) before returning to the thorny issue of nuclear arms control.

This conception of the appropriate sequencing of the relationship accounts in part for the desultory way in which the Soviets pursued the SALT II negotiations during the initial phase. It also helps to explain why Brezhnev and Gromyko pressed Nixon and Kissinger to conclude a second formal understanding on the nature of U.S.–Soviet political relations—the Agreement on the Prevention of Nuclear War—in time for the 1973 Washington summit, while manifesting only polite interest in achieving a breakthrough in SALT. The Soviets came to understand in the early part of 1974 that American policy-makers could not, as a practical matter, sanction additional movement on political and economic issues without fresh progress in arms control; only then did the Kremlin begin to advance SALT proposals of sufficient substance to engage Washington's interest.

Two meetings between American and Soviet officials during 1974 lend credence to this interpretation of events. When Kissinger met with Brezhnev in Moscow in March, the Soviet leader accepted the principle of unequal MIRVed missile limits, even as he rejected the precise numbers contained in the American proposal.[48] In his memoirs, Kissinger characterizes the Soviet concession as an important advance in the negotiations, a significant change in the Soviet position, which might have provided the impetus to break the deadlock in Geneva had the two sides persevered.[49] Instead, the negotiations stalled again during the spring, as the Soviets held back to await the outcome of the Watergate crisis, then entering its final phase.

The second indication that the Soviets were prepared to sanction the conclusion of a new arms control agreement in advance of concrete progress on political and economic relations with Washington was the September 1974 White House meeting between Ford and Gromyko. At that session, Gromyko conveyed the Kremlin's willingness to conclude a SALT agreement as expeditiously as possible along the lines proposed in the June 1974 summit communiqué: a ten-year treaty to limit strategic forces of the two sides, both quantitatively and qualitatively.[50] It is important to bear in mind that the Kremlin's strong endorsement of SALT came at a time of considerable uncertainty and some confusion in U.S.–Soviet relations, due in part to continuing problems over the interrelated issues of bilateral trade and Soviet emigration practices. In this instance, of course, Gromyko's intervention, coupled with the success of Kissinger's

October Moscow mission, did produce results, in the form of the Vladivostok accord.

The failure to translate the framework negotiated at Vladivostok into a formal treaty by the end of the Ford administration should not obscure the larger point that between the summer of 1972 and the fall of 1974, the Kremlin felt compelled to alter what it believed was the logical sequencing of its détente policy and that in the end it responded flexibly to that challenge. Soviet leaders did so despite their strong and well-advertised conviction that the ABM Treaty and the Interim Agreement constituted sufficient progress in arms control *for the time being* and that a follow-on agreement to regulate the two sides' strategic nuclear arsenals should await the further development of U.S.–Soviet political relations.

At the time, this subtle change in Soviet policy had little if any discernible impact on U.S. decision makers, who were themselves struggling in the midst of an intense domestic political crisis to define and implement a policy toward the Soviet Union that was without precedent in the American experience; that process had been, and would continue to be, time-consuming, divisive, and controversial. Nonetheless, Moscow's shift should be understood for what it was: an important departure in Soviet thinking, not easily or lightly sanctioned, that temporarily reinvigorated the superpower dialogue and contributed in a direct, if less than obvious, way to the conclusion of the SALT II Treaty in June 1979.

Soviet Preferences Regarding the Character of a New SALT Agreement

The Kremlin's movement away from its rather rigid conception of how the détente relationship was supposed to unfold necessitated extensive changes in the Soviet SALT strategy between 1972 and 1976. In the section that follows, the evolution of Soviet thinking about the structure of a new SALT agreement is assessed. Discussion of how Soviet authorities negotiated on the various substantive points at issue in SALT—on MIRVed missile limits, throwweight constraints, and forward-based systems, for example—is reserved for the third part of the analysis.

Before U.S. and Soviet authorities could engage one another on the specific provisions of any future SALT agreement, they had first to resolve three issues of a more general character: the duration of the agreement, its degree of complexity, and the balance between quantitative and qualitative constraints. The Soviet proposals of November 1972, which were modified only slightly during the ensuing fifteen months, addressed all three issues, after a fashion. According to the Soviet plan, the two sides would make permanent the five-year limits on ICBM and SLBM launchers contained in the Interim Agreement, while also undertaking a commitment to exercise "restraint" in the development and deployment of new strategic weapon systems. In addition, Soviet negotiators insisted on some form of compensation for U.S. forward-based nuclear-capable tactical aircraft and urged the withdrawal of U.S. ballistic missile submarines patrolling forward areas.[51]

The inclusion of the last two demands, particularly the second, suggests that Soviet policymakers felt under no great pressure to reach consensus in Geneva, reflecting the leadership's overall satisfaction with the results of SALT I, as well as its determination to focus Washington's energies on the political and economic aspects of the relationships and to defer serious negotiations on arms control to a later date. In this sense, the Soviet offer had the look of an opening gambit, an effort to stake out an extreme position that could be modified, at Moscow's discretion, in subsequent rounds. Leaving aside the problem of forward-deployed U.S. aircraft and missile-firing submarines, the November 1972 proposals also suggest, however, that the Soviets would have looked favorably on a simple ratification of the military status quo in that year, should the Americans have evidenced a willingness to go along. From the Kremlin's perspective, the numbers contained in the Interim Agreement were perfectly acceptable, as were the modest limitations governing ICBM silo modification and the deployment of large land-based missiles.

Throughout 1973, the Soviets remained faithful to the logic of their opening position: reaffirm the principle of unequal ICBM and SLBM launcher ceilings, avoid the complex formulas and negotiating minutiae to which Washington seemed drawn, and negotiate—in good faith but without much urgency—a new treaty of unlimited duration on strategic offensive forces. The Kremlin scored a partial victory on the last point at the 1973 Washington summit, when the two sides pledged to work toward the conclusion of a permanent accord to supersede the Interim Agreement. On balance, however, the Soviet proposals faced tough sledding. The United States made known early in the negotiations that the asymmetries contained in the Interim Agreement were unacceptable and would not be tolerated in a new SALT treaty. As noted, the administration also lobbied hard for provisions to equalize missile throwweight and to restrict the deployment of MIRVed ICBMs. In August 1973 Kissinger dismissed as inadequate and self-serving the one Soviet initiative of an ostensibly qualitative nature, namely, Ambassador Dobrynin's suggestion that the United States and the Soviet Union promise to forgo the deployment of "new" strategic weapon systems for a period of ten years, while permitting "modernization" of existing types to proceed unhindered.[52]

In 1974 the Kremlin modified its SALT strategy in several key respects, seeming to recognize that the fate of the negotiations—not to mention the future of détente more generally— hung in the balance. At the 1974 summit, the two sides, at U.S. urging, set aside the pursuit of a permanent agreement in favor of a ten-year treaty, to contain both quantitative and qualitative restraints. Of greater significance, in agreeing at Vladivostok to replace the asymmetrical launcher ceilings from SALT I with a new set of aggregates affording each side numerical equality, the Soviets abandoned their clear preference for a ratification of the military status quo; in signing the aide-mémoire of December 10, they had also taken a fateful step away from the notion of simplicity in SALT and in the direction of greater complexity— how much more complex they were to find out only in the months and years to come.

The Soviet retreat at Vladivostok was hardly a rout, however. For example, Moscow was able to negotiate a separate subceiling on MIRVed missile launchers that, at 1,320, was unlikely to restrain the Soviet MIRV program to any significant degree—an objective once at the heart of the American SALT strategy. In addition, the agreement said virtually nothing about qualitative measures to limit the arms race, such as restrictions on the introduction of new systems, on accuracy improvements, or on missile flight testing.

There is nothing remarkable about the fact that Soviet leaders revised their approach to SALT during 1974. Without such emendations on the part of negotiating partners, whoever they might be, no agreements would be possible. What *is* interesting about Soviet conduct between February and December 1974 is the abruptness of the Kremlin's turnabout and the facility with which the leadership seemed to sanction these adjustments. Clearly, the Soviets believed it necessary to produce a dramatic breakthrough in the negotiations. That they had come to this conclusion provides strong circumstantial evidence in support of the proposition that the Soviets had begun to see strategic arms control as the very core of the new relationship between the superpowers—the veritable engine of détente—and not, as they had written and said in 1972, as a kind of static celebration of the Soviet Union's arrival as Washington's military equal. For the Kremlin leadership, hardly the most flexible group of decision makers, such a shift in conception could hardly have come easily.

Negotiating the Particulars: Equal Security, FBS, and MIRVs

Reference has already been made to the Soviet Union's clear interest in perpetuating in SALT II the missile launcher ceilings written into the Interim Agreement. Kremlin negotiators offered elaborate justifications for maintaining the imbalance. The Chinese pointed their nuclear weapons at the Soviet Union; the British and the French did the same. The Americans had begun to deploy multiple warheads on their missiles; the Soviets had not. The United States had stationed hundreds of nuclear-capa-

ble aircraft within range of Soviet cities (and military installations); the Kremlin maintained no overseas bases. Soviet authorities cited these and other factors to rationalize and lend credence
to their demand that they be accorded numerical superiority in
ICBMs and SLBMs on a permanent basis. Such compensation,
they argued, was consistent with the principle of equal security.[53]
The Americans preferred the term "equality."

The source of the problem lay in the sharply different
geopolitical circumstances of the two superpowers, which gave
rise to an important definitional dispute. Washington held that
the negotiations were between the United States and the Soviet
Union; as such, they should focus only on the two sides' strategic
nuclear forces—long-range ballistic missiles, both land- and sea-
based, and heavy bombers. The Soviets eventually accepted the
first point, but they rejected the second throughout SALT I.
They argued that any U.S. or Soviet nuclear weapon capable of
reaching the territory of the other side should be considered
strategic, regardless of its range or external dimensions. What
mattered to Moscow, in other words, was not the origin of the
weapon, but its destination. According to the Soviet definition,
the American nuclear-armed F-4, A-6, and A-7 aircraft arrayed
around the borders of the USSR constituted no less a threat to
Soviet security than the Minuteman missiles deployed in the
continental United States. During the early rounds of SALT I, in
developing their case for an agreement based on the concept of
equal security rather than numerical equality, the Soviets advanced a similar argument, but without much conviction, concerning British and French nuclear systems—these were
weapons of the North Atlantic Treaty Organization, after all,
and as such should be considered part of an integrated Western
arsenal.[54]

When the SALT II negotiations began, the Soviets did not
renew their demand for explicit compensation in the form of
higher weapons totals because of British and French nuclear
systems. They did hold out, however, for the inclusion of U.S.
forward-based systems in the American weapons total. Just as
firmly, the United States declared FBS a nonissue. For two years

Washington and Moscow held their ground. Finally, in the fall of 1974, the Soviets yielded, agreeing not only to equality in strategic nuclear delivery vehicles (upon the expiration of the Interim Agreement in October 1977), but also to the exclusion from SALT of all U.S. forward-based systems. Setting the strategic weapons ceiling at 2,400 doubtless contributed to Moscow's newfound reasonableness on the issue; nonetheless, the concession was significant. When Paul Warnke, the director of the U.S. Arms Control Disarmament Agency, was in Moscow in March 1977 to help unveil a new set of strategic arms control proposals, a high-ranking member of the Soviet Foreign Ministry reminded him of the Soviet Union's previous concessions in SALT, citing, in particular, the senior leadership's willingness to dispose of the FBS issue in a manner favorable to the United States. "You shouldn't have disregarded the fact," the official is alleged to have said, "that Brezhnev had to spill political blood to get the Vladivostok accords."[55]

Soviet negotiators have never formally abandoned the position that all arms control agreements concluded by the superpowers should be based on the principle of equal security; as with other divisive issues in the relationship, the problem has been repeatedly finessed. In this case, the two sides' positions—equality and equal security—were simply placed side by side in the relevant documents. As a major obstacle in the negotiations, both then and now, however, the problem all but disappeared with Brezhnev's concession at Vladivostok.

If how to dispose of U.S. forward-based systems preoccupied Soviet leaders during the first two years of SALT II, how to limit MIRVs and MIRVed missile deployments troubled their American counterparts no less. In this instance, however, it was the United States that was repeatedly forced to redraw its proposals in order to overcome Soviet objections and to accommodate Moscow's demands.

From 1972 to mid-1974, the Nixon administration advanced a variety of plans to restrict the Soviet deployment of multiple warheads and MIRVed missile launchers. The proposals ranged from an outright moratorium on the testing and deployment of such weapons, to a limit on MIRVed ICBM throw-weight, to asymmetrical subceilings on missiles equipped with multiple warheads. Ultimately, Moscow rejected each of the U.S. initiatives as one-sided and prejudicial to Soviet security interests. The most promising of these proposals—to grant the United States a lead in the number of MIRVed missiles in exchange for Soviet superiority in the overall number of strategic nuclear systems—foundered in the early summer of 1974 as the Americans pressed for a greater asymmetry in MIRVed launchers than the Kremlin was prepared to tolerate. The issue was resolved only at Vladivostok, and then in a manner that signaled the essential collapse of the U.S. position, when the two sides agreed that each should be entitled to equal numbers of strategic nuclear delivery vehicles and to equal numbers of MIRVed weapons.

Moscow's refusal to go along with any of Washington's proposals to limit MIRV systems should have come as no surprise to U.S. policymakers. In November 1972, when the SALT II negotiations commenced, the American MIRV effort was in full swing; Soviet deployments had yet to begin. As suggested by Brezhnev's expression of interest in the principle of asymmetrical MIRV ceilings in the course of his March 1974 discussions with Kissinger, Moscow's tolerance for *any* agreement governing multiple-warhead systems that significantly departed from the notion of equality was extremely low. At that time, Brezhnev was prepared to sanction a U.S. margin of only 100 MIRVed launchers, to be counterbalanced by a Soviet advantage of 100 in the total number of strategic weapons. When the United States sought later that spring to widen the American MIRV lead, first to 150 systems and then to 300, the Soviets balked.[56] Given the extent of the USSR's investment in the procurement of a fourth generation of land-based missiles, two of which had been tested with multiple warheads ten months before Nixon and Brezhnev met for their third and final summit in June 1974, it is difficult to see how any plan that would have deprived the Soviet Union of rough equality in MIRVed systems could have been negotiated at any point during the initial phase of SALT II.

In the end, all of the major substantive issues that divided the superpowers in the period before Vladivostok were not so much resolved by the parties as they were accommodated. The United States insisted that the Soviets drop their demand on forward-based systems and agree to an equal aggregate weapons ceiling. The Kremlin did so, but in return secured a weapons ceiling that provided the Soviet Union with a de facto advantage of some 400 strategic launchers at the time of the agreement's signing. It also obtained Washington's agreement to extend the principle of equality to MIRVed missile systems.

Though hardly unique in the history of U.S.–Soviet arms control, this willingness to sanction an outcome based on the logic of the lowest common denominator had seldom been more explicit. One consequence of this approach, which neither side could have anticipated at the time, was a further erosion in the domestic U.S. base of support for strategic arms control, which, as Jimmy Carter was to discover in 1977, complicated the later negotiations. It also made the SALT II Treaty, once concluded, less rather than more appealing to the American public and to a skeptical Congress. What seemed, in other words, an entirely acceptable if imperfect solution to a vexing set of problems in November 1974 had taken on, within several months of its signing, a decidedly negative political cast, especially in the United States. It was one of the blows from which the SALT process never completely recovered.

The issues remaining *after* Vladivostok, cruise missiles and the Backfire bomber, could not be resolved in the same fashion. Despite repeated attempts throughout 1975 to devise a formula whereby concessions in one area might be offset by concessions in the other, compromise proved elusive. By then, of course, the overall deterioration in superpower relations, as well as the approach of the 1976 presidential election, had begun to have a negative spillover effect in SALT, depriving the Ford administration of the kind of negotiating latitude required to achieve consensus on contentious issues. The relative facility with which U.S. and Soviet negotiators were able to arrive at mutually acceptable compromises on Backfire and cruise missiles after 1977

68

suggests that the difficulties during President Ford's last two years in office had more to do with American domestic politics and the state of U.S.–Soviet relations than with any insurmountable technical problems.

The Rise of an Arms Control "Process" in the Soviet Union

Many U.S. analysts are persuaded that it was during the initial years of SALT II, from 1972 to 1976, as the negotiations grew progressively more complex, that Soviet decision makers began to assemble the elements of a political-governmental system to assist in the formulation and conduct of the Kremlin's arms control policies. Most are also agreed that no one outside the system, Western or Soviet, knew—or knows—very much about it: how and when it began, how it developed, how it evolved, and how it functioned, beyond the reasonable assumption that it was made up of both formal and informal structures that in some cases included and in other cases reported to the country's most senior officials. The traditional Soviet disinclination to acknowledge the existence of, let alone discuss, such sensitive arrangements requires that any characterization of this presumed system be largely speculative in nature, although additional insights may be forthcoming should the tendency toward greater openness concerning the workings of the Soviet decision-making process continue.

Relatively few elements of the Soviet national security decision-making structure were known to Western observers during the mid-1970s; moreover, those that were known provided only the sketchiest of insights into how the system actually functioned. It was not until the late 1970s, for example, that the West learned of the existence of the Defense Council, a small group of very senior Soviet officials with special responsibilities in the area of national security, chaired by the general secretary in his capacity as commander in chief of the armed forces and ranking Politburo member. To this day, the membership of the Defense Council remains something of a mystery, as does an exact understanding of its duties. U.S. analysts have assumed, however, that the members of this body make all key decisions regarding Soviet arms control policy.[57]

During the mid-1970s, the Ministry of Defense, the Foreign Ministry, the Party Secretariat, and various departments of the Central Committee staff are assumed to have shared primary responsibility for the consideration of negotiating options and the generation of Soviet arms control proposals. Other ministries, agencies, commissions, and ad hoc groups also may have played a part in the process, depending on the issues under review. Of these various bureaucratic actors, the Ministry of Defense and, in particular, the Soviet General Staff are believed to have had a special and privileged voice, in light of the implications of arms control for Soviet national security and defense policy. It is not known how the activities of these institutions were coordinated, nor who might have performed this function. We know of no direct Soviet analogue, for example, to the SALT Verification Panel, the committee chaired by Kissinger in his capacity as national security adviser, which was vested with these and related responsibilities in the Nixon White House.

Whatever the particular institutional arrangements that may have influenced the shape and character of Soviet arms control policies, one of the most interesting political developments during these years was Leonid Brezhnev's clear ascendancy within the Kremlin leadership as first among equals on matters relating to SALT. The evidence that can be marshaled in support of this assertion is compelling, though not definitive, and much of it is anecdotal. Many of the Americans who took part in the negotiations have written about Brezhnev's role in SALT and about his gradual but steady accumulation of power as the talks progressed.[58] Examples of the general secretary's special weight in the negotiating process, and in conduct of U.S.–Soviet relations more generally, figure prominently in the SALT literature. When Richard Nixon arrived in Moscow in May 1972, he was met at the airport tarmac by Nikolai Podgorny, chairman of the presidium of the Supreme Soviet. Upon Nixon's return to the Soviet capital, in June 1974, Podgorny was nowhere to be seen. Instead, Brezhnev welcomed the American president, despite the manifest breach in protocol.[59] The general secretary, who held no position within the state apparatus at the time, should have deferred either to Podgorny, as head of state, or to Alexei Kosygin, as head of government. He chose not to do so.

Kissinger recounts Brezhnev's central involvement in most aspects of the negotiations, including those occasions on which Kissinger traveled to Moscow, first as Nixon's personal emissary and later as secretary of state.[60] At many of these meetings, the two men negotiated directly and individually on sensitive and complex issues; at other times, they were joined by Foreign Minister Gromyko. As the relationship developed, Brezhnev's tendency to go it alone became more pronounced. At one particular fateful Moscow meeting, in March 1974, Kissinger leaves the distinct impression that it was Brezhnev, sorting through the relevant numbers, who made the key decision to accept, in principle, the U.S. proposal for unequal MIRVed missile limits. At the same time, Kissinger is careful to point out that Brezhnev appeared to operate as the Politburo's agent for SALT, the duly authorized and designated representative of the collective leadership, and not as an autonomous decision maker.[61] As powerful as he may have been, in other words, his authority was not unlimited. This interpretation conforms to the views of others who have studied Brezhnev's role in SALT, including Garthoff and Wolfe.[62]

A second interesting issue that arises from an analysis of this period in Soviet national security decision making is the nature of the relationship between senior political leaders, especially Brezhnev, and the uniformed military. Most Western scholars who have examined Soviet civil-military relations during the SALT decade agree that the partnership between ranking political and military figures was, for the most part, harmonious, though not without occasional strain. Contributing to the harmony, they argue, was the Politburo's generous allocation of resources to the armed forces, which made possible a steady expansion in Soviet military capabilities during the first half of the 1970s. The party also accorded high status and special privileges to senior officers, glorified the Red Army's accomplishments in war and peace, and emphasized the military's important and ongoing contributions to the building of socialism. Returning the favor, the military regularly reaffirmed the party's leading role as the vanguard force in Soviet society, refrained from overtly criticizing either the conduct or the directives of the political leadership, and acquiesced to the civilians on matters relating to the execution and implementation of national security policy, including arms control.[63] Such tensions as may have existed were resolved in camera and seldom, if ever, surfaced publicly.

The military press did publish a series of articles in 1974 focusing on the role of nuclear arms control in Soviet policy in which the authors struck a careful balance between support of the process and the continuing need for military vigilance.[64] The articles seemed to be an attempt to interpret for a military audience the function of arms control agreements within Soviet policy and to place such initiatives in a broader political-military context—as one increasingly vital component of the country's national security policy, which, under the party's guidance, could contribute directly to the safety and well-being of the entire socialist community. They also could be considered a subtle reminder to senior political leaders that negotiating with the Americans on the limitation of strategic nuclear forces stood to benefit the Soviet Union only to the extent that the resulting agreements served the country's security interests, leaving open the possibility that military and civilian authorities might not always have been of a single mind on what constituted "good" arms control. One would be hard-pressed, however, to extract from these writings such veiled warnings.

The most obvious manifestation of the military's high-level involvement in Soviet arms control policy was the active participation of uniformed officers in the negotiating sessions at both the third summit and the November 1974 meetings at Vladivostok. On the first occasion, Brezhnev was joined by Colonel General Kozlov of the General Staff, who, according to Garthoff, "actively assisted" the general secretary in describing to Nixon and Kissinger, in great detail, the American military threat as seen from Moscow.[65] At Vladivostok, events took a different and more interesting turn. Brezhnev was again the beneficiary of the military's assistance, in the form of two generals who sat at his side during most of the negotiations. In this instance, however, Kissinger and Dobrynin joined forces to reduce the size of the U.S. and Soviet delegations when they sensed toward the end of the meetings that the talks were becoming stalemated. As a result, therefore, of Soviet and American collusion, the two generals lost their places at the bargaining table. At key junctures, again according to Garthoff (quoting Kissinger), the Soviet side would call for a break in the negotiations, permitting Brezhnev to consult his military advisers and to contact Moscow.[66] Here, then, is the one public case in which the ostensible identity of interests between Soviet political and military leaders on SALT-related issues appears to have broken down. The fact that Dobrynin, rather than Kissinger, proposed the scheme to limit attendance at the meetings would tend to support this hypothesis. On the other hand, Kissinger, as well as others who have reported on this drama, may have been reading more into the episode than the evidence warrants; to a degree, at least, they may have seen what they wanted to see.

As is almost always the case in analyzing the internal dynamics of the Soviet political process, the ability to render firm judgments is limited by the relatively closed nature of the system. Analysts are left to draw conclusions from data that are often fragmentary, inconsistent, and less than completely reliable. As an exercise in Sovietology, assessing the military's role in SALT II negotiations is hardly immune to such limitations. What can one usefully say, then, about the state of Soviet civil-military relations during the years 1972–1976?

On balance, the impression that emerges is one of consensual decision making, in which the goals and objectives of the senior political and military leadership largely coincided. The civilians would negotiate arms control agreements to restrict at least some U.S. military programs and to foreclose various American military options, while at the same time permitting the modernization of Soviet weapon systems to proceed largely on schedule. Its essential interests served, the military would hold in check its deeply embedded suspicions about negotiated security arrangements with the principal adversary, support the political line, and provide such advice and assistance to ranking party and government officials as the latter deemed appropriate. Whatever differences might develop in the course of the negotiations would be resolved quietly and in a collegial manner, within the secure walls of the Kremlin. For all concerned, it appears to have constituted a workable and eminently sensible solution to what otherwise might have been a difficult and divisive situation.

The ongoing nature of superpower arms control negotiations also contributed to the development of a civilian-based community of experts on the United States and on U.S.–Soviet relations. It was during these years, for example, that the Academy of Sciences' Institute of the U.S.A. and Canada, established in 1968, first rose to prominence within the Soviet system. The Institute's director, Georgi Arbatov, wrote extensively on superpower relations at this time, including two particularly important articles in July 1973 and July 1974 that summed up and put into perspective for Soviet readers the results of the second two summit sessions.[67] Despite the passage of time, these and other of Arbatov's writings make for fascinating reading. Arbatov, along with Secretariat Aide Andrei Alexander-Agentov, a specialist on strategic arms control, was said to have enjoyed excellent access to the senior leadership and to have participated in many of the high-level meetings at which U.S.–Soviet relations were discussed and decisions reached. Several of the institute's deputy directors, including Vitaly Zhurkin, also achieved a degree of professional visibility both within and outside the USSR that at the time was unusual for Soviet academics. To a lesser extent, officials of the Institute of World Economics and International Relations (more familiarly known by its Russian acronym, IMEMO) were also tapped for duty, although they appear to have enjoyed neither the access to policymakers nor the influence on policy that was accorded their colleagues at the U.S.A. Institute.

Did representatives of these various party, governmental, and nongovernmental organizations—the Secretariat, the International Department of the Central Committee, the Defense and Foreign ministries, and the Academy of Sciences—make up during these years what might be thought of as a loosely constituted national security community within the Soviet system? If by the term "community" we mean a collection of individuals who, by virtue of their positions and expertise, directly and indirectly influenced both the character and the content of Soviet arms control policies, the question can be answered in the affirmative. If, on the other hand, we mean to imply something more, such as an officially sanctioned set of relationships cutting across various institutional and bureaucratic divisions to produce a distinct "cluster" of officials with special responsibilities in this area of Soviet policy, our answer must be more tentative. A more detailed understanding of how the Soviet national security decision-making process functioned between 1972 and 1976 lies beyond our reach. The most that can be said is that a small subset of senior officials—led by the general secretary, but including representatives of those Soviet bureaucracies with a recognized and sanctioned interest in the negotiations—made all critical decisions relating to SALT and that in this effort they appear to have been assisted by a set of advisers, drawn from a number of institutions, who may or may not have functioned as a collective, but who performed vital staff functions.

U.S. Domestic Politics and SALT: The Soviet View

In considering how the Soviets might have assessed the impact of domestic U.S. politics on the SALT II negotiations, and on the course of superpower relations more generally, it is important to distinguish between two quite different manifestations of what the Kremlin doubtless saw as a central and growing problem in the relationship.

On the one hand, arrayed in opposition to the Soviet policies of the Nixon and Ford administrations was a small but influential group of critics, made up of a handful of senators and representatives whose views coincided with those of a number of former government officials, foreign policy experts, professional commentators, journalists, and interested citizens. Their concerns ranged from a general unease over the direction of American foreign policy and the apparent erosion of U.S. political, economic, and military leadership in the world, to more concrete fears centering on the growth in Soviet strategic capabilities and the Kremlin's newfound willingness to assert its interests in distant geographic areas. Still others focused on the repressive character of the Soviet political system, as evidenced in its treatment of dissidents and its refusal to permit unrestricted emigration, especially for Jews wishing to settle in Israel or elsewhere in the West. The group's acknowledged leader was Senator Henry Jackson, Democrat of Washington.

Soviet leaders were surprised at neither the existence nor the influence of the opposition. For years they had charted the struggle in Washington between what they labeled the forces of reaction and the forces of realism for control of American foreign policy. Consistently, in their opinion, the "cold warriors" had prevailed—outtalking, outspending, and outvoting those within the U.S. political system who counseled some form of accommodation with Moscow. Nixon's advocacy of and support for détente had temporarily neutralized the power of the right in American politics, but in the Kremlin's estimation the "realist" hold on policy was as yet a tentative one. At no point during the early or mid-1970s were the Soviets prepared to argue that the proponents of détente had scored a decisive victory over the opposition. In the Soviet view, right-wing forces in the United States could draw on considerable political and economic reserves with which to obstruct the development of more positive relations between the superpowers.

On the other hand, with the Watergate scandal and its debilitating effect on the Nixon presidency, the Soviets also had to contend with something they had not anticipated, could not control, and never did seem to understand. This was confusing enough. To make matters worse from the Kremlin's vantage point, as the crisis unfolded and Nixon's authority eroded during 1973 and 1974, the domestic critics of détente acquired progressively greater influence over the direction and content of the administration's Soviet policies. Nixon's weakness emboldened Jackson and those allied with him to escalate their demands and to abjure compromise. The result was a policy impasse. In the weeks immediately preceding Nixon's resignation, the Kremlin watched as all forward movement in U.S.–Soviet relations ceased. The SALT negotiations, which had limped along through the spring, also ground to a halt.

Soviet leaders responded to these two challenges—the domestic U.S. opposition to détente and the Watergate crisis—in very different ways. To overcome the first, the leadership worked closely, if not always smoothly, with the Nixon and Ford administrations to appease at least some of the concerns expressed by détente's critics. Following the introduction of the Jackson and Vanik amendments to the Trade Reform Act in the spring of 1973, for example, the Soviets, even as they denounced the linkage between trade and economic issues and Soviet emigration practices, communicated to the administration their willingness to suspend the "exit tax" and to grant a larger number of exit visas than they had in previous years. Prolonged negotiations ensued—between the Kremlin and the White House, and between the White House and Senator Jackson. Some progress was achieved: emigration from the Soviet Union increased from 25,000 in 1972 to 35,000 in 1973.[68]

In the spring of 1974, however, relations suffered a setback, as Senator Jackson demanded a Soviet commitment to permit the emigration of at least 60,000 people per year. Kissinger, Dobrynin, and Gromyko labored to resolve the conflict on terms acceptable to both sides, but in the end their efforts failed. When the trade reform bill, containing Jackson's amendment linking most-favored-nation status to the abolition of the exit tax, finally passed the Congress in December 1974, the Kremlin reacted sharply, condemning the measure as an attempt to meddle in Soviet internal affairs. The following month, Soviet officials notified Washington that the 1972 U.S.–Soviet trade bill could not be brought into force "at this time."[69] In 1974, the number of individuals allowed to emigrate from the Soviet Union declined to 21,000; in 1975, the figure dropped to 13,000.[70]

The inability of the U.S. and Soviet officials to strike a deal on emigration is less important for purposes of this analysis than is the fact that for two years the Kremlin actively pursued a negotiated outcome to what was, and continues to be, an extraordinarily sensitive domestic issue for the Soviet regime; moreover, as the Soviets recognized throughout the process, it was an issue that had been defined, dramatized, and manipulated by American forces hostile to détente and to the Soviet Union for reasons that had only partially to do with concern for the plight of Soviet Jews.

The sophisticated and relatively deft manner in which Soviet authorities dealt with the problems generated by Senator Jackson and his allies was nowhere in evidence when it came to Watergate. The Kremlin understood the origins, the power, the objectives, and perhaps even the psychology of Washington's cold warriors. By contrast, the slow unraveling of the Nixon presidency, especially in the early phases of the crisis, seemed to baffle, confuse, and astound the Soviets. How could the most powerful man in American politics, reelected by a lopsided majority in 1972, be brought so low so quickly over something as mundane as a misdemeanor offense against property, authorized by midlevel members of his political staff?

It was only when the seriousness of the crisis could no longer be denied, when the political talk in Washington turned to impeachment, that the Soviets began to express both genuine unease and a profound interest in the proceedings. In April 1974, for example, Gromyko asked Kissinger about the constitutional mechanism to replace a sitting president.[71] Two months later, at the Moscow summit, Nixon toasted the continuing improvement in superpower relations, a phenomenon he attributed in part to "the personal relationship" that he had established "between the General Secretary and the President of the United States."[72] Brezhnev, looking toward the future, toasted Congress and the American people.[73]

By the time of Nixon's second presidential visit to Moscow, the Soviets had begun to sense that the end was near. They kept up appearances, nonetheless. In Arbatov's semiofficial commentary on the state of U.S.–Soviet relations, he left the distinct impression that the prospects for the further positive development of relations were good, despite the persistence of serious differences between Washington and Moscow on matters of policy.[74] The Soviets could say little else at the time, of course, given diplomatic courtesy and the uncertainties then attending the domestic American political scene. Six years later, as Garthoff has pointed out, they could write about the impact of Watergate on détente and arms control with many fewer constraints. Interestingly, one Soviet commentator, in explaining Nixon's fall, cited "the massive intrigues" of détente's opponents—the pernicious influence of the forces of reaction—in addition to the administration's "own abuses of power."[75]

The argument that Nixon was forced from office primarily by powerful and sinister opposition to the regularization of U.S.– Soviet relations, and only secondarily by his conduct in office, is a recurring theme among Soviet observers of American affairs, even fifteen years after the fact.[76] For the Soviets, never well attuned to the fine points of U.S. constitutional law and doctrine, Nixon had moved too far too fast against the interests of right-wing ideologues and their friends in the "military-industrial complex," who stood to lose valuable Pentagon contracts in the event of additional progress in arms control. Joining these forces, in the Soviet view, were American Zionists, servants of Israel, who detested the Soviet Union and stopped at nothing to secure the release of their coreligionists—even if their strategy of relentlessly pressuring Moscow endangered the very objective they were fighting so hard to achieve.

When Ford succeeded Nixon, the Soviet leadership saw an opportunity to revive détente's sagging fortunes, as suggested by Gromyko's assurance to the new president in September 1974 that the Kremlin was eager to sign a new arms control agreement as soon as possible, consistent with the terms that had been discussed in previous negotiating sessions. The Soviets may have anticipated that by doing so they might silence détente's critics in the United States, or place them on the defensive, at least temporarily. If so, their hopes were dashed by passage of the Trade Reform Act, less than a month after the signing of the Vladivostok accord.

The Soviets never sought to trivialize the substantive differences that complicated the SALT negotiations between November 1972 and the end of President Ford's term. They understood that resolving disagreements over forward-based systems, launcher limits, cruise missiles, and the Backfire bomber required time, skill, and patience. They also understood, however, that absent one additional ingredient, political will, no agreement was possible. In their assessment, it was precisely the lack of such will, due first to Nixon's preoccupation with Watergate and later to Ford's relatively weak domestic base, that prevented the two sides from completing a SALT treaty in 1975 or in the first part of 1976. It was a problem they would again encounter several years later under a different president and for different reasons.

REFLECTIONS

Every discrete period in the history of U.S.–Soviet arms control is to a greater or lesser degree an extension of what has come before and a preview of what lies ahead. SALT I determined many of the issues negotiated during the first four years of SALT II. At the same time, the latter negotiations directly influenced both the tone and the substance of strategic arms control from 1977 to 1979. It is also true, however, that each phase has unique features.

The SALT II negotiations between November 1972 and the spring of 1976 are no exception. They occupy a confusing and complex middle ground between the beginning of a process and its maturation, during which time the two superpowers sought— with only limited success—both to redefine their political relationship and to regulate various aspects of the strategic military competition. The negotiations are especially interesting for what they reveal about possible Soviet perceptions and motives. How did Kremlin leaders think about this period? What lessons did they learn from the experience of negotiating with the United States during these "years of upheaval"?

The evidence suggests that the Soviets were ill prepared for what they were about to encounter. Having successfully concluded the May 1972 agreements limiting anti-ballistic missile systems and the deployment of long-range ballistic missiles, the leadership seemed to believe that the most difficult and sensitive aspect to the restructuring of U.S.–Soviet relations was behind them. What could be harder than negotiating constraints on strategic nuclear weapons, the ultimate guarantor of national security and the very symbol of what it meant to be a superpower? As a consequence of that achievement, they seemed to anticipate the further positive development of relations with Washington both politically and economically. They were, it appears, building for the long term, eager to put in place the architecture to make détente "irreversible." To the extent they foresaw that additional negotiations on strategic forces would be required to advance this goal, they seemed to have convinced themselves that the Americans would accede to a codification of the quantitative military balance then in place and to a continuation of the qualitative competition, though at a somewhat reduced pace. They were wrong on all counts.

They soon discovered that the Nixon administration was either unwilling or unable to accept Moscow's somewhat mechanistic notions about the proper sequencing of détente. As a practical political matter, the Americans made clear, a second round of negotiations to limit the nuclear weapons arsenals of the two sides was central, not peripheral, to the further development of U.S.–Soviet relations. Moreover, a number of issues the Soviets thought resolved in 1972, such as aggregate launcher levels and the permissibility of strategic modernization, were suddenly back on the negotiating table. Soviet leaders resisted the American initiatives for the better part of two years, patiently explaining to their U.S. counterparts that while additional progress in arms control was indeed possible, what the relationship required in the aftermath of SALT I was a strong political impetus.

At this juncture the Soviets were faced with a difficult political decision. On the one hand, they could hold firm to their position and wait for the United States to amend its strategy. Such a decision on Moscow's part would hardly have been unprecedented. On the other hand, they could modify their SALT stance in order to invigorate the negotiations and to generate reciprocal concessions from Washington. In the late winter of 1974 they chose the second option. The negotiations, moribund for months, began to move off dead center. Allowing for the delay imposed by the final act of the Watergate drama, the movement toward agreement continued throughout the year, culminating in the Vladivostok accord.

The leadership's decision to alter its course signaled more than a tactical adjustment. It represented a sophisticated, if delayed, response to the shifting context of U.S.–Soviet relations brought about by the rising influence of détente's critics in the United States and the approaching collapse of the Nixon presidency, among other factors. By their willingness to sanction a new arms control agreement—even in the absence of satisfactory progress in political and economic relations—the Soviets demonstrated a degree of flexibility seldom associated with the Brezhnev regime. They also, and more importantly, demonstrated a relatively subtle understanding of the ways in which even modest changes in their behavior could redound to their political advantage by influencing the state of public and elite opinion in the United States. It was a lesson that was to serve them well in later years.

With their decision to press ahead in SALT despite the manifest political obstacles, the Soviets had still to resolve with Washington the several outstanding substantive differences separating the two sides. The manner in which the American and Soviet officials eventually overcame their differences should be of more than passing interest to arms control analysts; it strongly suggests that as late as the mid-1970s, the Kremlin believed it possible to combine agreements in SALT with the existing military strategy and prospective force deployments. Moscow's recourse to solutions based on the logic of the "lowest common denominator" enabled it to reach important agreements with the United States while, at the same time, continuing to develop and deploy strategic nuclear forces whose primary mission, should deterrence fail, was to limit damage to the Soviet Union. With the exception of the ABM Treaty, which they saw as essential to safeguard their strategic retaliatory capability, the Soviets rejected all U.S. efforts to employ the SALT negotiations to impart greater stability to the superpower military competition—preferring, it seems, to rely on the threat to prevail, rather than on the threat to avenge, to deter the outbreak of war with the West. This, too, seems to have changed, though neither as much nor as fast as some observers have proclaimed.

In retrospect, what is so striking about this first phase of SALT II is not how little the two countries achieved, but how much. Starting off with a firm conception of how it wanted détente to develop, which in 1972 did not include a lengthy second agreement to limit strategic offensive forces, the Soviets were forced to retreat and regroup as their negotiating partners offered at first a contrasting vision and then no vision at all. As they fell back, they also advanced, however, gaining valuable insights into the workings of the U.S. political process and the preoccupations of the American strategic community. For Brezhnev and his Politburo colleagues, the experience could hardly have been an unalloyed pleasure. Learning seldom is. Yet, as Lenin might have reminded his successors, all political struggles, be they domestic or international in character, unfold in an agonizingly nonlinear way. As the leadership was about to discover, the situation would get worse before it got better.

NOTES

1. Quoted in Raymond L. Garthoff, *Détente and Confrontation: American-Soviet Relations from Nixon to Reagan* (Washington, D.C.: Brookings Institution, 1985), p. 451.
2. Ibid.; William G. Hyland, *Mortal Rivals: Superpower Relations from Nixon to Reagan* (New York: Random House, 1987); Strobe Talbott, *Endgame: The*

Inside Story of SALT II (New York: Harper Colophon Books, 1980); and Thomas W. Wolfe, *The SALT Experience* (Cambridge Mass.: Ballinger, 1979).

3. Henry A. Kissinger, *Years of Upheaval* (Boston: Little, Brown & Co., 1982).
4. Garthoff, *Détente and Confrontation*, p. 307; and Kissinger, *Years of Upheaval*, p. 249.
5. Garthoff, *Détente and Confrontation*, pp. 309–310.
6. Bernard Gwertzman, "Little Progress Reported in U.S.–Soviet Arms Talks," *The New York Times*, January 9, 1973, p. 1.
7. Kissinger, *Years of Upheaval*, p. 267.
8. Ibid.
9. Gwertzman, "Little Progress," p. 1.
10. Garthoff, *Détente and Confrontation*, pp. 327–329; and Kissinger, *Years of Upheaval*, p. 270.
11. Kissinger, *Years of Upheaval*, p. 272.
12. Ibid., pp. 270–271.
13. Ibid., pp. 271–272.
14. "Basic Principles of Negotiations on the Further Limitation of Strategic Offensive Weapons," reprinted in *Survival* 15, no. 5 (1973), p. 244.
15. Kissinger, *Years of Upheaval*, pp. 1016–1017.
16. Kissinger attributed the lack of Kremlin initiative to the nature of the Soviet system. "Experience has shown," he wrote, "that the Soviet bureaucracy may be structurally incapable of originating a creative SALT position." See *Years of Upheaval*, p. 1007. Although Soviet arms control proposals since the advent of Gorbachev suggest otherwise, Kissinger's characterization of Soviet lethargy during both phases of the SALT negotiations is borne out by the evidence. See below.
17. Ibid., p. 1014.
18. Ibid., p. 1015.
19. Garthoff, *Détente and Confrontation*, p. 419.
20. Wolfe, *The SALT Experience*, p. 97.
21. Kissinger, *Years of Upheaval*, p. 1018.
22. Ibid., p. 1023.
23. Ibid., p. 1024.
24. Ibid., p. 1026.
25. Ibid., p. 1152.
26. Quoted in Garthoff, *Détente and Confrontation*, p. 423.
27. Ibid.
28. "Text of Nuclear Accords and Joint Statement," *The New York Times*, July 4, 1974, p. 2.
29. Ibid.
30. Garthoff, *Détente and Confrontation*, pp. 443–444.
31. Ibid., p. 444.
32. Ibid.; and Kissinger, *Years of Upheaval*, p. 1018.
33. Garthoff, *Détente and Confrontation*, pp. 445–446; and John Herbers, "Ford, Brezhnev Agree to Curb Offensive Nuclear Weapons; Final Pact Would Run to 1985," *The New York Times*, November 25, 1974, p.1. See also

"Text of Ford-Brezhnev Communiqué," *The New York Times*, November 25, 1974, p. 14.

34. Garthoff, *Détente and Confrontation*, pp. 446–447.

35. Ibid., pp. 447–448; and Wolfe, *The SALT Experience*, pp. 126–127, 177, and 200–202. These two are the best accounts.

36. U.S. and Soviet officials agreed that any long-range land- or sea-based ballistic missile tested with multiple independently targetable reentry vehicles would constitute a MIRVed system and that for counting purposes, any such system would be considered equipped with the largest number of reentry vehicles ever tested on that system.

37. Bernard Gwertzman, "Ford Says Accord Gives a Basis for Cut in Arms," *The New York Times*, December 3, 1974, p. 1; and John W. Finney, "Pentagon Chief Sees Pact Leading to Arms Buildup," *The New York Times*, December 7, 1974, p. 28.

38. Garthoff, *Détente and Confrontation*, p. 450.

39. Wolfe, *The SALT Experience*, p. 201.

40. Garthoff, *Détente and Confrontation*, pp. 540–543.

41. Ibid., pp. 543–544.

42. The Soviet literature on the correlation of forces is voluminous. For a discussion of its role in the shaping of Soviet foreign policy during the first half of the 1970s, see Coit D. Blacker, "The Soviet Union and Mutual Force Reductions: The Role of Military Détente in the European Security Policy of the U.S.S.R.," Ph.D. diss., Fletcher School of Law and Diplomacy, 1978, pp. 13–19. See also————"The Kremlin and Détente: Soviet Conceptions, Hopes and Expectations," in Alexander L. George et al., *Managing U.S.–Soviet Rivalry: Problems of Crisis Prevention* (Boulder: Westview Press, 1983), especially pp. 121–129.

43. See, in particular, Nikolai Podgorny, address in Riga, Latvia S.S.R., December 26, 1973 (translated in Foreign Broadcast Information Service, *Soviet Union*, January 3, 1974, p. R11).

44. Throughout the period under review, the doctrinal pronouncements of senior Soviet military officials continued to emphasize the undiminished utility of robust strategic offensive and defensive military forces to "frustrate" the military objectives of the West, should deterrence fail despite Soviet efforts. Explicit references to "victory" in the event of a strategic nuclear war between the superpowers were infrequent during these years (though not absent entirely), but the implication—that through proper preparation, timely warning, and near-flawless execution, victory could be attained—was unmistakable. Precisely why the Soviet military was prepared to argue in these terms, given the reality of mutual nuclear deterrence (powerfully affirmed in the 1972 ABM Treaty), as well as the evident willingness and demonstrated capacity of the United States to maintain the deterrent relationship, is more difficult to determine. Several explanations come to mind. Soviet military planners may have believed, in light of the record of the preceding half-decade, that they could continue to make incremental improvements to the Soviet Union's military posture without arousing a forceful U.S. response, eventually garnering enough of an edge to produce decisive military advantage. They may also have concluded that

whatever the long-term future, the near-to-medium term looked quite favorable militarily, and thus may have been encouraged to proceed with plans to increase particularly the counterforce potential of their most advanced strategic nuclear systems. Finally, to ensure the uninterrupted flow of resources to the defense sector, the military may have argued to the political leadership that the traditional goals of Soviet military strategy could still be realized within the kind of arms control regime likely to emerge from the negotiations with Washington, permitting the Kremlin simultaneously to achieve two sets of objectives—better relations with Washington and victory in the event of war. Senior political leaders, encouraged by the seemingly beneficial consequences of the worldwide shift in the correlation of forces to Moscow's advantage, may have found the military's logic both reassuring and compelling—at least for a time.

45. See, for example, G. Arbatov, "Sila politiki realizma k itogam Sovetsko-Amerikanskikh peregovorov na vysshem urovne," *Izvestia,* June 22, 1972, pp. 3–4. See also "Sovetsko-Amerikanskie otnosheniya na novom etape," *Pravda,* July 22, 1973, p. 4; and M. A. Mil'steyn and L. S. Semeyko, "Ogranichenie strategicheskikh vooruzhenii: problemi i perspektivi," *SShA: ekonomika, politika, ideologia,* no. 12, 1973, pp. 3–13.
46. Kissinger, *Years of Upheaval,* p. 1253.
47. See, in particular, Ye. Primakov, "Disarmament: Paramount Task," *New Times,* no. 33, 1975, p. 22; D. Proektor, "Urgent Problems of Security and Cooperation in Europe," *International Affairs* (June 1974), p. 70; and Ye. Primakov, "Politicheskaya pazryadka i problemi razoruzheniya," *Mirovaya ekonomika mezhdunarodniye otnosheniya,* no. 10, 1975, p. 4.
48. Kissinger, *Years of Upheaval,* p. 1253.
49. Ibid.
50. Garthoff, *Détente and Confrontation,* pp. 442–443.
51. Kissinger, *Years of Upheaval,* pp. 267–270.
52. Ibid., pp. 1014–1015.
53. Ibid., p. 1014.
54. Gerard Smith, *Doubletalk: The Story of the First Strategic Arms Limitation Talks* (Garden City, N.Y.: Doubleday, 1980), pp. 132–133, 145; and John Newhouse, *Cold Dawn: The Story of SALT* (New York: Holt, Rinehart and Winston, 1973), p. 175.
55. Quoted in Garthoff, *Détente and Confrontation,* p. 465.
56. Wolfe, *The SALT Experience,* p. 101; and Kissinger, *Years of Upheaval,* pp. 1157–1158.
57. See the following in Jiri Valenta and William Potter, eds., *Soviet Decision Making for National Security* (London: George Allen & Unwin, 1984): Ellen Jones, "Defense R&D Policymaking in the USSR," pp. 124–125, and Raymond Garthoff, "The Soviet Military and SALT," p. 144.
58. Kissinger, *Years of Upheaval,* pp. 1164, 1170; and Garthoff, *Détente and Confrontation,* pp. 421, 428–429, 465–466.
59. Kissinger, *Years of Upheaval,* p. 1161.
60. Ibid., pp. 1021, 1024–1025, 1164.
61. Ibid., p. 1023.

62. Garthoff, *Détente and Confrontation,* pp. 429 and 465; for a more complete discussion, see Wolfe, *The SALT Experience,* pp. 50–70.
63. Garthoff, *Détente and Confrontation,* pp. 430 and 433. See also David Holloway, "War, Militarism, and the Soviet State," Working Paper 17, World Order Models Project (New York: World Order, 1981).
64. See, in particular, the analysis contained in Wolfe, *The SALT Experience,* pp. 72–77.
65. Garthoff, *Détente and Confrontation,* p. 429.
66. Ibid., p. 430.
67. Arbatov, "Sovetsko-Amerikanskie otnosheniya," and "Novie Rubezha Sovetsko-Amerikanskikh otnoshenii," *Izvestia,* July 13, 1974, pp. 3–4.
68. Adam B. Ulam, *Dangerous Relations: The Soviet Union and World Politics, 1970–82* (New York: Oxford University Press, 1983), p. 122; and Garthoff, *Détente and Confrontation,* p. 461.
69. Garthoff, *Détente and Confrontation,* p. 460.
70. Ibid., p. 461; see also Kissinger, *Years of Upheaval,* pp. 246–255 and 985–998.
71. Kissinger, *Years of Upheaval,* p. 1026.
72. Ibid., p. 1162.
73. Garthoff, *Détente and Confrontation,* pp. 431–432.
74. Arbatov, "Novie Rubezha," p. 4.
75. Quoted in Garthoff, *Détente and Confrontation,* pp. 434–435.
76. Author's conversations with Soviet scholars, principally those associated with the U.S.A. and Canada Institute and IMEMO, beginning in 1979.

3

MOSCOW'S INF EXPERIENCE

Andrew C. Goldberg

The signing and subsequent ratification of the agreement banning intermediate-range nuclear forces (INF) from Europe symbolized the close of an era in U.S.–Soviet relations. The treaty stands as a demonstration of the "new thinking" in Soviet foreign policy. As much as any event in the recent history of relations between the superpowers, the process of achieving an agreement on such a contentious issue reflected the coming of age of a new generation of Soviet leadership and foreign policy elite with new ideas on strategy and foreign policy. The agreement symbolized a new cycle in the Kremlin's approach to the management of diplomacy toward and military affairs with the United States and Western Europe.

This thesis—that the INF negotiations became a test case for what was to become Mikhail Gorbachev's policy of new thinking and can be understood only as part of a broader process of change in Soviet perceptions, attitudes, and tactics—may seem somewhat overstated when one considers just the substance of the treaty itself. In contrast to a potential agreement on strategic nuclear weapons (the Strategic Arms Reduction Talks, or START), the INF Treaty achieved no real reduction in the magnitude of the threat facing the United States and Western Europe, and made only a small cut in the overall nuclear arsenal facing the USSR. Only by placing the INF process against the backdrop of evolution in Soviet strategy can one appreciate its political and strategic importance, which transcends the numbers of weapons involved. At the end of the process, Soviet leaders turned a diplomatic debacle into a triumph.

Assessing the INF experience requires looking backward to a period that seems, in the light of Gorbachev's recent foreign policy initiatives, very distant. The standard chronology of the INF episode spans a decade, encompassing the first deployment of Soviet multiple independently targeted reentry vehicle (MIRV) SS-20 missiles in 1976–1977, the U.S. decision to deploy ground-launched cruise missiles (GLCMs) and Pershing II intermediate-range ballistic missiles (IRBMs) in 1979, and the final agreement to abolish these weapons completely in 1987–1988.

Yet, important antecedents of these events lie in the preceding decade. The political-military decisions surrounding INF weaponry follow a path from the regimes of Nikita Khrushchev and Leonid Brezhnev in their primes, to the paralytic interregnum of the early 1980s, and ultimately to the ascendancy of Mikhail Gorbachev. Moscow's INF experience thus spans two generations of evolving Soviet perceptions of the relationship between military power and political purpose.

THE CHRONOLOGY IN BRIEF

The key events of the INF episode may be divided into four periods. The first is the two or more decades of Soviet military expansion leading up to and culminating in the deployment of the SS-20 that commenced in 1977. Anxieties over this trend expressed within the North Atlantic Treaty Organization (NATO), particularly by the West German government of Chancellor Helmut Schmidt, led the United States to consider a variety of responses. In the second phase, NATO's deliberations led to the 1979 "dual track" approach of deploying weapons while negotiating reductions. Following the dual track decision was a period of proposals and counterproposals from 1980 to 1983. Finally, there were the major Gorbachev initiatives of 1985–1987, which ultimately embraced the "zero option" proposed by President Ronald Reagan and led to the INF Treaty in December of 1987.

The first phase of the INF episode has its roots in the 1949–1960 period, when the United States and USSR deployed crude tactical and medium-range missiles in Europe. In the early 1960s, U.S. and Soviet nuclear forces developed quite differently, with the United States withdrawing land-based missiles from Europe and instead relying on its expanding strategic nuclear superiority over the Soviet Union. Technological failures in the Soviet missile programs meant a continued reliance on aging SS-4s and SS-5s for the next two decades. The Soviets, however, continued an active IRBM development program throughout the 1960s and into the 1970s, while the first set of Strategic Arms Limitation Talks (SALT I) in 1972 failed to address Soviet theater ballistic missile programs. The Soviets eventually developed and deployed the three-warhead SS-20 mobile missile after 1977. The SS-20 deployment occurred against the background of steady growth in Soviet conventional and tactical nuclear arsenals, and was viewed by many in the West as a primary tool of political intimidation during a crisis, as well as a flexible system for fighting a nuclear war in Europe.

After a period of debate within the alliance, NATO responded to the deployment of the SS-20 with the dual track decision of December 1979. The first track was the deployment of 464 GLCMs and 108 Pershing II missiles in five countries, to commence in 1983; the second track involved arms control negotiations with the USSR to establish INF ceilings.

The period of 1980–1983 featured a succession of U.S. and Soviet proposals for limiting long-range theater nuclear forces. The most notable of these, the Reagan zero option of November 1981, was proposed to and rejected by Brezhnev in February 1982, but would eventually be the cornerstone of the INF agreement. In March 1982 Brezhnev announced a unilateral moratorium on the SS-20, which would remain in effect until NATO began deployment of GLCMs and Pershing IIs. Private conversations between the chief U.S. negotiator, Paul Nitze, and his counterpart, Yuli Kvitsinsky, in mid-July 1982 resulted in what could have been a major breakthrough: U.S. and Soviet INF launchers and nuclear-capable aircraft in Europe limited to equal levels—70 and 150, respectively.

In May of 1983 General Secretary Yuri Andropov launched a new initiative: limiting Soviet INF weapons in Europe to existing French and British levels—which were below the Soviet level of 1977, when SS-20 deployments began. Negotiations ended without success in July, and NATO began deploying INF systems in November 1983. On November 23, the Soviets walked out of negotiations and ended the moratorium on the SS-20.

In March 1985 Mikhail Gorbachev succeeded Konstantin Chernenko, ushering in a much publicized reappraisal of Soviet strategic thinking under the banner of new thinking. Gorbachev began with a unilateral moratorium on new INF systems in Europe to continue until December of that year.

In an initial bargaining ploy, he linked all proposed reductions of nuclear forces to the banning of testing and deployment of space weapons. Faced with continued U.S. opposition, in October 1985 he delinked INF systems from negotiations on strategic offensive and defensive weapons and space weapons. By the October 1986 Reykjavik meeting with President Reagan, Gorbachev had abandoned the prevailing Soviet position of using British and French nuclear forces as the sizing criteria for Soviet forces; his eventual embrace of the U.S. concept of total elimination of American and Soviet forces culminated in the December 1987 INF agreement.

This brief synopsis disguises a complex interplay of international and domestic factors over a period of almost three decades. First and most important were the Soviets' perceptions of the Western military challenge, their "net assessment" of the strategic relationship between the two opposing alliances. Affecting this was the pace of military technological development in Soviet nuclear programs, whose political significance each side interpreted differently. Finally, the psychological profile of the Soviet leadership changed dramatically during the period under consideration, with the almost complete replacement of the geriatric Brezhnevite "old guard" by a fresher group of political leaders.

INF IN THE SOVIET PERSPECTIVE: THE EARLY YEARS

Now that it is fashionable and politically expedient to criticize the "years of stagnation" under Leonid Brezhnev, Soviet publicists openly castigate Gorbachev's predecessors for bringing about

Moscow's INF travail. Retrospective Soviet commentaries not only suggest that the Brezhnev regime mishandled the arms control diplomacy of INF weaponry, they also assert that the original decision to deploy the SS-20 IRBM was a fundamental and avoidable error.[1]

Recent Soviet criticisms, of course, echo the questions that Western commentators raise. Could Brezhnev and his colleagues not have foreseen that the deployment of modern, MIRVed IRBMs would exacerbate East-West relations? Were these capabilities so important for Soviet foreign and military strategy that they were worth risking a Western counteraction? Why did the Soviets believe that the challenge of the SS-20 would go unanswered?

The contrasting actions of the Gorbachev regime are also rather peculiar. Having expended so much diplomatic capital and such extensive economic resources on developing the SS-20s, why were the Soviets suddenly willing to abandon these weapons? During the protracted negotiations over INF systems, there were often hints that the United States and NATO would accept far less than zero as a compromise, leaving a potent Soviet INF deployment still in place. Did Gorbachev's response reflect a new vision of radical disarmament, or had the SS-20s become militarily irrelevant to Soviet planners?

The answers to these questions can be found in the events that preceded the deployment of the SS-20 and the turmoil it provoked. Once the geostrategic setting from Moscow's vantage point is reconstructed, it is harder to dismiss the original Brezhnev decisions as the product of a shortsighted leadership excessively enamored of military instruments and besotted by the expansion of its military power and influence. Equally dubious is the image of Gorbachev as a totally "new" thinker, whose ideas on security are a fundamental departure from those of his predecessors. While it is apparent that Gorbachev initiated tremendous changes in the Soviet approach to arms control, it is important not to lose sight of major policy continuities.

It is sometimes easy to forget that today's older Soviet leaders, the last holdouts from Brezhnev's generation, were once young. The "new men" of the post-Stalin era were socialized in a foreign policy environment critically affected by the dissolution of the traditional prenuclear continental threats to Soviet security and the rising importance of nuclear weapons—in which the United States was superior for two decades.

For Brezhnev's generation, the dominant preoccupation was the neutralization of the West's nuclear advantages, thereby reinforcing Soviet political and military preponderance in Eurasia. Countering U.S. nuclear might was extraordinarily difficult, for the USSR suffered from numerous technological and geographic disadvantages. It is in this context that Moscow's INF experience took shape.

The Soviets have aimed nuclear weapons at Western Europe since the early 1950s. At first the USSR, like the United States, possessed a crude and limited arsenal of warheads carried by bombers of relatively short range. Unlike the United States, it had no allies to provide bases close to the territory of its primary opponent. From the vantage point of Stalin's successors, the zone of U.S.–Soviet nuclear engagement from 1949 to nearly 1960 began and ended for the most part in the theaters adjacent to the USSR. It was dominated by U.S. forward-deployed bombers that could attack targets throughout the USSR and Soviet bombers that could pose a threat primarily to targets around its periphery.[2] As time went on, this bomber-dominant balance was altered by tactical and eventually medium-range missiles, such as the American Thor and Jupiter (deployed in 1958 and 1959, respectively) and the Soviet SS-4s and SS-5s.

From the outset, these Soviet and American theater ballistic missiles were extremely cumbersome to use. Liquid-fueled and of poor accuracy, they required as much as 12–18 hours to ready for launch and therefore had only limited survivability against a first strike. Nevertheless, from the Soviet perspective, they had the virtue of being immune to U.S. air defenses. Given sufficient preparation, they could be highly useful first-strike weapons against targets such as industrial sites, NATO airfields, and command centers whose destruction did not require great accuracy.[3]

During the 1950s, an era in which NATO's military policy called for the prompt use of nuclear weapons in wartime, the SS-4s and SS-5s emerged as a subordinate part of Moscow's search for weapons that could erode Western confidence in the ability to use nuclear weapons in a crisis. Once war was inevitable, INF weapons might be used to reduce the weight of NATO's nuclear onslaught. Thus, they provided some limited psychological leverage over NATO leaders in peacetime and a potent war-fighting ability should deterrence fail.

By the early 1960s, however, the conditions that gave birth to a theater-centered nuclear posture for both powers had changed. For the United States, at least, forward-based capabilities were supplanted by those of substantially greater range, particularly land-based intercontinental ballistic missiles (ICBMs) based in the continental United States, Polaris submarines, and B-52 bombers.

The deactivation of American Thors and Jupiters in 1963 signaled the end of the U.S. capability to target the USSR with missiles based in Europe. A nominal capability to bombard the Soviet Union and its allies with nuclear weapons from air bases or aircraft carriers in the European region did remain in the form of NATO dual-capable strike aircraft; but this was not the actual mission of these aircraft, since they would be needed for the defense of the European front.

The Soviet Union took a separate path, one dictated primarily by technological deficiencies. Moscow began to deploy ICBMs during the early 1960s, but encountered severe problems with guidance systems and propellants. Of necessity, the Soviets continued to rely on intermediate-range missiles to target Western Europe. The SS-4s and SS-5s were to remain in service for almost two more decades, while the search for a more efficient replacement for these weapons was included in Soviet research and development (R&D) programs.

Different U.S. and Soviet experiences with nuclear weapons development therefore led to alternative perspectives on the prospect of nuclear war fighting in the event of a European war, and also to disparities in each side's nuclear programs. Washington took an early lead in the deployment of a large, flexible, intercontinental force. Not only did this create a gross superiority over the Soviets, it also meant that American ICBM and submarine-launched ballistic missile (SLBM) forces could promptly cover a sizable number of targets in Eastern Europe and the USSR. Meanwhile, shorter-range NATO nuclear forces, such as artillery and tactical bombers, were retained for use against Soviet frontline divisions. From the perspective of Robert McNamara's Pentagon, central strategic forces had made longer-range forward-based nuclear systems in Europe superfluous.[4]

By contrast, technological advances in Soviet forces proceeded extremely slowly, thereby constraining not only the overall quality of Soviet strategic forces but also their size. By 1965, the USSR possessed 224 ICBMs, fifteen SLBMs (of which fewer than 15 percent were on station at any one time), and a crude bomber force.[5] Since the Kremlin's nascent strategic force was dedicated entirely to deterring the United States, it made a great deal of sense to maintain a secondary force that could be assigned in-theater responsibilities.

Both the Khrushchev and the Brezhnev regimes attempted to replace the vulnerable SS-4 and SS-5 missiles with mobile, solid-fuel successors that would be easier to keep on alert and more difficult for Western nuclear forces to attack. Development of the SS-x-14 medium-range missile and the SS-x-15 IRBM commenced between 1958 and 1961. Had the designs been successful, these missiles would have begun to replace the SS-4s and SS-5s between 1965 and 1968. The failure of these systems, however, eliminated an entire generation of IRBMs. Consequently, when the Soviets fielded their first successful mobile IRBM in 1976, its appearance created a good deal more political surprise in the Western world than would otherwise have been the case.

As a stopgap measure, the Soviets placed the SS-4s and SS-5s in harder silos and began to replace some of these weapons with the newer, variable-range SS-11 ICBMs. Thus, the momentum of Soviet modernization, although substantially slowed, never stopped.

In contrast to the plodding but determined Soviet effort to maintain a regional ballistic missile force was Washington's approach to IRBM modernization. The earliest zero option, President Kennedy's 1962 political trade of U.S. Thor and Jupiter missiles for Russian missiles in Cuba, tacitly acknowledged keep-out zones for such weapons in areas adjacent to the superpowers' homelands. The decision to deactivate U.S. IRBMs and not to replace them had, in fact, already been on the Kennedy administration's agenda before the missile crisis. This decision reflected the indifference to INF weapons of the American government (particularly McNamara's Defense Department) at the beginning of the 1960s.

Before Kennedy took office, plans were under way to replace the Thor and Jupiter weapons, possibly with land-mobile Polaris missiles under the operational control of Supreme Allied Command Europe (SACEUR), but subject to the final concurrence of the American president. McNamara, however, had little enthusiasm for follow-on land-based IRBMs. Modern, solid-fueled Minutemen—which maintained high states of alert, were easy to communicate with, and could be used without Allied consultation—were the weapons the administration preferred for responding to Soviet aggression in Europe.[6]

European leaders were exercised about Soviet intermediate- and medium-range missiles and the prospect of what would later be called decoupling. Decoupling would occur if the United States decided not to use its strategic nuclear forces in response to Soviet attack in Europe. The Europeans feared that if the Soviets felt that U.S. leaders were deterred from a strategic response, Moscow might come to believe that a theater nuclear strike against Europe would not provoke retaliation against the Soviet homeland.

There was no NATO consensus on what the appropriate response to Soviet long-range nuclear missiles ought to be. During the early 1960s, the United States did attempt to ease European anxieties over decoupling by offering to help develop a token multilateral force (MLF) of sea-based weapons that could attack Soviet targets.[7] This effort was initially envisioned as a submarine deployment, but for the sake of cost considerations and political visibility was later changed to a surface ship option that was at the same time quite vulnerable to Soviet preemptive attack.

Ultimately, the MLF foundered in a welter of crosscutting NATO policies and lack of U.S. resolve. The French and the British, of course, eventually fielded their own national SLBM forces, but by the late 1960s the collective weight of alliance decisions was to abandon the search for a NATO missile distinct from the American arsenal based in North America or at sea.

Numerous Soviet observers, analyzing the NATO nuclear debates of the early 1960s, believed that the United States intended to abandon its commitment to use strategic nuclear forces in the defense of the alliance. This opinion triggered a debate within the Soviet military on the changing characteristics of U.S. and NATO military doctrine. By the mid-1960s the preponderant view expressed in civilian journals and in the military media was that the United States was retreating from a willingness to use nuclear weapons rapidly in a war for Europe. The removal of U.S. IRBMs, the failure of the MLF, and repeated U.S. calls after 1961 for measures to extend the nuclear threshold in Europe by increasing NATO's conventional defenses raised the possibility that a future war could be contained at the nonnuclear level.[8]

This new strategic concept gave birth to a number of Soviet military programs designed to wage war at the nonnuclear level. It also added impetus to a new Soviet arms control policy at the end of the 1960s, the objective of which was to regulate U.S. nuclear modernization and growth and further erode American interest in pursuing nuclear superiority.

By the start of the SALT era, all the basic elements shaping Soviet perceptions of the new European nuclear balance were in place: a lack of U.S. support for long-range theater nuclear weapons; Allied anxiety over asymmetries in the IRBM balance, exacerbated by an inability to decide on a response; and, in contrast, a relatively consistent Soviet commitment to the modernization of long-range theater missiles.

INF AND SALT

The MLF episode left an impression in the minds of many Soviet observers of a divided alliance and contradictory Western commitments where the intermediate-range nuclear balance in Europe was concerned. The Soviets perceived that U.S. policy had consciously allowed the continuation of asymmetrical IRBM deployments. This assessment was reinforced in U.S.–Soviet bargaining maneuvers over SALT.

At the opening round of SALT I in 1969, the United States tabled a proposal to put a cap on the number of Soviet medium- and intermediate-range ballistic missiles. According to Henry Kissinger, the goal was to "give us a positive public posture of having favored comprehensive limitations" in order to allay European concerns about the separation of the European nuclear balance issue from SALT.[9]

The Soviet negotiator, Vladimir Semyenov, rejected this position, but took the opportunity to raise the issue of forward-based systems (FBS)—principally the American FB-111 long-range aircraft based in England, which could reach Soviet targets. He insisted—as Soviet negotiators would a decade later—that "all delivery systems which could be used to hit targets in the other country should be covered in SALT, regardless of whether their owners called them strategic or tactical."[10] Under the Soviet definition, their medium-range ballistic missiles (MRBMs) and medium-range bombers were not to be constrained; U.S. FB-111s and a sizable portion of long-range tactical aircraft based on land and sea would, by contrast, be included under SALT ceilings. The Soviets, in a move that would characterize their bargaining tactics in SALT, refused to offer their own counting rules for FBS, instead insisting that the United States offer one, to which they would react.

Rather than snapping at this bait, the United States sought to protect FBS entirely by offering to defer demands for a Soviet IRBM freeze "in exchange for the Soviets' agreeing that American FBS not be included."[11] Instead, the Soviet negotiators continued to press their demands on FBS. Eventually they would agree to defer discussions on it when Brezhnev felt that holding out for American concessions would wreck the treaty. The contrast between the two negotiating positions is crucial. Even as SALT I was being concluded in 1972, the Soviets continued to characterize U.S. FBS as "strategic," and to insist that SALT II would deal with these weapons.

Despite its desire to assuage European concerns about the SS-4 and SS-5 missiles, the United States was reluctant to trade NATO long-range aircraft for Soviet missiles out of fear of eroding NATO's tactical nuclear position in Europe. The assumption made by the Nixon administration (and its successors) was that NATO conventional defenses on the ground would be too weak to resist a Soviet offensive. These long-range aircraft would therefore be required either to bolster NATO's conventional defense or to deliver nuclear payloads against Eastern Europe should conventional defense fail. The bombers were deemed too precious to eliminate. Unwilling to relinquish these systems, U.S. negotiators simply abandoned any further effort at limiting Soviet long-range theater weapons.

The result of the SALT episode was to reinforce the environment of permissiveness for future Soviet MRBM deployments. By first raising the issue of IRBM limits, and then rapidly dropping it, U.S. arms control negotiators left open a gray area for increasing the numbers of long-range theater launchers or warheads.

DEPLOYING THE SS-20

The collapse of Western efforts to deploy weapons analogous to the SS-4 and SS-5, and the concomitant failure to eliminate such weapons through arms control, set the stage for the political turbulence surrounding the deployment of the SS-20. R&D flight testing of the SS-20 had commenced in 1974. Unlike those of the SS-14 and SS-15, these trials were successful, and final development proceeded at a rapid pace.

As the full-deployment decision neared, however, signals concerning the international environment were becoming increasingly contradictory and difficult for the Soviets to read. On one hand, the Soviet military buildup and the policy of détente had occasioned unprecedented international influence for the USSR. The rather exuberant Brezhnev foreign policy speeches of the twenty-fourth and twenty-fifth congresses of the Communist Party of the Soviet Union (in 1971 and 1976, respectively), trumpeting an inexorable change in the global "correlation of forces" in favor of Moscow, were the proud statements of a politician raised in an environment of inferiority who had achieved unprecedented success.[12] That this perception was shared by others in the leadership, and throughout the Soviet elite, is apparent from the journals and statements of the period.

Yet, against this backdrop were conflicting trends to which the Soviets were not blind, but for which the solutions were not obvious. By 1976, American euphoria over détente had given way to intense debate over prevailing strategy toward the global Soviet threat. The U.S. policy establishment was still a year away from the hysterical debate over the significance of growing Soviet nuclear capabilities that would culminate in the widespread conviction that a so-called window of strategic vulnerability existed. Nonetheless, internal discussions in the Department of Defense highlighting the Soviet nuclear threat were becoming public, occasioning heated congressional calls for modernizing and augmenting U.S. nuclear forces at home and in Europe.[13]

As a response, the American government began a review of the existing targeting policy designed to increase the range of military options that could be used in a controlled manner. This initiative, known as NSDM-242, or the doctrine of limited nuclear targeting, was directly related to growing anxieties within the Nixon and Ford administrations over the erosion of U.S. nuclear credibility. The United States also began developing more accurate strategic capabilities that could be used to attack hardened military assets.

The Soviets were aware of these trends, arguing in their own journals that right-wing elements in the U.S. policy community were deliberately misrepresenting Soviet military policies in order to resuscitate an American drive for nuclear superiority.[14]

They began to take extraordinary pains in their public statements to point out the defensiveness of their nuclear doctrine. At the same time, they started to tone down references in their writings indicating that Soviet nuclear weapons would be used preemptively in a nuclear war. Such provocative statements had been characteristic of Soviet military media for years and had become the focus of comment in the West during the mid-1970s.

In what would ultimately be called the Tula line, after a 1977 Brezhnev speech in that central Asian city, Soviet declaratory policy proclaimed that nuclear war could be neither limited nor won, and asserted an unshakable commitment to the control of nuclear armaments.[15]

The Brezhnev regime never linked its conciliatory policy line on nuclear weapons to the sorts of sweeping arms reductions that would have allayed intensifying Western fears. This is explicable only in terms of the collective mentality of the mature Brezhnev establishment at its high-water mark during the mid-1970s.

After a decade of determined efforts to reverse its perceived military inferiority, the Soviet elite developed a conviction that the West, particularly the United States, had been coerced into treating the USSR as a political equal. According to a wide variety of Soviet commentators, the contradictions that had emerged in the capitalist camp bore a direct relationship to the loss of American military superiority.[16]

During the early 1970s, the Soviets interpreted U.S. reactions, such as congressional opposition to SALT I, as the work of elements within the United States and in Europe that would not submit to military parity and political equality without a fight. Yet, Soviet policymakers, like their counterparts elsewhere, rarely budge from a proven formula. In this case the formula consisted of a policy of combining political and economic détente, continued arms control efforts aimed at moderating the nuclear competition, and a steady buildup of conventional power in the theaters adjacent to the Soviet Union. Consequently, Soviet statements of the period sidestepped the prospect that the USSR's military buildup would lead to countervailing Western efforts, emphasizing instead the positive aspects of global transformation.

Moreover, in terms of the European balance, the prospect of significant additions to NATO's nuclear force structure was still quite dim. Much could happen to hinder any new NATO initiatives, as the MLF episode had demonstrated. Since decision makers generally tend to assume that the political future will be much like the past, the Soviet calculus may have been that whatever the Americans' eventual response, they would not deploy intermediate-range systems that had been abandoned in the preceding decade.[17]

Therefore, lacking constraints in the foreign policy arena, and committed to a proven recipe of military growth and modernization, the Soviets continued developing IRBMs. This suggests that the Brezhnev regime had no qualms about fielding the new system and that it did not assign any unusual political significance to the deployment beyond demonstrating the will to improve Soviet forces, whatever the cost.

During the early and mid-1970s it would have been easy for the Soviet military to make the case for going forward with a mobile replacement for the SS-4 and SS-5. Soviet military writings in the classified journal *Military Thought* emphasized the importance of survivable nuclear systems to frustrate an opponent's first strike.[18] Lacking easy access to the open oceans for their submarine fleet, the Soviets' only viable long-term solution to the vulnerability of their missile forces was to deploy them on mobile launchers.

Moreover, their reading of Defense Secretary James Schlesinger's limited nuclear targeting doctrine, along with anticipated improvements in U.S. ICBM accuracy, probably fostered the conclusion that the United States included the rapid elimination of Soviet theater nuclear capabilities in any limited first-use options of a European war. The SS-4s and SS-5s were more than ever a wasting asset.

The choice of the modified SS-16 as a replacement for the SS-4 was therefore logical. The missile was available for procurement and was highly survivable because of its road-mobile launcher. It was also efficient, since a multiple-warhead system would produce more survivable warheads than the old single-warhead Soviet systems.

FROM THE NEUTRON BOMB TO THE DUAL TRACK

Well before Helmut Schmidt's now famous 1977 address at the International Institute for Strategic Studies in London, in which he called for redressing the imbalances posed by new Soviet nuclear weapons such as the SS-20 and the Backfire medium bomber, American defense officials had begun to fret about the potential impact of continuous Soviet theater nuclear moderni- zation. As early as 1974, Secretary Schlesinger's report to Con- gress noted that the "development of the Backfire and SS-x-20 and deployment of improved tactical aviation units" reinforced the need to review the theater nuclear balance. Schlesinger as- serted that "even though NATO now maintains a formidable array of nuclear forces . . . the Soviet peripheral attack force will soon present such an improved capability that we must review the needs and structure of NATO INF."[19]

Not only did Schlesinger and succeeding defense secre- taries, Donald Rumsfeld and Harold Brown, highlight the need for modernized U.S. theater nuclear forces, but ongoing devel- opmental programs for INF, including a longer-range successor to the short-range Pershing I ballistic missile, continued apace. Much of U.S. diplomacy toward the Western Allies concerning nuclear weapons during this period involved, in fact, a scramble to find modernization plans that would be militarily useful and politically acceptable.

Despite the increasing attention paid by Western policy- makers to the Soviet buildup, the available Soviet literature of the 1974–1979 period shows no evidence of Soviet anticipation of the December 1979 decision to deploy the Pershing II and ground-launched cruise missiles. Soviet articles did suggest that "right-wing" elements within the Carter administration were seeking to persuade the president to deploy new nuclear weapons in Europe. But the expectation was that these would be battlefield systems.

The Soviet logic, based upon analyses that were consistent with assumptions developed in the 1960s, was that Western military planners envisioned "an opening escalatory strategy in which the exchange of nuclear strikes will not touch the territory of the USA or of its enemy, which possesses strategic nuclear weapons." That long-range theater ballistic forces did not figure in Soviet analytic assessments of U.S. policy was reinforced by the careful wording of U.S. Defense Department statements that described the purposes of INF in geographically limited terms: "primarily for use in selected or limited operations *short of the Soviet Union.*"[20]

Instead of long-range weapons, Soviet writers anticipated new initiatives in short-range nuclear modernization, principally in the form of the enhanced-radiation warhead (ERW) teamed with the Lance, a short-range ballistic missile that the Carter administration sought to deploy in 1978–1979. The ERW offered a relatively low-cost riposte to the dramatic growth in Soviet frontline armor capabilities. This program fed Soviet preconceptions that the United States was still searching for a graduated nuclear response to a conventional offensive that would not necessarily trigger general nuclear war.

The massive European public opposition to the "neutron bomb" and the subsequent failure of the United States to deploy even these weapons bolstered prevailing lessons of the past within the Soviet policy community. The first was that the United States would still prefer to deploy weapons that left the USSR a sanctuary, while trying to offset unfavorable trends in the theater balance. The second was that the United States could not deploy any new nuclear weapons without an Allied consensus, and that this would be difficult to achieve. Finally, the episode fostered the belief that the European publics, particularly in Germany, could and would force their governments to back away from NATO commitments. Although the first assumption would be abruptly shaken by the 1979 INF deployment decision, the other two would linger beyond the Brezhnev regime's waning years.

INF AND THE SOVIET INTERREGNUM

NATO's INF deployment decision of December 1979 seemed to come as a surprise to Soviet observers. Until very late in the year, most Soviet commentators expected a reprise of the neutron warhead episode and continued to focus attention on this issue, rather than on the deployment of long-range missiles. The announcement of the dual track decision to deploy 572 NATO INF while negotiating on equal U.S.–Soviet ceilings met with three months of silence as the Brezhnev regime mulled over an appropriate response.

That regime, its leader aged and ailing, was by now beset with a general erosion of its foreign and domestic policies. The economy had entered a period of stagnation, a Western buildup in armaments had commenced, and the USSR was embroiled in a number of conflicts in Africa and Asia. Eastern Europe was also unsettled, with political unrest mounting in Poland. Overloaded by this avalanche of challenges, Brezhnev initially responded to the announcement of the NATO deployments by attempting to make some limited concessions that would not be interpreted as a Soviet retreat.

Between 1980 and Brezhnev's death in October 1982, Moscow floated a series of proposals that, while hardly meeting the requirements of the Western alliance, were designed to make the Soviets look conciliatory in the eyes of the European publics. In the meantime, Soviet propaganda and public diplomacy tried to give the impression that American policy was turning Europe into a nuclear lightning rod. The approach sought to revive the contradictions among the Allied governments that had been so apparent in the earlier MLF and neutron bomb episodes.

From the Soviet standpoint, two questions were central. First, how serious was the military threat posed by the eventual deployment of NATO missiles? Second, how strong was the Allied political consensus in support of these weapons?

Soviet military media discussion during the early 1980s appeared intensely concerned about the military threat from NATO INF. Although the numbers were small in relation to the overall U.S. arsenal facing the Soviets, the deployment had some special characteristics that were particularly worrisome. The Pershing II missile's speed and proximity to the USSR gave it a roughly 7–15-minute flight time to its targets (as opposed to thirty minutes for an ICBM), which made it a potential first-strike weapon that would decrease the warning time for Soviet defenders. Furthermore, Soviet spokesmen argued, numbers of INF could increase once the initial development was successful, thus allowing the United States to evade SALT limitations in a new and more militarily effective manner.

Western analysts questioned the credibility of the Soviet assertions. If the Soviets were so worried, they asked, why did they not offer more sweeping concessions at the outset to block the deployment?

The probable reason was tied to Soviet assessments of the European consensus. Soviet official and quasi-official organs alike tended to characterize the deployment as having been foisted on the Europeans. While to some extent such statements were propagandistic, they also reflected the Soviet view that divisions within NATO were very serious. Consequently, a strategy that combined minimal concessions, coercive statements, and public diplomacy aimed at alienating Europeans from the United States was probably deemed sufficient for Moscow's purposes during the opening round of bargaining with the West.

Given this logic, Brezhnev stuck to a minimalist negotiating strategy that embraced three principles. First, NATO and Soviet long-range theater systems were not comparable and should not serve as the basis of a trade. INF, in the Soviet characterization, was simply a more potent augmentation of forward-based systems that allowed the United States to circumvent the existing SALT understandings. Second, the Soviet Union had not changed the theater balance with the SS-20, but simply had replaced superannuated launchers with modern weapons on a one-for-one basis. The United States, by contrast, was deliberately introducing first-strike systems under the pretext of modernization. Third, the Soviets argued that they needed IRBMs as a counterweight to existing nuclear forces in Europe and the Far East, particularly the independent French and British nuclear forces. Therefore, the SS-20 was a legitimate matching deployment, based upon the Soviet definition of strategic equivalence.[21]

Subsequent Soviet proposals flowed directly from these claims, each succeeding one being a variation on the same theme: out of deference to Western concerns, the USSR would freeze its deployments of INF, but only if the United States would not deploy any missiles. The final numbers of Soviet INF would be included under equal levels of existing NATO and Warsaw Pact weapons, but would be based on counting rules that balanced Soviet forces with French and British systems and U.S. forward-based aircraft.[22]

Soviet faith in the efficacy of its position was reinforced during the early 1980s by the ground swell of popular opposition to INF throughout Europe. Demonstrations of ever increasing scale, particularly in the Netherlands and the Federal Republic of Germany, encouraged the Soviets to believe that over time, key members of NATO would respond to this opposition and defect from the December 1979 agreement. Until the Soviets were convinced that the momentum for the NATO deployment was irresistible, they were under little pressure to offer significant concessions.

The Kremlin leadership nonetheless did not abandon the search for some negotiating formula to stabilize the deteriorating East-West relationship and forestall the NATO deployment. Despite the self-serving nature of early Soviet INF proposals, it was clear that Brezhnev, Foreign Minister Andrei Gromyko, and Defense Minister Dmitri Ustinov hoped to salvage the fabric of détente, at least in Europe. Having publicly insisted on the noncomparability of the SS-20 with the Pershing II and SLCMs, however, the Soviet leadership found it difficult, perhaps impossible, to present a negotiating package that was much more attractive.

President Reagan's zero option of November 1981 was an almost certain nonstarter for Brezhnev. The Reagan position was simple—NATO would deploy no INF if the Soviets eliminated all of their existing long-range missiles, including their SS-4 and SS-5 weapons. An incredulous Soviet leadership could not accept the idea that it should eliminate existing systems that the West had left out of all previous negotiations for nonexistent U.S. weapons, let alone abandon modern replacements.

Still, it was under Brezhnev that the Soviets advanced their first reductions package. Soviet negotiators tabled a proposal calling for a phased reduction in NATO and Warsaw Pact missiles and nuclear-capable aircraft in Europe down to 600 systems by 1985 and 300 by 1990.

During 1982, this shift in Soviet arms proposals was followed rapidly by two new developments: the announcement in the spring of a moratorium on SS-20 deployments in the western USSR and, in July, the floating of the "Walk in the Woods" compromise proposal that would have equalized the number of U.S. GLCMs and Soviet IRBMs at seventy, with the allowance of an additional ninety SS-20 launchers in the eastern USSR.

The Walk in the Woods is one of the most obscure episodes in the history of U.S.–Soviet arms control talks. INF negotiations had stalled, and the chief American negotiator, Paul Nitze, had become increasingly distraught at what he saw as the administration's aversion to any form of arms reductions. In response, Nitze, on his own initiative, opened private discussions with his Soviet counterpart, Yuli Kvitsinsky.

The exact details of the conversations that day are murky, but it is well established that they produced a "joint exploration package" for the consideration of both governments. By Nitze's admission, the contents of this package were 80 percent his own and 20 percent Kvitsinsky's. Nitze took the proposal home and engaged his bureaucratic ally, Arms Control and Disarmament Agency (ACDA) Director Eugene Rostow, to help him sell it to the White House through National Security Adviser William Clark.

Back in the United States, the proposal set off furious bickering over what Secretary of State George Shultz called "freelancing" by Nitze. After heated discussions, the White House assigned the Joint Chiefs of Staff to study the necessity of the Pershing IIs. They concluded that since the Soviets greatly feared the Pershings, the United States could use these weapons as an effective bargaining chip for SS-20 limits in Asia and reductions in Europe. Secretary of Defense Caspar Weinberger quashed the original report, added some revisions, and sent a memo of his own to the president. Subsequently, President Reagan issued a directive that the zero option was still preferred, thereby implicitly rejecting the Walk in the Woods formula.

As for the Soviets, the record is cloudier because of the hidden character of their bureaucratic decision making. As opposed to Nitze, Kvitsinsky was obsessed with accountability for any informal negotiations. He apparently told Nitze that he had consulted with Foreign Minister Gromyko, who had authorized him to keep the private discussions going through the Walk in the Woods. After the walk, Kvitsinsky did not make contact with Nitze again until the end of September, when the Soviets publicly rejected the offer. Kvitsinsky told Nitze that his superiors had given him a hard time for his part in the Walk in the Woods. He put Nitze on notice that if their back-channel dealings were to advance further, Nitze would have to be speaking for Secretary Shultz as well as for himself.

One might speculate that it was Gromyko, through Kvitsinsky, who was freelancing during what was a period of Soviet leadership succession. Well before the spring Brezhnev was certainly physically, and perhaps mentally, incapacitated. His soon-to-be successor, former KGB Chief Yuri Andropov, had increased in stature within the Politburo hierarchy when Premier Alexei Kosygin and Party Ideology Chief Mikhail Suslov died, but the level of policy coordination during this period is uncertain.

Andropov's rise set in motion a short-lived effort to break the INF deadlock. Although both sides rejected the daring Walk in the Woods proposal, by the beginning of 1983 Andropov had aired some comparatively attractive proposals. One of these would have reduced Soviet warhead levels in Europe to the number of British and French forces, actually reaching a number lower than that of the 1978 period. Again, the flexibility was too little and too late. The process of conciliation was halted by Andropov's death.

Between 1980 and 1984, the Soviets had developed a negotiating strategy and public diplomacy predicated on assumptions that turned out to be wrong. NATO leaders made a determined effort not to repeat the deployment failures of the preceding two decades and remained more cohesive than the Soviets had expected. European public opposition had proven a less potent force in blocking the deployment. Soviet arms proposals, adequate to an old reality, failed in new conditions.

GORBACHEV'S RADICAL SOLUTION

Toward the end of the Brezhnev period and Andropov's brief tenure, the criteria upon which the Soviets had been making their decisions began to change. NATO INF were no longer a distant prospect but an increasingly imminent reality.

Also, confidence in the political benefits of Soviet military preponderance was also starting to crumble: the Soviet economy was stagnant, and a more benign West seemed increasingly necessary; the Reagan military buildup showed no signs of abating, and a new round of competition in military high technology was in the offing. The pressure for a reconsideration of existing strategic policy on many fronts was considerable.

The complexities and pitfalls of the succession, however, stymied the decision-making process. It was only after the interregnum that the Soviets could again pick up momentum. Mikhail Gorbachev, a man less bound than his predecessors to past practice and hungry for new initiatives, was determined to break the deadlock on arms control. Like Brezhnev and Andropov, he recognized the need to resuscitate détente and brake the Western military buildup, of which the INF deployment was a prominent symbolic expression. Unlike Brezhnev, he was not emotionally and conceptually wedded to preserving all of the existing military capital of the preceding era.

By 1985 the military need for the SS-20 was not what it had been when the weapon was first designed in the mid-1960s. The Soviets' central strategic forces were now so large and diverse that it would be easy to devote a small fraction of their land- and sea-based forces to the limited number of targets in Western Europe.

While the SS-20s were certainly welcome to Soviet commanders because they add flexibility to war plans, the weapons were made less desirable by the qualitatively new threat posed by NATO's missiles. The escalatory dangers posed by the short-warning attack capabilities of the Pershing II were uncomfortably potent. Thus, once efforts to forestall the U.S. deployment had failed, arguments against agreeing to asymmetrical cuts in Soviet forces in exchange for eliminating these American ones weakened.

Gorbachev seized the initiative immediately upon coming to office. Not a month after succeeding Chernenko, he announced a unilateral moratorium in the deployment of new INF in Europe (to last until December 1985), reduced the number of SS-20s in Europe to the level they had reached when talks broke off in November 1983, and announced an interest in summit talks. He continued to link INF negotiations with space weapons and strategic offensive and defensive weapons until just prior to the November 1985 Geneva summit, at which he and Reagan agreed to support the idea of an interim INF agreement.

In his January 1986 disarmament plan, Gorbachev for the first time excluded French and British forces, the inclusion of which had blocked all prior negotiations. For the next twenty-three months, Gorbachev and Reagan would wrangle over different versions of the zero option, originally proposed by Reagan in 1981; the final version of the INF agreement was signed in December 1987.

It is clear from commentary appearing after the signing of the treaty that many within the Soviet party apparatus were unhappy with the ultimate Soviet acceptance of the zero option.[23] In most cases the opposition reflected the conviction that the USSR should not show weakness by caving in to Western pressure. Gorbachev's new leadership was, however, clearly working from a different assessment of the requirements of East-West relations.

An important part of Gorbachev's ability to free himself from the shackles of past policy in the arms control arena had to do with the shifts in party and state personnel that began under Andropov and rapidly accelerated under Gorbachev's aegis. These new individuals in the Foreign Ministry and Central Committee Secretariat staff were no longer committed to maintaining and justifying policies that had originated with the old leadership.

The more relevant issue for Gorbachev and his colleagues was how to take advantage of the U.S. zero option without appearing to capitulate to American pressure.[24] After a period of political reappraisal in 1985, the Soviets began in 1986 to transform the zero option from a proposal identified with the United States to an integrated component of Soviet new thinking on arms control.

Without question, Gorbachev made a dramatic difference in the Soviet Union's INF position, as he did in so many aspects of Soviet policy. Yet it would be a mistake to underestimate the continuities between the Gorbachev approach to arms control and its antecedents in the Brezhnev period. The arms control diplomacy of the current Soviet regime is in many ways an evolutionary outgrowth of Brezhnev's earlier commitment to détente and arms control as means of regulating the superpower competition and maintaining an open door to Western trade and technology. Gorbachev's trade of military systems like the SS-20 would probably have been impossible had Brezhnev not created such an enormous margin of military superiority and bargaining capital.

The Gorbachev leadership inherited a long history of Soviet efforts to negate the U.S. nuclear commitment to Europe. This meant a declaratory stance that emphasized nuclear stability and an operational policy that sought to contain war below the nuclear threshold. On the other hand, Gorbachev was bequeathed domestic economic problems and a military apparatus that was reeling from the combined effects of economic backwardness, fiscal overextension, and Western military-technological competition.

Gorbachev and his colleagues had therefore come to realize that the abatement of external pressure—the so-called breathing spell (*peredyshka*) in the East-West competition—could be purchased at lowest political cost by dramatic steps in the arms control arena. INF, therefore, lay at the very heart of a policy resuscitating Soviet political, economic, and military influence.

CONCLUSION: EXPLAINING SOVIET INF DIPLOMACY

As a historical episode, the INF example illustrates some important features of Soviet strategic thinking and diplomatic style. It demonstrates the changing character of the Soviet leadership's perceptions of the West since the 1950s. For two generations of Soviet leaders, the INF issue was a major force in modifying some old policy assumptions and reaffirming others.

Perhaps the first lesson is that the pace of military modernization has a pervasive influence on Soviet political choices. During the 1960s enormous pressure built up on the Kremlin's leaders to resolve the vulnerability of their medium-range missile forces caused by the ongoing failure of existing MRBM development programs. This vulnerability was as much political as technical, since Brezhnev and his colleagues were determined to erode the appearance of U.S. military superiority in as many areas as possible as part of their drive for increased global influence.

By the time the SS-20 was ready for deployment, in the mid-1970s, U.S. nuclear strategy was taking on a more assertive cast, involving traditional counterforce plans and programs. This trend simply reinforced the decade-old requirement for a mobile system.

Ironically, by the time U.S. long-range theater nuclear forces were deployed in the mid-1980s, the military rationale for preserving the Soviet intermediate force had weakened, if not evaporated. Andropov and, subsequently, Gorbachev found themselves negotiating largely for the sake of prestige rather than because of military need.

The second lesson of the INF experience is that Soviet strategic objectives maintained basic continuity despite changes in immediate political circumstances. Brezhnev and Gorbachev were socialized in different political environments, one of strategic inferiority, the other of parity and global reach. While Brezhnev had a vested interest in specific programs and policies supervised over a period of two decades, Gorbachev did not. Yet in both cases the fundamental objective at the nuclear level remained to remove weapons that would allow NATO to escalate to nuclear attacks on the USSR in the event of conventional war in Europe.

In the Brezhnev era this was not considered possible without substantial growth and modernization of offsetting Soviet nuclear capabilities, combined with some broader structure of arms negotiation to regulate the military competition. For Gorbachev, the modern, diverse, and survivable nuclear weaponry that Brezhnev had accumulated provided the military slack needed to accommodate sharp theater nuclear reductions.

This, then, leads to the third lesson. Soviet perceptions of NATO's cohesion, particularly in terms of nuclear strategy, often lagged behind actual change. This disparity had little to do with rigidity or a lack of intelligence on the part of Moscow's political elite. Rather, the Soviets confronted an alliance whose politics were often difficult for its own members to understand and a NATO record of failed deployments and conflicting negotiating positions in MLF, SALT, and the neutron weapons imbroglio. NATO's track record reinforced the appearance of Western uncertainty on deployment issues. Soviet leaders therefore predicated their INF diplomacy in the 1970s and early 1980s on what they believed to be the dominant lessons of each previous episode, overlooking the fact that NATO's determination and cohesion might intensify after defeats.

The Soviet reading of U.S. nuclear strategy also tended to lag in the period after the McNamara era. Soviet analysts tended to assume that any U.S. nuclear improvements within the NATO context would involve short-range weapons, such as the Lance and Pershing I ballistic missiles and nuclear-capable artillery, rather than long-range systems, such as the Pershing II. Short-range systems, while threatening to Soviet forces in Europe, could not directly harm the USSR. Some impetus for developing an intermediate-range ballistic missile in the form of an enhanced Pershing II bubbled to the surface when James Schlesinger was secretary of defense, from 1973 to 1975; however, the emphasis from the Kennedy administration through the end of the Carter administration was on short-range improvements, a trend confirmed by the abortive ERW initiative. This was consistent with the Soviet strategic view that the United States was determined to avoid rapid escalation in Europe in an effort to leave the territories of the two superpowers as sanctuaries.

The Soviets were inflexible when most of their core assumptions collapsed in the wake of the December 1979 dual track decision. By then, bureaucratic gridlock, ill health, and a general erosion in foreign policy prevented the leadership from making the sweeping gestures necessary to forestall the long-range theater nuclear deployment that it feared.

It is certainly true that Gorbachev moved radically and forthrightly to clear away the existing deadlock. Yet, it is difficult to see what alternative he had, except perhaps to revive the rejected Walk in the Woods formula. Gorbachev's dynamic personality may have had a great deal to do with his dramatic embrace of Ronald Reagan's zero option. Another factor, however, may simply have been that given the existing nuclear balance, any number of long-range nuclear weapons would have been useful in reinforcing NATO's nuclear policy of flexible response, while the small number of remaining SS-20s would have been irrelevant to the Soviet military position. With the passing of the old guard, the zero option made strategic sense so long as it could be rationalized in political terms that favored the USSR.

It is noteworthy in this regard that the lingering Soviet criticism of the INF Treaty surfacing in the Soviet press in 1987 and 1988 focused not so much on the net military result in operational terms but rather on the symbolism of having exchanged so many more Soviet weapons for so few on the Western side. Gorbachev's great strength was in understanding how large his margin of superiority was and being willing to make cuts for the sake of political advantages.

Mikhail Gorbachev, therefore, did not simply fling off a bankrupt policy. Instead, he encouraged the shedding of timeworn assumptions that no longer responded to contemporary conditions. His INF strategy was ultimately a repudiation not of Brezhnev's overall goal of reducing the nuclear threat facing the USSR, but of the superannuated policies that supported it.

NOTES

1. Deputy Foreign Minister Alexander Bessmertnykh commented that "technology rather than political analysis often influenced many decisions" when it came to nuclear forces, including the SS-20. Quoted in *The Washington Post*, November 29, 1987. See also Vitaliy Zhurkin, "Meeting in Washington," *SShA: ekonomika, politika, ideologiia*, no. 1, 1988, as reported in JPRS *USA*, July 6, 1988; G. Dadyants, "The Echo of the Saryozek Explosions," Foreign Broadcast Information Service (FBIS), August 19, 1988, pp. 1–3 (on the INF policy decision); and O. Bykov, "The 19th Party Conference and Problems of Peace," *Pravda*, August 11, 1988 (translated in FBIS, August 19, 1988).
2. An arcane but important technological ambiguity remains as to whether Soviet Bear bombers (deployed in the mid-1950s) could reach the United States. This author's impression, based upon the evidence, is that they could not, even on one-way missions, until about 1960. By that time, Soviet forces had mastered midair refueling. See Robert P. Berman and John Baker, *Soviet Strategic Forces* (Washington, D.C.: Brookings Institution, 1982), pp. 45–46.
3. See Stephen M. Meyer, "Soviet Theater Nuclear Forces," pts. 1 and 2, *Adelphi Papers* 187 and 188 (London: International Institute for Security Studies, 1984), pp. 1–6; and Berman and Baker, *Soviet Strategic Forces*, pp. 113–124.
4. See William Kaufman, *The McNamara Strategy* (New York: Harper & Row, 1964); John Steinbrunner, *The Cybernetic Theory of Decision* (Princeton: Princeton University Press, 1974); and Desmond Ball, ed., *Strategy and Force Levels* (Ithaca: Cornell University Press, 1986).
5. See Berman and Baker, *Soviet Strategic Forces*, p. 138.
6. Steinbrunner, *Cybernetic Theory*, pt. 2.

7. The initial deployments were to involve Polaris submarines under NATO control with a European crew. Technical concerns about submarine communications shifted the project to surface ships, which were more vulnerable, but also more compatible with prompt first use.

8. Differences of opinion remain about this chronology and about the character of the actual debate. For perspectives that support this argument, see Michael MccGwire, *Soviet Military Objectives* (Washington, D.C.: Brookings Institution, 1987). A more detailed discussion may be found in Andrew C. Goldberg, *New Directions in Soviet Military Policy* (Washington, D.C.: Center for Strategic and International Studies, 1987).

9. Henry Kissinger, *The White House Years* (Boston: Little, Brown & Co., 1979), pp. 543–544.

10. Gerard Smith, *DoubleTalk* (Lanham, Md.: University Press of America, 1985), p. 91.

11. Ibid., p. 146.

12. Brezhnev speeches suggesting the "changed correlation of forces" may be found in the following issues of *Current Digest of the Soviet Press*: April 20, 1971; May 4, 1971; and March 24, 1976.

13. Richard Pipes, "Why the Soviet Union Thinks It Could Fight and Win a Nuclear War," *Commentary* 64, no. 1 (1977). The rationale for the nuclear war-fighting view of Soviet policy may be found in Joseph D. Douglas, *The Soviet Theater Nuclear Offensive* (Washington, D.C.: U.S. Government Printing Office, 1976); this study by the Pentagon was influential at that time. For further discussion, see Andrew C. Goldberg, "Western Analysts Reappraise Soviet Strategic Policy," *Washington Quarterly* 12, no. 2 (1989), pp. 201–213.

14. For example, see Georgi Arbatov and Alexei Arbatov, "Schlesinger's Ideas in Form and Content," *Novoye Vremya*, July 25, 1975 (translated in FBIS, August 14, 1975).

15. See Leonid Brezhnev, "Outstanding Exploits of the Heroes of Tula," speech delivered on January 19, 1977, in *Current Digest of the Soviet Press*, February 16, 1977. For discussion and analysis, see Andrew C. Goldberg, "New Developments in Soviet Military Strategy," *Significant Issues* 9, no. 7 (Washington, D.C.: Center for Strategic and International Studies, 1987); Raymond L. Garthoff, "New Thinking in Soviet Military Doctrine," *Washington Quarterly* 11, no. 3 (1988), pp. 131–158; and Gerhard Wettig, "Europe after the INF Treaty," *Aussenpolitik*, January 9, 1988, p. 30.

16. This period of Soviet foreign policy has been heavily studied. For a sampling, see Raymond L. Garthoff, *Détente and Confrontation* (Washington, D.C.: Brookings Institution, 1985); and Thomas W. Wolfe, "Military Power and Soviet Policy" in William E. Griffith, ed., *The Soviet Empire: Expansion and Détente* (Lexington, Mass.: Lexington Books, 1976). Stephen S. Kaplan, *Diplomacy of Power* (Washington, D.C.: Brookings Institution, 1981), is also helpful.

17. Robert Jervis has noted this phenomenon of structured learning in the habits of elites. See his *Perception and Misperception in the International System* (Princeton: Princeton University Press, 1976); and Lloyd S. Etheredge,

"Thinking about Government Learning," *Journal of Management Studies* 20, no. 1 (1983), pp. 41–58.

18. See Meyer, "Soviet Theater Nuclear Forces," pt. 1, pp. 17–21.

19. James Schlesinger, *Report of the Secretary of Defense to the Congress, FY 1975* (Washington, D.C.: U.S. Government Printing Office, 1974), p. 147.

20. Harold Brown, *Report of the Secretary of Defense to the Congress, FY 1979* (Washington, D.C.: U.S. Government Printing Office, 1978). Emphasis added.

21. See Raymond Garthoff, "The SS-20 Decision," *Survival* 25, no. 3 (1983), pp. 110–119.

22. Arms Control Association, *INF Background and Negotiating History* (Washington, D.C.: 1988).

23. See Zhurkin, "Meeting in Washington"; Dadyants, "The Echo of the Saryozek Explosions"; and Bykov, "The 19th Party Conference."

24. See Garthoff, "New Thinking"; and Andrew C. Goldberg, "The Present Turbulence in Soviet Military Doctrine," *Washington Quarterly* 11, no. 3 (1988).

4

LIMITED ADVERSARIES, LIMITED ARMS CONTROL: CHANGING SOVIET INTERESTS AND PROSPECTS FOR ENHANCED SECURITY COOPERATION

Cynthia Roberts

In anarchy, even adversaries sometimes cooperate. The postwar U.S.–Soviet relationship is a case in point. Recognizing their common interest in avoiding a nuclear war, the superpowers gradually came to realize that some level of cooperation to advance this objective was desirable. As the preceding chapters recount, arms control became the primary mechanism for joint action, although neither side considered it an end in itself nor likely to provide more than a partial solution to its security problems. Not only were the basic political interests of the superpowers still irreconcilable, but as negotiations progressed, it was evident that differences in their strategic approaches and the composition of their arsenals would be a serious complicating factor. Thus, even during the heyday of the Strategic Arms Limitation Talks (SALT) in the 1970s, political, strategic, and ideological competition continued largely unabated, reflecting the limited nature of accommodation between the United States and the Soviet Union.

Given that refraining from the use of nuclear weapons was virtually the only matter on which the superpowers could agree, theirs was what Marshall Shulman termed a "limited adversary relationship."[1] In this context, it is hardly surprising that more than three decades of various superpower negotiations have produced only a few, modest arms control agreements. In fact, except for the Anti-ballistic Missiles (ABM) Treaty and the Inter-mediate-range Nuclear Forces (INF) accord, both sides have preferred to rely more on unilateral measures to provide security than on cooperative agreements that constrain their freedom to pursue policies they perceive as necessary to their respective self-interests. Only recently has it appeared, owing primarily to developments on the Soviet side, that the common ground between them may be expanding, thereby brightening the prospects for cooperative measures to enhance security.

Since Mikhail Gorbachev assumed power in 1985, the Soviet Union, through a series of dramatic concessions, negotiating initiatives, and unilateral force reductions, appears to have radically transformed its approach to arms control. The Gorbachev approach is being driven not only by the emergence of a new coalition of more sophisticated political elites and the need to respond to serious political and economic challenges at home and abroad. A third, and potentially more profound, impetus may be at work. There is evidence that the Gorbachev leadership is redefining Soviet political and security interests in ways that markedly reduce the sources of confrontation with the West. If this redefinition takes root and becomes the basis for long-term Soviet policy, it could contribute to the establishment of an entirely new framework of security cooperation and a more stable military balance.

A framework of cooperation between adversaries is not inconceivable if one or both sides redefine core interests in ways that diminish fundamental disagreements. Moreover, in rare instances, the process of changing basic goals, values, and institutions, if extensive and enduring, may even radically transform the nature of the adversarial relationship. Developing more cordial bilateral relations and a broader range of mutual interests, of course, is no guarantee that cooperation will result.[2] But eliminating the main sources of confrontation may greatly expand the possibilities for cooperative endeavors.[3] At this juncture, it is perhaps premature to envision such a transformation in U.S.–Soviet relations in the near future. However, this is apparently just what Gorbachev and his supporters have in mind when they talk about restructuring the Soviet system and denying the West to be a threat.

CHANGING SOVIET ARMS CONTROL STRATEGIES OR SECURITY INTERESTS?

Such developments raise important questions about the factors that lead to change in the definition of Soviet security interests and the role of arms control in promoting those interests. The connection between the two is significant because more extensive security cooperation depends heavily on both superpowers concluding that seeking advantage in the military competition is futile and that achieving stable deterrence at lower levels would be mutually beneficial.[4] On the Soviet side, this would require changing many of the long-standing political and security objectives that have fostered aggressive behavior and legitimized sustained investment in military forces designed for nuclear counterforce and large-scale offensive operations.[5]

As a consequence, in reviewing the record, it makes a difference whether Soviet leaders usually have altered the arms control strategies by which they pursue their interests or whether they have been open to modifying fundamental goals and values. One would expect the first to encourage limited or peripheral arms control agreements, whereas the second should contribute to the achievement of more meaningful security cooperation.[6]

The preceding case studies offer useful starting points for examining such issues. For instance, the chapters on the SALT II and INF negotiations by Coit Blacker and Andrew Goldberg, respectively, suggest that Soviet leaders have been more prone to shift their arms control strategies for various political purposes than to change their conceptions of basic security interests. These findings conform to the expectation that cooperation between adversaries usually results from a narrow convergence of otherwise antagonistic state strategies. In short, joint action would likely be considered a more effective means for pursuing each side's original goals.

By comparison, Rebecca Strode's description of the test ban negotiations implies that Khrushchev's conception of Soviet security interests was not immutable, and that at least in part as a consequence, agreement was eventually reached on the limited test ban. Other milestones, such as the ABM Treaty and the dramatic initiatives undertaken by Gorbachev, offer even more convincing evidence that Soviet security interests have evolved in the nuclear age.

Admittedly, distinguishing one from the other is no easy task, especially since the Soviet process of adjusting to changing realities is still unfolding, and available historical evidence remains limited. However, the alternative approach of searching only for strategic or geopolitical explanations for Soviet arms control behavior may generate erroneous conclusions and missed opportunities for Western policymakers. In the competitive international environment, great powers have strong incentives to be "sensitive to costs" and therefore often find it useful to alter the strategies by which they pursue their interests.[7] But this core assumption of the realist approach to international politics ignores the fact that interests themselves may also evolve in response to changing environmental and domestic conditions, interdependence and transnational relations, and altered perceptions and beliefs policymakers hold about the world and the role their state should play in it.[8]

Whether such factors have affected Soviet conceptions of their political and security interests, or whether there has generally been continuity in interests and changes in arms control strategy, is the central question explored in this essay. The analysis proceeds chronologically, suggesting that a combination of motivations—including perceived strategic imperatives, institutionalized ideological biases, and erroneous policy expectations—stifled incentives for successive Soviet leaders to redefine their security interests. This was the situation until the mid-1980s, when a new generation of better-educated political elites, who see reality differently, were elevated to positions of influence with the Gorbachev succession. Meanwhile, between Stalin and Gorbachev, important changes emerged in Soviet thinking about the role of nuclear weapons, in military doctrine, and in foreign policy concepts that, implicitly or explicitly, encouraged some flexibility in the Soviet approach to arms control. But these were differences of degree. The argument of this chapter is that only since Gorbachev's qualitative break with old definitions of Soviet interests have opportunities been created for far more extensive arms control than ever before within a new framework of security cooperation.

THE FIRST POSTWAR DECADE: STRATEGIC AND STALINIST IMPERATIVES

Although it is tempting to dismiss Stalin's advocacy of peace and disarmament measures in the postwar years as merely propaganda, in fact, such proposals also served concrete policy objectives. The obstacle to agreements, therefore, was not a lack of Soviet attention to what is now (at least in the West)[9] commonly referred to as arms control, but rather the overriding importance of competing East-West political and security interests. As in the interwar period, Soviet disarmament proposals were designed in the late 1940s to divert hostile forces during a time of weakness and potential danger. Faced with a U.S. nuclear monopoly, Stalin agitated for disarmament while simultaneously striving to develop his own nuclear arsenal. The Soviet Union wanted not only to buy time to redress its position of weakness, but also to "stigmatize nuclear weaponry" so that American leaders would be inhibited from "contemplate[ing] its use against the USSR."[10]

During this period, it should also be recalled, Soviet political and security interests were expanded to include the protection of the enlarged Soviet empire and the creation of satellites in key adjacent countries. Stalin sought safety not only from military attack, but also from the political and ideological challenge that capitalism posed to the stability of the empire. Of course, the USSR's military and political insecurity was largely a product of its own making. By establishing subservient regimes in Eastern Europe and encouraging the political fragmentation of Western

THE OTHER SIDE OF THE TABLE

Europe, Stalin stimulated a larger U.S. role in the recovery and defense of Europe than might otherwise have been the case and increased Western unity on security matters.[11]

Given the American lead in nuclear technology and deepening U.S. involvement in Europe, the Soviet Union pursued its European interests in a calculated and risk-averse way.[12] Nevertheless, Stalin apparently underestimated the impact of Soviet behavior on Western policy, while overestimating the possibilities for exploiting popular antiwar sentiment to disrupt Western rearmament efforts and encourage an abatement of cold war tensions. The latter efforts probably stemmed in part from his evolving belief that war between socialism and capitalism was avoidable. He apparently held this view despite acknowledging the contradictions and hostility that divided the two camps, and despite his idée fixe that a future war would somehow be decided by certain "permanent operating factors" that neglected the implications of the nuclear revolution.[13]

In any event, Soviet diplomacy was directed at rallying support within the Western peace movement, which was engaged, inter alia, in attacking German remilitarization and collecting signatures for the 1950 Stockholm Appeal to "ban the bomb."[14] By one count, the Soviet leadership itself advanced fifteen sets of disarmament proposals between 1945 and Stalin's death in 1953. These included some early inconsequential efforts, such as an effort to ban the use and production of the atom bomb and, in October 1950, a proposal to conclude a peace pact between the United States, Great Britain, France, China, and the Soviet Union.[15]

Given the level of Western threat perceptions during the late 1940s, which increased dramatically after the outbreak of the Korean War and the establishment of a communist regime in China, it was unlikely that the West would accept any of Stalin's disarmament gambits. Moreover, since they lacked adequate verification measures, which were a sine qua non for Western leaders, it is reasonable to assume that Moscow was either counting on its ability to circumvent any potential treaty or more interested in the political benefits to be derived from promoting peace and disarmament. In any event, disarmament was never a substitute for military power, and thus the main purpose of Soviet security efforts was to remedy the nuclear imbalance and ensure a favorable "correlation of forces."

Stalin's approach to security also had two important domestic implications. First, it legitimized continued priority to the military-industrial sector of the Soviet economy, thereby further entrenching the influence of those individuals and institutions that supported the Stalinist approach to running the bureaucracy and dealing with the outside world. Second, Stalin's strategic ideology, and the policies and propaganda it generated, had an enduring effect on the mind-set of a generation of Soviet policymakers. Above all, it reinforced the traditional Bolshevik predisposition to see the world in Manichaean terms. Despite Stalin's peace tactics and veiled acknowledgment that war with the West was unlikely, the party line typically branded "Western imperialism" as the aggressor, while emphasizing tireless Soviet efforts aimed at preventing the threat of war. Over the years, this twisted and self-serving logic tended to settle, as one Soviet historian put it, "into stereotyped, clichéd thinking in the psychology of leading officials, who became, for all intents and purposes, prisoners of their own propaganda."[16]

THE KHRUSHCHEV ERA I:
STRATEGIC ADJUSTMENTS

Despite his de-Stalinization campaign and his own particular ideas about the Soviet force posture, Nikita Khrushchev did not radically depart from the Stalinist emphasis on military power as the primary means to ensure Soviet security. What did change, however, by the late 1950s was the strategic outlook. Finally, the Soviet Union possessed a significant intermediate-range missile and bomber force, its first intercontinental bombers were operational, and Moscow was rushing to test the world's first intercontinental missile, the SS-6.[17] Although the United States maintained quantitative superiority, Soviet nuclear weapon programs were proceeding on a broad front. Moreover, Khrushchev believed that the correlation of forces—embracing the strength of the socialist camp and the overall balance of political, military, and economic power—was shifting in the Soviet Union's favor.[18]

The USSR's entry into the nuclear-rocket age may have coincided with a revised approach to arms control. For the first time, Rebecca Strode suggests, Soviet negotiating proposals implied a serious interest in certain types of restraints on the development and proliferation of nuclear weapons.[19] At a minimum, the new leadership probably decided that continuing Stalin's reliance on antinuclear agitation would be counterproductive, given the Soviet Union's own programs and the risks of incurring undesirable political costs.[20] On the other hand, like Stalin, his successors did not view arms control as an alternative to Soviet military power. In fact, Khrushchev anticipated that nuclear weapons would become the mainstay of the Soviet force posture. How, then, should Soviet proposals for a comprehensive test ban be explained?

One explanation emphasizes the impact of strategic and international developments during the mid-1950s. Accordingly, Soviet arms control strategy was refocused largely to curtail American military programs and frustrate the efforts of China and other states, notably France and Britain, to develop nuclear arsenals. The Soviet Union also sought to avert the stationing of American nuclear weapons on the territory of such countries as the Federal Republic of Germany.[21]

At the same time, the Soviets may have concluded that a test ban would not impose severe constraints on their own nuclear weapon program. Although some uncertainty regarding the feasibility of new weapon designs would inevitably result from a comprehensive test ban, Khrushchev seemed to value nuclear weapons particularly for their political and psychological impact. Thus, as Strode hypothesizes, he may have considered such uncertainty tolerable.[22]

Soviet leaders may also or alternatively have initiated their campaign for a comprehensive test ban agreement to reap the propaganda benefits, and only after the Cuban missile crisis decided that some form of agreement (providing it did not compromise defense requirements) would help ease tensions.[23] Khrushchev himself reportedly lectured one of his subordinates in 1960 about "the appeal that the idea of disarmament has in the outside world. All you have to do is say, 'I'm in favor of it,' and that pays big dividends."[24] After the Cuban missile crisis, however, Khrushchev was more willing to accommodate U.S. concerns about verification, suggesting that the crisis triggered a more serious commitment to concluding a test ban treaty. According to Raymond Garthoff, at this point, Khrushchev accepted in principle three on-site annual inspections "despite the stiff opposition of some of his colleagues."[25]

Finally, it is not inconceivable that the Soviets believed they could violate a test ban agreement with impunity, given their initial stand against intrusive verification measures and Khrushchev's subsequent refusal to allow more than three on-site inspections per year. The last two explanations, of course, are bolstered by their ability to accommodate the Soviet military's concerns about the reliability of the USSR's nuclear weapons and the prevailing numerical imbalances between U.S. and Soviet nuclear forces. While each of these explanations has some merit, a definitive solution to this puzzle must await additional information.

THE KHRUSHCHEV ERA II: STRATEGIC BELIEFS AND DOMESTIC IMPERATIVES

Although the Soviet Union's changing strategic calculus appears to have influenced a modest redirection of Soviet arms control policy under Khrushchev, three broader political and economic considerations weighed more heavily in his approach to security problems. First, in accordance with past Soviet practice, Khrushchev's disarmament proposals were designed to serve the USSR's foreign policy interests as much as they served military requirements. In particular, the arms control process was expected to help moderate aggressive U.S. behavior. This view followed logically from Khrushchev's dual assumptions that "reasonable" elements existed in the United States and that the changing correlation of forces supported those elements, helping to deter the outbreak of a world war and constrain American defense efforts.[26]

A second foreign policy objective that arms control was supposed to serve stemmed from the Soviet preoccupation with being recognized as a coequal superpower. Notwithstanding the nuclear imbalance that existed when he was in power, Khrushchev frequently bristled about this issue, insisting that "President Kennedy once admitted that our strength is equal . . . and it is high time that . . . American leaders should come to correct conclusions and pursue a reasonable policy."[27] Undoubtedly, Khrushchev recognized the Soviet Union's objective strategic weaknesses and this probably influenced his decision to station nuclear weapons in Cuba.[28] However, his inflated expectations about the USSR's ability to redress its strategic inferiority and rapidly overtake the United States in the systemic competition blinded Khrushchev to America's determination to maintain its superior position.

The United States plainly was supposed to adjust to the new correlation of forces and accept the progression of the historical process toward the ultimate victory of socialism over capitalism.[29] American restraint and cooperation in maintaining the peace were, in the Soviet view, logical corollaries. Never mind that the Khrushchev leadership pursued self-serving political gains by alternating between the use of "rocket rattling" (to create the impression of nuclear strength) and overtures for détente.[30] Nor was the United States supposed to take countervailing steps in response to Khrushchev's creation of the Strategic Rocket Forces in 1959 or his announcement that the next war (while not inevitable) would assuredly be nuclear.

Soviet expectations that American policymakers could be lulled into accepting such an arrangement were based not only on the prevailing image of the United States and the shifting correlation of forces, but also on the traditional view of peaceful coexistence as embracing both cooperation and struggle between the two social systems. Hence, the Khrushchev leadership believed that the superpowers could cooperate to lessen the chances of war while the Soviet Union, as Feodor Burlatskii, Khrushchev's speech-writer and aide, then put it, used "the existing situation to the maximum in the interests of the struggle for world socialism."[31]

In effect, the Khrushchev leadership refused to choose between projecting Soviet influence and expanding Soviet military might, on the one hand, and improving East-West relations, on the other. But the very fact that the Soviet leadership cared about maximizing its relative power and position vis-à-vis the West mitigated the prospects for serious negotiations to reduce nuclear arsenals.[32] As one Soviet observer explains, Khrushchev and other leaders of his generation emerged as political figures during the Stalinist years and therefore were prone to view international relations as a "gladiators' stadium." These leaders strove "not so much to ensure genuine security as to achieve momentary tactical advantages in this planetary skirmish."[33]

This perspective helps explain why Soviet policymakers consistently viewed the test ban negotiations as primarily a political, rather than a technical, issue. They probably believed that a comprehensive test ban would have constrained American weapon modernization efforts and improved bilateral relations while allowing the Soviet Union to proceed with its own nuclear programs.

Finally, it is important to consider the extent to which economic factors influenced the Soviet approach to arms control. At first, Khrushchev may actually have believed that arms control would allow the Soviet Union to reduce the defense burden without sacrificing security.[34] He calculated, erroneously as it turned out, that negotiating a nuclear test ban would help alleviate the external threat, thereby freeing needed resources for other sectors of the economy.

In reality, the test ban issue was but one part of a larger, more complex strategy by which Khrushchev attempted to link other arms control and foreign policy initiatives to his domestic policy agenda.[35] As Burlatskii recounts, Khrushchev believed that it was his destiny "to bring peace and prosperity to the Soviet people." However, although he frequently spoke of this as his

131

main objective, Khrushchev's conception of the means by which these goals would be realized was problematic.[36] For instance, Soviet economic progress was partially tied not only to the assumption that Soviet defense expenditures could be capped, but also to Khrushchev's belief that East-West trade and technology transfer could be greatly expanded. Such expectations depended in turn on a constellation of dubious assumptions including the USSR's ability to rely primarily on nuclear weapons for defense, the superior dynamism of Soviet technology and the Soviet economy, and the success of Khrushchev's bold foreign policy moves.[37] In the end, Khrushchev's ambitious juggling act failed to bring about the desired results, and he was deposed.

KHRUSHCHEV'S ARMS CONTROL POLICY REAPPRAISED

In one important respect, the Khrushchev experience lends support to the argument that even antagonists can recognize their common interest in avoiding a nuclear war and cooperate to this end. Khrushchev's chief contribution to furthering Soviet recognition of this principle came at the Twentieth Party Congress, in February 1956, when he decisively abandoned Leninist doctrine, declaring that war between the two social systems was no longer inevitable. This departure, while not entirely new, imparted doctrinal significance to the common interest of the superpowers in averting a nuclear war, for both sides recognized that it would bring disastrous consequences.

Yet, it does not necessarily follow that arms control, however desirable, was or is a necessary means for preventing war. Starting with Khrushchev, Soviet leaders seemed to believe that the arms control process could meaningfully contribute to this goal.[38] But as some leading Western academics have maintained, the superpowers pursue the prevention of war primarily unilaterally, by maintaining nuclear forces capable (at a minimum) of inflicting unacceptable retaliation.[39] Although it would be unwise to discount the Soviet view entirely (since arms control could lead to smaller retaliatory forces), it has squared more neatly with the role of Soviet diplomacy in averting war than with limiting offensive capabilities. After all, if Khrushchev had not yet developed a credible deterrent capability, he was surely committed to obtaining one.

It is also true, as Professor Alexander George and his colleagues note, that a shared superpower fear of Armageddon is not a sufficient condition for U.S.–Soviet security cooperation.[40] According to George, two additional factors are required: first, the superpowers must perceive that each is dependent to some extent on the other's behavior (in this context) to prevent the outbreak of war; second, both must conclude that "strictly unilateral measures, however important and necessary, will either not suffice to deal [with this threat] . . . or are too expensive or risky."[41] Although the first was obtained while Khrushchev ruled, neither superpower unambiguously drew the second conclusion.[42] In fact, on the Soviet side, Khrushchev believed almost precisely the reverse—namely, that reliance on cheap, nuclear weapons reinforced the changing correlation of forces, and that both mitigated the likelihood of war.[43]

That the superpowers were able to bring about a limited test ban in spite of these factors was probably a consequence of both the peripheral importance of the agreement to central security concerns and a shared recognition that some concrete form of mutual reassurance was desirable after the shock of the Cuban missile crisis.[44] Other considerations, such as appeals from Soviet scientists to put an end to atmospheric testing for environmental reasons, appear to have had at most a minimal impact on Soviet policy decisions.[45]

Thus, except for the important doctrinal innovation refuting war's inevitability, which coincided with a new awareness of mutual vulnerability, the Khrushchev era did not see the necessary modification of Soviet political and security interests for more extensive cooperation in arms control arrangements. In the last years of Khrushchev's rule, there were signs of a reappraisal of the traditional zero-sum approach to international politics and an evolution in Soviet perceptions of the respective interests of the superpowers. But this trend did not develop far enough to improve the prospects for arms limitations, and it was reversed as the new leadership consolidated its power in the mid-1960s.[46] On balance, therefore, Soviet policy under Khrushchev was still based essentially on self-interest defined as defense of the empire and the expansion of global influence. Moreover, to the extent that Khrushchev's foreign policy differed significantly from Stalin's, the differences stemmed mainly from the former's own particular "misguided and provocative" offensive strategy, which, for most of his tenure, was predicated on the "deceptively bright prospect of Soviet superiority" in the relative balance of power.[47]

THE BREZHNEV ERA: DÉTENTE AND COMPETING SUPERPOWER INTERESTS

Like Khrushchev, Brezhnev placed a high priority on displacing the United States in the competition for power and influence, and defined successful cooperation with the West as preventing war and achieving joint enterprises favorable to the Soviet Union. Khrushchev's impetuous and often shrill style was replaced by greater reliance on traditional diplomatic interaction, as well as by a more steady pursuit of foreign policy gains. But as one scholar has observed, the Brezhnev leadership "did not learn that offensive détente was an inherently self-defeating policy."[48]

During the early 1970s, Soviet leaders were even more convinced that the correlation of forces was shifting to the Soviet Union's advantage and that this would compel the United States to embrace détente. An important turning point was the enunciation of the Nixon Doctrine, which encouraged the Soviets to believe that the United States was finally retreating from its "aggressive globalism."[49] They concluded that U.S foreign policy was constrained by a variety of factors, including the polarization of American society, the loss of a foreign policy consensus during the Vietnam War, and discord within the North Atlantic Treaty Organization (NATO).[50] Above all, the Soviets stressed their achievement of parity, which, as Coit Blacker emphasizes, convinced them that Washington would now have to behave in a more conciliatory manner and engage Moscow "as a political and military equal."[51]

In fact, the Nixon administration only reluctantly acknowledged the loss of America's strategic superiority and sought to limit its political consequences.[52] Then and afterward, the United States resisted the idea that the Soviet Union was entitled to an equal global role. If at the outset of détente there was some hope that the Soviet Union would exercise restraint in its foreign policy, it became clear that the superpowers could not precisely define the contours of a mutually acceptable code of conduct either in the text of the 1972 Basic Principles agreement or in practice.[53]

For its part, the Soviet Union throughout the 1970s denied that any "deal between the two superpowers" would impede Soviet actions elsewhere. In a 1972 article in *Pravda,* Nikolai Inozemtsev, then director of the Institute of World Economic and International Relations (IMEMO), pointedly insisted that "the Soviet Union has been, is and will always remain a true friend of peoples struggling for national independence . . . and against imperialism and colonialism."[54] According to the high-ranking Soviet defector Arkady Shevchenko, the Kremlin considered it important that Brezhnev's policy line on détente not be construed (by either domestic or foreign audiences) as signaling a "cessation of the ideological struggle." On the contrary, he reports, it should be seen as "a great victory" and "'convincing proof' of the 'powerful rise of Soviet influence throughout the world.'"[55]

Subsequently, Soviet officials and public figures frequently complained that the problem was not Soviet behavior but Washington's inability to accept the logical implications of equality. Thus, while Soviet political objectives had historically been ambitious, the Brezhnev leadership increasingly demonstrated that it associated growth in military power with a new sense of entitlement for the USSR to pursue its interests wherever it deemed necessary or desirable.

135

As the decade unfolded, conflicts in Angola, the Horn of Africa, the Middle East, and elsewhere offered promising opportunities for the expansion of Soviet influence, and in such places Moscow often made effective use of its new military reach.[56] Apparently, the changing correlation of forces had encouraged the Brezhnev leadership to redefine its definition of acceptable risks vis-à-vis the United States. While eschewing Khrushchev's adventuristic behavior, Brezhnev and his colleagues seemed to believe that the combination of parity and détente allowed the Soviet Union to steadily expand its global position beyond the point that previously might have provoked a strong U.S. response, if not a dangerous confrontation.[57]

In certain respects, Brezhnev's détente strategy attained the desired results and thus appeared to confirm the validity of the Soviet leadership's ambitious agenda. Clearly, Soviet foreign policy scored many successes in the Third World during the 1970s, primarily by actively supporting left-wing opposition forces, and also by fostering the image of the Soviet Union as a proponent of positive change and the United States as the guarantor of an oppressive status quo. At the same time, Brezhnev and his colleagues made more headway than Khrushchev had on the cooperative track, obtaining not only a series of much desired security agreements (including the 1969 Nuclear Non-Proliferation Treaty and the 1973 Prevention of Nuclear War Agreement), but also Western acceptance of the postwar division of Europe.

Ironically, such international triumphs seemed to reinforce the Brezhnev leadership's conviction (which was identical to Khrushchev's view) that choosing between competition and cooperation with the United States was unnecessary. Consequently, Soviet leaders were ill disposed to reconsider their basic assumptions as U.S.–Soviet relations nevertheless steadily deteriorated. Instead, Moscow preferred to blame Washington for exaggerating the pernicious effects of competition in the Third World, for blocking cooperative enterprises critical to the bilateral relationship, and for failing to accommodate the Soviet view on how to manage European security issues. Even after the Carter administration, responding to the Soviet invasion of

Afghanistan, shelved the SALT II Treaty and initiated a defense buildup, the Brezhnev leadership was disinclined to believe that competing superpower interests would block security and other types of cooperation for long.

THE ROLE OF ARMS CONTROL IN BREZHNEV'S DÉTENTE STRATEGY

By all accounts, Soviet observers in the early 1970s did not foresee the possibility that détente could unravel in such a relatively brief time frame. In fact, as Coit Blacker suggests, some Soviets were so encouraged by the early trends in U.S.–Soviet relations that they began to believe détente would be irreversible.[58] In part, this perception reflected the package of agreements concluded under the 1972 SALT I framework, which was hailed by both sides as a significant milestone in bilateral relations.

Although the Brezhnev leadership attached special importance to the agreement on "basic principles of relations" between the superpowers,[59] the ABM Treaty was jointly recognized as the centerpiece of SALT. By effectively prohibiting the deployment of nationwide ballistic missile defenses, the treaty represented an unprecedented departure from the peripheral types of agreements negotiated under Khrushchev; it remains to date the superpower accord with the greatest military significance.

If, as some Western observers have suggested, the ABM Treaty also signified Soviet acceptance of mutual deterrence, evidently this was not a notion that all members of the Soviet leadership (or some in the American, for that matter) embraced enthusiastically.[60] Because of their World War II experience, the Soviets regarded defense of the homeland as both a sacred task and an objective national security requirement. Thus, it was not easy for them to acknowledge, even implicitly, that for the foreseeable future the USSR could mount no effective defense against nuclear attack and that an ABM competition with the technologically superior United States would likely leave the Soviet Union in an even worse position. As many Americans came to realize, the idea that strategic defenses were destabilizing and thus best prohibited required some hard "new thinking." Yet, according to a former high-ranking Soviet Foreign Ministry official, "Not everyone in our leadership was able to do that." Consequently, the negotiations generated "a fierce struggle, internal [that is, within the Soviet Union] and bilateral," even to the point that a Soviet diplomat who had been among the first advocates of the ABM Treaty was regarded by a high Soviet official "as almost a 'US agent.'"[61]

Nonetheless, SALT I was signed. And as part of the bargain, the Soviet leadership fully expected that the Brezhnev approach to détente with the United States would soon bring about its main objectives, namely, a tempering of Western behavior, restraints on American weapon developments, and an expansion of economic ties and technology transfers. What the Soviets did not expect, or appreciate, according to Blacker's account, was the U.S. insistence on resuming arms negotiations without delay. The arms control process unexpectedly became the central focus of détente, thereby forcing the Soviet Union, as Blacker notes, to alter what Moscow considered "the logical sequencing of its détente policy."[62]

Brezhnev and his colleagues went along grudgingly, no doubt hoping that other parts of their political and economic agenda would soon bear fruit. Meanwhile, the content of Soviet proposals, not to mention Moscow's response to American initiatives, revealed that the Soviet Union—like the United States—placed a higher priority on protecting essential strategic programs than on achieving mutual reductions. This attention to military requirements never flagged, even as the Soviet Union was drawn into a long, complex series of discussions about various weapons ceilings and possible trade-offs. Throughout the twists and turns of the SALT II negotiations, each superpower attempted simultaneously to constrain the other and obtain a favorable position for itself.[63] As a consequence, it was hardly surprising that the Vladivostok agreement, reached in the autumn of 1974, and the SALT II accord, signed in June 1979, were both essentially based on "the logic of the 'lowest common denominator.'"[64]

For its part, the Soviet Union retreated very little from its principal security concerns.[65] In the fall of 1974, after two years of standing firm on the need to include U.S. forward-based systems (FBS) in the negotiations, Moscow finally yielded. At the same time, the Soviets agreed to an equal ceiling on the number of strategic nuclear delivery vehicles (SNDVs), despite their concern that this left them with *"less* than equal security," given the prevailing geopolitical situation.[66] However, such concessions diminish in significance when viewed in the context of the high launcher ceiling of 2,400 SNDVs established at Vladivostok. Even accounting for the fact that the Soviet Union dedicated a percentage of its ballistic missile force to cover targets on the Eurasian periphery, such a ceiling would seem to have allowed adequate coverage of North America, as well as some room for modernization. It is also notable that in 1974 the Soviets began flight tests of the SS-20 intermediate-range ballistic missile (IRBM), which, when deployed, would alleviate concerns about regional target coverage.[67]

If, therefore, as ACDA Director Paul Warnke reports, "Brezhnev had to spill political blood to get the Vladivostok accords,"[68] it is likely that the main issue involved political considerations. Undoubtedly, Soviet military leaders were displeased about the switch from SALT I to equal numerical levels in the Vladivostok accord, since the Soviet Union faced more potential enemies (in addition to American FBS) and thus, according to their assessment, required greater nuclear potential. But judging from the fact that senior Soviet military advisers had at one point been excluded from the Vladivostok deliberations, Brezhnev either did not fully share this worst-case outlook or overruled his military, believing the numerical ceiling adequate and the political need for agreement paramount.[69]

In any event, the real issue was probably that by 1974, Brezhnev had chalked up relatively few concrete successes in his American policy to be able to comfortably justify to domestic critics the need for such apparent concessions. Certainly, Soviet economic problems were not being helped either by the Jackson-Vanik and Stevenson amendments, passed by Congress in 1974, or by the fact that U.S. weapon modernization programs continued, albeit at a slower pace and on a smaller scale than their Soviet counterparts.[70] Both factors challenged critical elements of Brezhnev's strategy: the first undermined the assumption that East-West economic ties would help alleviate the need for domestic economic reforms, while the second, coupled with the Schlesinger Doctrine, was predictably interpreted by the military and other members of Brezhnev's coalition as evidence that America was still a threat to be reckoned with, thereby justifying a continuation of the Soviet defense buildup.[71]

Ultimately, however, Leonid Brezhnev prevailed, and the Vladivostok agreement was hailed as another political measure contributing to the prevention of war. But despite subsequent foreign policy successes, this was by no means the end of either Brezhnev's struggle to achieve détente with the West on Soviet terms or his political and economic difficulties at home. The struggle toward détente was aggravated by the continuing delays and incessant U.S. demands for Soviet concessions in the SALT II negotiations; by NATO concerns about European security, culminating in the 1979 dual track decision to deploy intermediate-range nuclear forces while negotiating with the Soviet Union; and by President Carter's decision to shelve the controversial SALT II treaty in the wake of the Soviet invasion of Afghanistan.

Meanwhile, Soviet political and economic problems continued to build, despite Brezhnev's reported ability to curtail military procurement in 1974 and reduce real growth in defense spending in 1976, when Dmitri Ustinov succeeded Andrei Grechko as minister of defense.[72] As Soviet reports now confirm, these halfway measures actually did little to improve the economic outlook. This suggests that Brezhnev was willing to reassess economic priorities,[73] but unprepared or unable (because of domestic political opposition) to undertake a major policy reorientation.

According to the late Soviet foreign minister and president, Andrei Gromyko, it would have been possible to have stopped the accumulation of nuclear weapons and reduced expenditures on their development, since the side with fewer nuclear weapons could still have inflicted a destructive retaliatory strike on its numerically superior opponent. "But this was not done," he maintains, because the complicated nature of Soviet-American relations did not promote "a sober appreciation" of the situation, and because in such conditions "no one could even hint at the necessity of reducing expenditures on nuclear armaments."[74] Conceivably, Brezhnev thought he was already accomplishing a great deal, given opposition to his incremental modifications of Soviet military doctrine (discussed below) and his insistence on holding the line on defense outlays even after the Reagan administration—having made clear its distaste for détente, the Soviet Union, and arms control—began a defense program of sizable proportions.

Toward the end of the 1970s and into the early 1980s, as the costs of Brezhnev's policies steadily mounted, additional incentives to rethink the larger picture presented themselves. At home, the hypercentralized Stalinist economic system, still oriented toward military-industrial production and ill-suited to the tasks of intensive economic development, was stagnating. Meanwhile, the Communist Party had suffered a serious loss of initiative and was unable to stem the rampant corruption, inertia, and abuses of power by *apparachiki*. Abroad, the stalemate in Afghanistan, closer political and military ties between the United States and China, and the diminishing returns garnered from support for revolutionary movements and radical regimes in the Third World provided ample inducements to reconsider Brezhnev's policy approach.

To a certain degree, Soviet intellectuals considered the implications of such foreign developments and began to adapt traditional assumptions about international relations.[75] Moreover, military officials now claim, the General Staff had opposed the decision to intervene in Afghanistan, and some professional Soviet analysts report a burgeoning skepticism about the wisdom of such international ventures even while Brezhnev was still in power.[76] Whatever the validity of such reports, neither the subcurrents in intellectual concepts nor advice from lower levels seem to have had any discernible impact on policy decisions. It appears that the Soviet leadership, which had earlier "over-estimated . . . [its] possibilities and underestimated . . . the resistance of the environment,"[77] had not yet come to terms with changing international conditions.

Another telling example was the fumbling Soviet approach to dealing with the INF issue, which current Soviet officials and analysts are examining.[78] Once again the opportunity to find a mutually beneficial solution existed even before NATO's dual track decision in 1979. As former First Deputy Foreign Minister Georgi Kornienko has maintained, there was a "real chance" that a dialogue could have been initiated to "search for a compromise" when West German Chancellor Helmut Schmidt visited Moscow in the summer of 1979. Moreover, in Kornienko's view, the Brezhnev leadership's most serious mistake was not to have reached a mutually acceptable solution soon after the Carter administration entered office in 1977.[79] According to another Foreign Ministry official, such opportunities were lost because "[the Soviet] conveyor belt was running, the stagnation period was at its height, and we thought and acted out of inertia."[80] The inertia in Soviet policy probably stemmed in part from the Brezhnev leadership's continuing assessment that the SS-20 was needed for regional target coverage (in light of SALT II ceilings for strategic forces) and from its mistaken assumption that European public opposition would block new NATO deployments of intermediate-range missiles.

After insisting for several months that it would not negotiate unless the NATO decision was canceled or officially suspended, the Soviet leadership finally withdrew its quid pro quo during Schmidt's visit in late June 1980.[81] But as Kornienko reveals, the Soviets had not yet changed their position on including British and French nuclear forces in the negotiations. Brezhnev, who by now was having difficulties in conducting meetings (presumably because of his declining health), at one point in the discussion implied to Schmidt that the Soviet Union might be prepared to revise its view on counting these systems. However, according to Kornienko, this was not an accurate reflection of the official

Soviet stance (at least at that time), and it therefore further complicated the ensuing negotiations.[82]

When the talks finally began, first Brezhnev, then Andropov (before a humbling Soviet walkout) tried to palliate Western concerns by offering increasingly attractive concessions in successive negotiating packages. But these same leaders still expected that they would be able to protect some proportion of the SS-20 deployments, thereby ensuring "Soviet security by military-technological means."[83] They also hoped, as Andrew Goldberg points out, to "salvage the fabric of détente" as Brezhnev defined it, but could not accept that the price of détente was now much higher.[84] The changing circle of Soviet leaders in Moscow obviously did not anticipate that Western resolve would strengthen rather than weaken over time. Consequently, Soviet negotiating gambits, while perhaps "adequate to an old reality, failed in new conditions."[85] It was only after Gorbachev assumed office that a major policy reversal occurred, leading to the conclusion of the INF Treaty in December 1987.

In these instances—as well as others, such as Brezhnev's disinclination to bite the bullet on reducing defense outlays—the signs of a strong Soviet reluctance to undertake a major policy reorientation are clear.

BREZHNEV'S RELUCTANCE TO SQUARE THE CIRCLE: CHANGES IN MILITARY CONCEPTS, CONTINUITY IN POLITICAL INTERESTS AND STRATEGY

Why, exactly, the Brezhnev leadership could not bring itself to change course and address the multiple external and internal challenges facing the Soviet Union is a question that cannot yet be answered definitively. However, besides Brezhnev's need to keep his political coalition intact,[86] and beyond the matter of his reportedly shallow mind and declining health,[87] two factors seem to form a significant part of the explanation.

First, as the history of the Brezhnev era reveals, the Soviet leadership was not entirely lacking in good fortune. After all, Brezhnev's détente strategy did produce a number of international successes, especially in the security sphere and in the Third World. Moreover, given the experiences of their generation, Brezhnev and his colleagues were inclined to insist that the Soviet people were living better than ever before. (Brezhnev was, of course, sheltered from the difficult living conditions confronting average Soviet citizens by the traditional privileges accorded to high officials and, reputedly, by his proclivity to believe the falsified Soviet economic statistics.) However, as Frederick the Great observed, "good fortune is often more fatal than adversity." Under Brezhnev, evidently success led to overconfidence and, in turn, to failure.

Second, like its predecessor, the Brezhnev leadership tended to define Soviet interests not only according to strategic imperatives but also according to an ideology heavily colored by traditional Bolshevik assumptions about the nature of "imperialism" and the international system. This ideology encouraged exaggerated threat perceptions and a reluctance to make more than tactical compromises in pursuing joint enterprises, such as arms control. It also contributed to the Brezhnev leadership's overly ambitious strategy and to its mistaken assumptions both that American leaders could be maneuvered into accepting détente on Soviet terms and that, as a consequence, the Soviet Union did not have to choose between competition and cooperation.

The impact of these considerations on Soviet security policy was clear. On the one hand, Soviet leaders could not bring themselves to redefine fundamental interests such that the East-West competition (let alone the global confrontation between socialism and capitalism) would no longer be the main determinant of policy. But at the same time, their approach to nuclear war showed signs of significant adjustment.[88]

Like Khrushchev, Brezhnev often emphasized the catastrophic consequences of a global nuclear war and the overriding need to avoid it. Yet, his government made even more far-reaching statements: in particular, it disavowed the goal of military superiority; repudiated assertions about the possibility of victory in a nuclear war; and proclaimed its intention to refrain from the first use of nuclear weapons. Although such innovations in Soviet declaratory policy may simply have been propaganda ploys to lull Western audiences, it is likely that real change of some importance was gradually taking root in the Soviet approach to war; otherwise, Brezhnev would not have faced an uphill battle to make such moves.[89]

That the Soviet Union was gradually adjusting to the new challenge of achieving security in the nuclear age is evident from the context in which these changes emerged. During the mid-1960s, and especially after Khrushchev's ouster, Soviet leaders came to the conclusion that nuclear weapons could not be regarded as ordinary means of warfare because the growing arsenals of both sides posed the threat of mutual annihilation. Although Khrushchev himself had earlier given signs of a similar understanding, he had established general nuclear war as the central planning requirement for military doctrine. His successors, however, abandoned this approach, along with Khrushchev's overemphasis on nuclear weapons. By the end of the decade, the new leadership believed that the Soviet achievement of strategic parity would deter the United States from starting an all-out nuclear war. Meanwhile, the buildup of a more balanced Soviet force posture would enable the USSR to cope with a variety of limited and regional scenarios below the level of general nuclear war.[90]

During the late 1960s and through the 1970s, as former Chief of the Soviet General Staff Nikolai Ogarkov has noted, a further, "radical reevaluation" of the role of nuclear weapons led the Soviets to conclude that a future war might be waged without their use.[91] Though this was rapidly becoming the preferred Soviet military strategy if war broke out (given the Soviets' growing confidence by the mid-1970s in their capability to wage war at this level), there remained concern about the threat of escalation, as well as about the worst possible case, however remote, of an unlimited U.S. surprise attack. At the same time, Soviet leaders recognized by the end of the 1960s that despite their long-standing preference for unilateral efforts to achieve security, defense against nuclear attack was not a realistic option for the foreseeable future.[92]

Thus, in order to reduce the likelihood of either escalation or surprise attack, the Brezhnev leadership committed itself to two objectives: maintaining strategic parity at all costs, and securing the cooperation of the United States to lessen the threat of war. In the Soviet view, the SALT I agreement and subsequent endeavors, such as the Prevention of Nuclear War Agreement, contributed to the latter objective, while the continuing modernization of Soviet strategic nuclear forces ensured the former.

In an effort to further the cooperative track, Brezhnev renounced the goal of military superiority, first during the SALT process by embracing the notion of "equality and equal security," and subsequently and more decisively in a 1977 speech in Tula.[93] During the 1970s, Brezhnev also attempted to enlist American cooperation in promoting a joint pledge not to be the first to use nuclear weapons, and even proposed an "understanding" that the two sides be considered sanctuaries from nuclear attack in the event of war.[94] Given the U.S. commitment to extended deterrence, this was obviously out of the question; hence, a watered-down compromise was reached in the 1973 Prevention of Nuclear War Agreement. But according to Raymond Garthoff, the Soviet leadership believed so strongly that such a decision would help reduce the prospect of war that it issued a secret directive to the military to make plans on the assumption that the Soviet armed forces would not be authorized to use nuclear weapons first, although they should be prepared for the possibility of escalation.[95] Soviet military leaders later implied that a change had been made when both Ustinov and Ogarkov claimed that the USSR's military doctrine does not provide for preemptive nuclear strikes (*uprezhdaiushchie udary*) and that despite the possibility of nuclear escalation, the Soviet Union will not be the first to employ nuclear weapons.[96] Finally, after additional efforts to obtain Western acceptance of no first use floundered, Brezhnev formally announced the Soviet Union's unilateral decision at the United Nations in June 1982.[97]

As in the Vladivostok deliberations, the military showed evidence of discontent over this move, given its implication that the Soviet Union would cede the first blow to the adversary.[98]

146

Undoubtedly, this created heightened concerns about the survivability of Soviet nuclear forces, which, in turn, reinforced the commitment to deploy (and protect from arms control) the mobile SS-20 IRBM. Soviet military leaders were evidently even more displeased with Brezhnev's repudiation of the possibility of victory in a nuclear war. This not only ran the risk of undermining morale and interfering with combat training, it also provided the political rationale for scaling back the development and procurement of what many in the military leadership considered to be essential systems.[99] At a time when new technological advances seemed to favor the West, Soviet military analysts became increasingly uneasy about their country's ability to provide the necessary high-technology components for future weapon systems. Such concerns provoked a prolonged and sharp debate, apparently over defense allocations and military requirements in general. Brezhnev insisted throughout, as in the final speech before his death to a special convocation of the military brass, that the military was getting everything it needed.[100]

Although Brezhnev apparently was unwilling to *reduce* defense allocations, the innovations he introduced in military doctrine had important implications for the Soviet approach to war and peace. In particular, they contributed to a greater emphasis on the need to promote strategic stability, while diminishing the earlier Soviet focus on a nuclear war-fighting strategy oriented toward damage limitation. Moreover, through the interaction of U.S.–Soviet relations and the conclusion of arms control arrangements, the Brezhnev leadership agreed to alter its political strategy and relinquish a small measure of unilateral control over decisions on strategic weapon deployments.

Still, these were halting steps, especially in comparison with the major transformation of political and security preferences that was to come later and more rapidly after the Gorbachev succession. They were halting because the Brezhnev leadership never fully reconciled the inherent incompatibility between its commitment to parity, as a means of ensuring a credible deterrent and advancing Soviet political interests, and its promotion of superpower cooperation to lessen the threat of a nuclear war.

Thus, despite progress in arms control, Soviet nuclear and conventional military capabilities were simultaneously increased well beyond the modernization programs initiated under Khrushchev.

To some extent, it may be argued, the Soviets were responding to Western defense initiatives.[101] Hence, because of their definition of parity, like the Red Queen in *Through the Looking-Glass,* they had to keep running in order to stay in the same place. Moreover, the influence of the USSR's military during the period undoubtedly helps to explain the scope and parameters of its defense buildup. But on both counts, it would be a misreading of the Brezhnev era to underestimate the larger commitment to military power of the Soviet political leadership. In fact, according to a recent Soviet analysis, the Brezhnev leadership created a kind of "parity 'cult,'" whereby parity became not only a means of safeguarding security but also a goal in itself.[102] In part, this was Moscow's way of compensating for its relative lack of economic power. But even more importantly, it stemmed from the growing proclivity of Soviet leaders to equate military power and political influence.

If, therefore, a degree of strategic readjustment and some small measure of learning is evident in the Brezhnev approach to security problems, the results were nonetheless limited, and they must have seemed disappointing to Moscow. In so many respects, both at home and abroad, the Soviet Union was worse off at the end of Brezhnev's long rule than when he achieved his position of primus inter pares in the early 1970s. Paradoxically, the Brezhnev leadership, having invested tremendous effort and resources in the accumulation of raw military power, was unable to translate this strength into a durable superior position for the Soviet Union in world politics.

Moreover, as Soviet observers now acknowledge, "never in its history did the Soviet Union have such a mighty defense potential as in the late 1970s–early 1980s, yet . . . concern over security heightened constantly."[103] Contrary to Soviet expectations, the United States did not accommodate itself to the strategic situation emerging at the end of the decade, but rather responded to the momentum of the Soviet arms buildup with its own extensive modernization program. Meanwhile, having placed a top priority on neutralizing external threats to its security, the Brezhnev leadership neglected, and thereby compounded, the political, economic, and social problems that were intensifying at home. Consequently, as one Soviet scholar has observed, through both its external behavior and its internal actions, the Soviet Union was actually "eroding its [own] security."[104]

THE UNDERLYING BASIS FOR GORBACHEV'S POLICY REORIENTATION

Responding to the failures of Brezhnev's strategy (continued to varying degrees by his immediate successors, Yuri Andropov and Konstantin Chernenko) and the systemic crisis created by several decades of dogmatic and centralized Communist rule, Mikhail Gorbachev initiated a radical reorientation of Soviet policy after he assumed the top leadership position in 1985.[105] Although Gorbachev evidently did not come to power with his own clearly defined strategy, he and his supporters rapidly learned that the external and internal challenges facing the Soviet Union required much more than simply vigorous diplomacy abroad and increased discipline combined with marginal economic reforms at home.[106]

Along the way, Gorbachev skillfully maneuvered to replace many of the Brezhnev holdovers and staunch conservatives on the Politburo. Gradually, he forged a new coalition of political elites who, like himself, were not tied either by shared generational experiences or by intellectual predispositions to many traditional assumptions about the nature of international politics or the requirements of the Soviet system. By the end of 1987, particularly after the embarrassment caused by the Matthias Rust affair, Gorbachev had also managed to renovate the military leadership, installing officers more responsive to the need for military reform.[107]

While the Gorbachev leadership has not yet reconciled all of the contradictions inherent in past Soviet strategies for dealing with the West and remains committed to ensuring the USSR's role as a global power, it has already cast aside many of the old premises and preconceptions that guided Soviet foreign policy for decades. In their place are quite different ideas and propositions, including a new emphasis on the political instruments of foreign policy rather than the military ones, mutual security rather than the pursuit of unilateral advantage, and universal human values rather than intense ideological confrontation.

To develop such ideas and translate them into viable policy concepts, Gorbachev and other leading officials have had to grapple with the political and ideological roots of past Soviet behavior. Though this process has been wrenching and not without opposition, the Soviet leadership has managed to shed many of its predecessors' xenophobic and dogmatic strategic beliefs. Partly as a consequence, the underlying basis of Soviet political and security interests is undergoing a fundamental transformation.

Three changes in basic Soviet premises are especially notable. First, Gorbachev and his supporters have plainly reconsidered standard Soviet ideas and formulas for achieving security in the nuclear age. Emphasizing the possibilities for a new level of East-West cooperation, Gorbachev himself asserted at the Twenty-seventh Party Congress, in 1986, that security can only be mutual because the insecurity of one side will lead to actions that diminish the security of both. He also insisted that no state can hope to defend itself "by military-technical means alone" and that political accommodation is the preferred solution to security problems.[108]

Gorbachev applies the same logic to the threat and use of force, which he repeatedly has claimed "should not be instruments of foreign policy."[109] Explaining the impulse behind this assertion, Soviet Foreign Minister Eduard Shevardnadze has said that "reliance on military force does not strengthen, but ultimately weakens national security."[110] While shunning force, Gorbachev maintains that states should respect the sovereignty, independence, and territorial integrity of other countries, including "friends and allies"; should tolerate political differences; and should orient diplomacy toward a "balance of interests."[111]

Both of these premises reveal the lessons the Gorbachev leadership has learned from such mistakes as the intervention in Afghanistan, an excessive reliance on military means (such as the SS-20) to ensure security, and, as Shevardnadze has put it, a "door-slamming" approach to diplomacy and negotiations. In fact, according to the foreign minister, "the disparity between the military and political areas" of policy during the Brezhnev era was "one of the worst phenomena" that acted "negatively on our international positions."[112]

Gorbachev delivered an even more severe indictment of the Brezhnev leadership's failures, first in his keynote speech to the Nineteenth Party Conference, in June of 1988, and then at a televised session of the Congress of People's Deputies the following spring. In both instances, he pointedly asserted that "arbitrary actions" encouraged by the "command-based system and secretive decision-making" had caused "serious harm" to the Soviet Union and "had a negative impact on its international prestige."[113] In the first address, Gorbachev also questioned whether his predecessors had defined the requirements of parity beyond what was necessary. Clearly, in his view, "fundamental changes in the world" had made possible political methods of ensuring security. But because these methods were not always employed, the Soviet Union had become enmeshed in a costly arms race that had eroded both its economy and its international position. Gorbachev further contended that the long-standing Soviet struggle for peace and disarmament had lost its persuasiveness under Brezhnev, and that this, in turn, raised the danger of military confrontation.[114]

A third departure from past premises is Gorbachev's apparent assumption that global interdependence has curbed the most aggressive aspects of imperialist behavior. In his view, this factor, coupled with heightened Western appreciation of the danger of war, explains why current international conditions are substantially different from those of the past.[115] Other prominent officials, such as Politburo members Alexander Yakovlev and Shevardnadze, have echoed this theme, and some Gorbachev supporters have even completely redefined the Soviet threat assessment, suggesting that it is difficult to imagine any goals that the West might achieve by an armed attack.[116]

Instead, the Gorbachev leadership and many professional Soviet analysts believe that the danger of war is rooted primarily in the threat of inadvertent escalation due to accident or policy miscalculations during a crisis. Such fears have reinforced their proclivity to regard nuclear deterrence as counterproductive to security. Besides contributing to an escalating arms competition and allowing unrestrained behavior toward nonnuclear countries, Gorbachev contends that deterrence is not "failsafe or of endless duration."[117] As a consequence, he argues that "security cannot indefinitely be built on fear of retaliation, that is, on the doctrines of 'deterrence' [sderzhivaniia] or 'intimidation' [ustrasheniia]."[118]

The Gorbachev leadership clearly understands the prevailing Western view that nuclear weapons have played a stabilizing role in the postwar era. But it rejects this argument as illusory and dangerous.[119] To be sure, some Soviet academic specialists have expressed views closer to Western notions of deterrence and stability, noting, for instance, that the very destructive power of nuclear weapons has minimized the likelihood of war.[120] On the other hand, many within both the political and the military bureaucracies have voiced their support for Gorbachev's perspective. Thus, one army general extolled Soviet efforts to do "everything possible to get out of the situation of 'mutually assured destruction.'"[121] Still others, including a senior General Staff analyst, maintain the old line that however catastrophic nuclear war would be, "the forces of militarism and the . . . threat they pose compel the Soviet Armed Forces to prepare for action involving conventional and nuclear weapons." Hence, it is still justified to regard the possibility of Soviet nuclear retaliation as "an enforced means of deterring a nuclear attack."[122] Interestingly, the author of these words further noted that war might start not only because of "unsanctioned use" of nuclear weapons, but also by aggressors whose "imaginary or real suc-

cesses" in developing novel weapons "can delude them into believing in their impunity and provoke them into carrying out a
surprise strike on their adversary."[123] Although he clearly had in
mind the impact of the Strategic Defense Initiative (SDI) on
American strategic calculations, the larger point about the danger of spurious strategic beliefs is important, if rarely discussed
by Soviet specialists.

Another reason Soviet leaders discount the Western view on
deterrence arises from their belief that American allies have
never fully relied on the U.S. nuclear guarantee. "Had nuclear
weapons really been a deterrent," Shevardnadze maintains,
"they would logically have curbed the race in conventional armaments. Actually the reverse happened."[124] Nonetheless, Gorbachev has demonstrated a willingness to search for a middle
ground, as evidenced most recently by his suggestion in
Strasbourg, in July 1989, that it would be "worthwhile to look
into what is behind the 'minimum' notion [of deterrence] and
where is the limit beyond which the potential for nuclear retaliation turns into an attack potential." He added that "the lack of
clarity [on the Western side] is a source of mistrust."[125]

Combined, these new premises advanced by the Gorbachev
leadership have profound implications for the Soviet approach
to security. Given concerns that war might occur as a result of
technical failures or other irrational causes, such as mispercep-
tions, Soviet leaders seem to have concluded that they must take
measures to establish mutual confidence and to reassure the
West that the Soviet Union does not harbor aggressive inten-
tions. As demonstrated by recent developments, such measures
include changes in Soviet military doctrine and force posture,
greater flexibility in arms control negotiations, and what
Yakovlev has called *preventive diplomacy . . .* to prevent the escalation of crises."[126]

NEW DIRECTIONS IN MILITARY DOCTRINE
AND ARMS CONTROL

Soon after Gorbachev assumed power, apparently one of his first
moves was to call for the Defense Council to reevaluate Soviet

strategic doctrine and the threat of nuclear war. According to some accounts, the decision to initiate a policy review was approved at the April 1985 plenum.[127] Interim steps were taken at the Twenty-seventh Party Congress in early 1986; a year later, in May of 1987, the Political Consultative Committee of the Warsaw Pact formally adopted a revised military doctrine that emphasized the task of preventing war.[128]

Although Soviet military doctrine was always said to have a defensive character, prior to Gorbachev's accession it was consistently defined in authoritative publications as the state's official view on "the nature of modern wars" and the requirements for "the preparation of the country and its armed forces for war."[129] The new definition, by comparison, emphasizes the "prevention of war" as the state's highest objective and, in lieu of the earlier wording, refers to official views on "military development, on the preparation of the country and its Armed Forces to repel aggression, and on the methods of conducting armed struggle for the defense of socialism."[130] In fact, the lead editorial in the January 1988 issue of the authoritative General Staff journal, *Voennaia mysl'* (Military Thought), emphasized that the principle of preventing war is now phrased more sharply and directly, and that in this new form it is included in "the definition of our military doctrine for the first time."[131]

This change in doctrine is significant because it allows Gorbachev to subordinate other relevant dimensions of Soviet policy to the goal of preventing war. In particular, these include both arms control initiatives and decisions concerning the size and orientation of the Soviet armed forces. With respect to the former, Gorbachev began in January 1986 to press his case for complete nuclear disarmament by the year 2000. However unrealistic, this proposal should not be taken as simply a propaganda ploy. This was a mistake the Reagan administration made nine months later, when Gorbachev advanced similarly breathtaking proposals at the superpower summit in Reykjavik.[132] After the fiasco there, it should be clear that Gorbachev genuinely believes the world would be a safer place without nuclear weapons and the need to rely on deterrence.

However, revealing that he is more a radical reformer than a utopian dreamer, Gorbachev introduced an intermediate option in 1987, proposing that force levels be based on the concept of "reasonable sufficiency" and that this could be achieved at much lower levels of armaments.[133] Several Soviet specialists have interpreted this concept to mean that the requirement for inflicting unacceptable damage could be met with fewer nuclear weapons (an idea that Ogarkov espoused earlier), and that nuclear arms reductions would pave the way for still lower levels of sufficiency.[134] More recently, some bolder analysts have suggested that the Soviet Union consider moving unilaterally to a minimal deterrent capability.[135] Still others have stressed the importance of ensuring the ability to inflict a retaliatory strike at lower cost to reduce the strain on the Soviet economy.[136]

At the same time, the Gorbachev leadership apparently hoped that the concessions it made to conclude the INF agreement—particularly, giving up more weapons than the United States, forgoing reductions in French and British nuclear arsenals, and agreeing to unprecedented on-site inspection measures—would give strategic arms negotiations a forward push. That START has progressed only marginally from the reductions agreed upon at Reykjavik must therefore be a source of some consternation to Gorbachev.[137]

At the December 1987 summit in Washington, the United States and the Soviet Union agreed to a sublimit of 4,900 ballistic missile warheads within the overall ceiling established at Reykjavik of 6,000 warheads, bombs, and air-launched cruise missiles. They also agreed to a sublimit of 1,540 warheads on heavy intercontinental ballistic missiles (ICBMs), which would require a 50 percent reduction in the Soviet force of SS-18 missiles. However, Washington and Moscow remain at odds over how to deal with the problem of sea-launched cruise missiles, as well as over the issue of mobile ICBMs, which the Soviet Union wants to allow but the Bush administration has sought to ban. Moreover, the Soviet side has insisted that reductions in offensive strategic weapons be linked to sharp limits on the testing and deployment of space-based ABM systems. In a somewhat ironic twist, ever since President Reagan launched SDI, Moscow, not Washington, has been the stauncher advocate of preserving the ABM Treaty. The Gorbachev leadership has also exhibited the same flexibility on intrusive verification measures that helped bring about the INF agreement.

While the U.S. presidential transition, the Bush administration's long policy review, and its difficulty in developing new positions delayed movement in START, Gorbachev was not idle. Building on such earlier initiatives as the unilateral moratorium on nuclear testing (from August 1985 to February 1987), the Soviet Union delivered an array of proposals and unilateral initiatives on a host of other issues. Moreover, in line with Gorbachev's policy of building mutual trust, various informal verification experiments involving American experts were permitted at Soviet test sites and on board a Soviet navy missile cruiser, and Westerners visited chemical weapon facilities, the Kyshtym nuclear complex, the Sary Shagan missile proving ground, the Krasnoyarsk phased array radar, and several other military installations previously closed to foreigners. Although many of these events involved public relations gestures, they nonetheless demonstrated that the Gorbachev leadership was willing to use *glasnost* to advance its arms control agenda and diminish Western fears and hostility.

ARMS CONTROL IN EUROPE:
THE SWITCH TO UNILATERAL INITIATIVES
AND NEGOTIATING CONCESSIONS

Of the Soviet Union's many arms control initiatives, the most significant to date concern reductions in and the restructuring of NATO and Warsaw Pact forces. That Europe is the region in which the cold war started and where the arsenals of the two sides are a concrete measure of continuing political differences is a fact Gorbachev obviously understands. Thus, he recognizes that the problem of conventional forces in Europe must be resolved in a mutually satisfactory manner if he wants to ease the Western concerns that underlie NATO nuclear and conventional modernization programs. As a consequence, the Soviet leadership proposes that the armed forces of NATO and the Warsaw Pact be restructured on a strictly defensive basis, that an equilibrium be reached in the military balance, and that both alliances adopt military doctrines "of an exclusively defensive character."[138] According to the Berlin communiqué, issued at the end of the May 1987 meeting of the Warsaw Pact Political Consultative Committee, a key objective of these proposals is that "none of the sides in ensuring its defense would have the means for a surprise attack on the other side and for mounting offensive operations generally."[139]

In a measure designed to demonstrate Moscow's interest in serious negotiations, Gorbachev announced in a December 1988 speech at the United Nations that by 1991 the Soviet armed forces would be reduced by 500,000 personnel (about half from the European part of the USSR and groups of forces in Eastern Europe); that six Soviet tank divisions would be withdrawn and disbanded from three front-line East European states; that existing divisions would be reconfigured on a defensive basis; and that several thousand pieces of other combat equipment, including artillery, combat aircraft, and air-assault units, would be withdrawn along with their forces.[140] A month later, Gorbachev went one step further, telling members of the Trilateral Commission that Soviet defense spending would be reduced by 14.2 percent, and defense production by 19.5 percent.[141] According to a subsequent report by Prime Minister Nikolai Ryzhkov, Soviet defense expenditures for 1989 and 1990 would be reduced by nearly 30 billion rubles, and Soviet leaders would seek to cut annual defense spending by one-third to one-half by 1995.[142] Meanwhile, several other Warsaw Pact countries announced similar plans to reduce forces and defense appropriations.[143]

Despite the generally positive reaction accorded to Gorbachev's dramatic unilateral initiatives, several Western experts (both governmental and nongovernmental) countered that such reductions, representing about 10 percent (12 percent by the Soviet count) of Soviet numerical strength, would not eliminate the Warsaw Pact's quantitative edge over NATO. By some calculations, the proposed cuts reduce long-standing Western fears that the Soviets could attempt a standing-start attack without reinforcing forces in place. However, given continuing statements by Soviet military leaders about the importance of qualitative factors and the need to preserve a counteroffensive capability, it remains unclear whether or to what extent overall Soviet combat potential will actually be lowered.[144] Such statements, in fact, raise the disturbing possibility that the restructuring of Soviet forces could eventually produce a leaner and more capable military machine, rather than one more oriented toward defense. Further offsetting Gorbachev's initiatives were reports by U.S. government sources that Soviet defense spending has continued to grow by roughly 3 percent annually in recent years (despite a staggering budget deficit equivalent to over 10 percent of gross national product), and that annual tank production would allow the USSR to replace roughly two-thirds of the tanks withdrawn within two years.[145]

Significantly, the Gorbachev leadership has moved to address Western concerns. Thus, Shevardnadze has instructed his subordinates that "'innocent' questions for clarification," such as "which kinds of tanks will be destroyed and when," must be answered honestly and precisely. He has insisted that an accommodating Soviet response is "absolutely necessary," given the importance of establishing "mutual confidence."[146] In January of 1989, the Soviet leadership published for the first time disaggregated data on the East-West military balance; in subsequent months, the government reaffirmed its intention to publish a new, and presumably more accurate, version of its defense budget.[147] In a further departure from past practices, the Gorbachev leadership has also promoted exchanges between Soviet and Western military officials to observe Soviet military exercises and widen the scope of mutual understanding.

Still more important, since the March 1989 opening of the Vienna negotiations on reducing conventional forces in Europe, the Gorbachev leadership has repeatedly demonstrated its willingness to modify the Soviet Union's original proposal for a three-stage reduction process.[148] Seeking to narrow the differences between the two sides, Moscow moved to embrace the basic Western framework for establishing regional force ceilings and geographic deployment zones. Some of the recent flexibility evidenced in Soviet positions has followed new proposals tabled by the Bush administration and its NATO allies, such as the concession in the spring of 1989 to negotiate limits on manpower and combat aircraft.[149] But such reciprocal gestures should not obscure the fact that Gorbachev's readiness to compromise in order to advance the conventional arms control negotiations represents a radical departure from the rigid stance adopted by the Brezhnev leadership in the earlier, ill-fated Mutual and Balanced Force Reduction talks.

Of course, it remains to be seen how the Soviet Union will address other serious Western concerns, such as providing a more detailed and accurate accounting of Warsaw Pact forces and equipment than is presently available, and ensuring that the combination of arms reductions and force restructuring results in a decrease rather than an increase in Soviet combat potential.[150] Moreover, Gorbachev's continuing campaign for nuclear disarmament in Europe—featuring successive unilateral cuts in the numerically superior Soviet arsenal of tactical nuclear weapons—has clearly troubled rather than reassured some Western leaders.

TRANSLATING PROPOSALS INTO PRACTICE: MILITARY AND CIVILIAN ROLES

Even granting Gorbachev's interest in achieving a balanced agreement, numerous obstacles remain to be surmounted. Besides the difficult stumbling blocks that confront both sides in the negotiations, Gorbachev must contend with continuing domestic opposition to his strategy of engagement with the West. Several party conservatives and military leaders have publicly expressed strong reservations about both the underlying premises of Gorbachev's approach to security policy and the wisdom of making extensive unilateral concessions. In their view, the threat posed by the West has not diminished, and determined

Soviet efforts to counter Western defense preparations are thus required.[151]

Prominent among those efforts, according to some leading military planners, is improving the capability to conduct operational and tactical maneuvers on a rapidly developing battlefield. This is the reason why the Soviet minister of defense, Dmitri Yazov, the new chief of staff of the Warsaw Pact, Vladimir Lobov, and other military officials envision a restructuring of forces that preserves the option of conducting decisive counteroffensive operations. Military logic, they contend, suggests that defense alone is not sufficient for the task of destroying the enemy.[152] While these military officers recognize the need to prepare for both offensive and defensive actions, their doctrinal formulations clearly contradict Gorbachev's goal of switching to a "strictly defensive doctrine."

As matters now stand, Gorbachev can consider himself fortunate that the Soviet military is not of one mind on such issues. Not only do some prominent defense leaders favor streamlining the Soviet armed forces, but elements within the military establishment clearly recognize that near-term budget cuts are essential for improving economic conditions and that economizing by the military could enhance efficiency as well as eliminate "overindulgence and mismanagement" in the Ministry of Defense.[153] However, it is one thing for Gorbachev to instruct the General Staff to put in place a nonoffensive defense, and quite another matter (assuming that such a posture is even feasible) to have that requirement implemented. Soviet political leaders have the decisive role in determining the main direction of military doctrine and national security policy in general; like political leaders elsewhere, however, they usually lack the requisite expertise and time to shape military operational matters directly. As a consequence, they generally must rely on indirect policy levers—such as power over budgets, organizational structure, and personnel appointments—to implement changes in defense policy. Such mechanisms may ultimately prove sufficient for Gorbachev to accomplish his stated objectives but some significant slippage in implementation is virtually inevitable along the way.

Thus far, Gorbachev has outmaneuvered his opponents and succeeded in getting his positions adopted, despite a battle over the unilateral cuts in conventional forces.[154] Yet, during Defense Minister Yazov's confrontational confirmation hearings before the Supreme Soviet in July 1989, Gorbachev revealed that "radical reconstruction" of the military was "more difficult than in society," given entrenched opposition from the General Staff and elsewhere, and still far from complete.[155] To overcome such opposition, Gorbachev has co-opted the support of like-minded political elites and intellectuals, who increasingly counterbalance the foreign and security policy views of conservatives in the party apparatus and defense establishment.

From almost the beginning of Gorbachev's tenure, Shevardnadze, Anatoly Dobrynin, former chief of the International Department of the Central Committee, and other officials have encouraged civilian specialists to contribute "serious new works" on national security issues.[156] Many of these specialists have interacted with their Western counterparts, exchanging information and ideas. Some have also developed contacts with members of the Soviet defense establishment. Thus, despite complaints about lack of access to important Soviet military data, the level of sophisticated analysis is growing rapidly.[157] The development of a cadre of civilian security specialists is important not only to offset the military's long-standing monopoly of expertise, but also because some civilian experts, as well as certain institutions—the Foreign Ministry and others—are becoming more influential in the national security decision-making process.[158]

A change of potentially even greater magnitude would be the establishment of some arrangement for checks and balances on the party leadership's decisive role in formulating foreign and security policy. Although the democratization process under way in the Soviet Union is still far from developing such an arrangement, let alone institutionalizing it, both Gorbachev and Shevardnadze have spoken in favor of increased participation in foreign policy decisions by the reconstituted Congress of People's Deputies and the Supreme Soviet.[159] Moreover, Yazov's conten-

THE OTHER SIDE OF THE TABLE

tious confirmation process, the creation of a Supreme Soviet committee to oversee the military and KGB, and calls for a justification of and debate on Soviet strategic programs and military strategy demonstrate a widespread interest by political elites in promoting greater accountability.[160]

THE SIGNIFICANCE OF THE GORBACHEV REVOLUTION FOR SECURITY COOPERATION

In the context of past Soviet policy orientations, Gorbachev's changes are striking. Wedded to strategic ideologies heavily influenced by traditional Bolshevik assumptions about the nature of the world and driven by the requirements of the centralized communist political system, Gorbachev's predecessors defined Soviet interests in ways that encouraged self-serving and confrontational policies. However, at the same time, they gradually adapted to the compelling realities of the nuclear age. Recognizing the vital imperative of avoiding a nuclear war, Stalin's successors concluded that some level of cooperation with the United States was desirable to avert such a catastrophe.

This recognition paved the way for limited changes in Soviet military doctrine, such as Brezhnev's renunciation of the goal of military superiority and the possibility of victory in a nuclear war. But given the overriding pressures exerted by the Soviet political system—including the entrenched influence of the military establishment—these changes were only partially reconciled with other dimensions of national security policy. The threat of a nuclear catastrophe also encouraged past Soviet leaders to conclude a series of arms control agreements that, with the exception of the ABM Treaty, imposed only modest constraints on U.S. and Soviet nuclear arsenals, and had no impact whatsoever on the accumulation of conventional military strength. Scaling back the military competition proved an impossible task because the basic political interests of the superpowers remained wholly irreconcilable. Rather than attempt to ease their ideological and geopolitical rivalry with the West, successive Soviet leaders encouraged it, thereby diminishing the prospects for more meaningful superpower cooperation in security arrangements.

By comparison, the main significance of the Gorbachev revolution for Soviet security policy lies in the leadership's recognition that the establishment of an entirely new framework of political and security cooperation requires a dramatic change in the Soviet definition of its interests, just as an end to the cold war, and the vast armies it fosters, requires a radical reduction in the sources of East-West confrontation.[161] In fact, after more than four years of sweeping changes in both concepts and policies, Soviet political and security interests are being fundamentally transformed. The emphasis has clearly shifted from the previously ambiguous balance that Khrushchev and Brezhnev defined between competition and cooperation to a clear preference for cooperation. This is evident both in the way leading Soviet officials define such concepts as "peaceful coexistence" and in the dramatic change in Soviet behavior around the world.[162]

No longer does the Soviet Union seek arms control and other cooperative ventures with the West while actively supporting revolutionary movements in the Third World. And no longer does it establish domestic priorities that favor the military-industrial complex and the steady accumulation of military power. Instead, the new emphasis is squarely on reducing the sources of confrontation by political accommodation and defining the priorities of Soviet domestic policy primarily in socioeconomic terms rather than military-industrial ones. If this transformation continues and is combined with an institutionalization of the reform process, it could provide the basis for a durable moderation of Soviet foreign policy and greatly expanded East-West cooperation. Already the Gorbachev leadership has demonstrated through unilateral reductions and concessions in the conventional arms talks in Europe that it is prepared—in ways that its predecessors were not—to address the *central* security concerns of the West.[163]

The ongoing transformation of Soviet interests is advanced by Gorbachev's initial success in discrediting the institutions that support militant competition with the West and in discarding many of the old ideological biases and strategic misconceptions that guided past Soviet policies. As a consequence, the Gorbachev leadership is better placed and better equipped to make realistic assessments and establish foreign and domestic priorities.

This fresh injection of realism into Soviet policy may be seen, for example, in Shevardnadze's acknowledgment that the Soviet deployment of SS-20s triggered "a second strategic front against us" and that the entire situation "could have been avoided if our *genuine national interests* at the time had been correctly evaluated."[164] So, too, is it evident in Moscow's willingness to agree to intrusive verification measures while making unilateral concessions in arms control negotiations. Whereas his predecessors attempted to ensure security primarily by military means, Gorbachev believes that Soviet interests require greater reliance on political methods.

Gorbachev has even gone a long way toward repudiating the "Brezhnev Doctrine" and is gradually disengaging the Soviet Union from its imperial relationship with Eastern Europe. As evidenced from both his Strasbourg speech and the communiqué issued from the July 1989 Bucharest meeting of the Political Consultative Committee of the Warsaw Pact, Moscow now recognizes the right of its socialist allies to make policy "without outside interference." Moreover, as Gorbachev explained in a television interview after the Bucharest meeting and subsequently in a speech to the Supreme Soviet, the easing of East-West confrontation in Europe has led the members of the Warsaw Pact to conclude that their alliance should be transformed from "a military-political organization to a political-military one," until such time that both NATO and the Warsaw Pact can be disbanded.[165] While radical reformers in Hungary and Poland may well have encouraged, and surely welcomed, such a shift in the alliance's objectives, the proposal clearly reflects Gorbachev's stress on political means of ensuring security.

Of course, the process of redefining Soviet political and security interests is still under way and therefore could be disrupted or reversed by certain domestic or international developments. At home, two problems, in particular, threaten the consolidation of this process. One is the economy. It is in dire straits and by some reports could collapse.[166] The other is the possibility that separatist fronts in the Baltics and in other republics and political opposition movements, such as the Inter-Regional Group composed of radical reformers elected to the Congress of People's Deputies, could spiral out of control.

The March 1989 general elections and the political turmoil and wave of strikes that swept the country the following summer suggest that the Communist Party has already lost a great deal of control over society.[167] Continuing acceleration of radical change—including the development of intra-party factions—will further erode the party's authority over policy, leading either to genuine political pluralism, to anarchy, or to a major confrontation between reformers and conservatives with unpredictable consequences. By early autumn, the explosion of political participation had so heightened concerns about the threat of anarchy or a coup against Gorbachev that even advocates of Western democratic values were suggesting that Gorbachev be granted special emergency powers to stabilize the reform process.[168] Yet, the possibility remains that liberals—like Feodor Burlatskii, the historian Roy Medvedev, and Georgi Shakhnazarov, a personal aide to Gorbachev—who seek fundamental but gradual reforms, will help the Soviet leader moderate growing pressures from radical groups and lesser challenges from conservatives who, to date, have lacked a realistic alternative program.

A related, daunting challenge stems from Gorbachev's attempt to preserve the legitimacy of Marxist-Leninist ideology and the one-party Soviet political system while pursuing sweeping political and economic reform and while dramatic changes unfold in Eastern Europe. This is arguably an impossible task, and thus it is hardly surprising that Gorbachev has opted to skirt important contradictions in Soviet doctrinal and policy formulations. For instance, when he says, as in his Strasbourg speech, that every nation has the right "to choose a social system according to its own discretion" and that "attempts to limit the sovereignty of states . . . are inadmissible," this is countered by his insistence that "differences among states are not removable" and that ending the cold war in Europe does not mean "overcoming socialism."[169] Perhaps Gorbachev and others in his circle will radically redefine what is meant by "socialism" (drawing on the experience of social democrats in Western Europe), as they have already redefined the traditional Soviet meaning of "peaceful coexistence" to stress (in its "new" Leninist form) political accommodation and "universal human values" over class struggle.[170]

Gorbachev's alter ego on the Politburo, Alexander Yakovlev, has already discarded cardinal Marxist-Leninist precepts by claiming that "the idea of violence as the midwife of history has outlived itself, just as has the idea of the power of dictatorship relying directly on violence."[171] Reflecting on the 200th anniversary of the French Revolution, Yakovlev further observed that the lesson for the Soviet Union was not the Revolution's cruelty and terror, but its encouragement of free thinking, personal initiative, and separation of powers. However, Yakovlev's advocacy of the primacy of reason and of the principles from the European Renaissance and Enlightenment contradict established orthodoxy concerning the leading role of the Communist Party, just as Gorbachev's statements about tolerating political diversity in Europe call into question the legitimacy of the requirement to defend the "gains of socialism."[172] One way or the other, developments in Eastern Europe and within the Soviet Union are bound to affect how these contradictions are resolved.

If such contradictions and other obstacles to the reformulation of Soviet interests seem formidable, so are the forces supporting it, and they are likely to be ascendant in the foreseeable future. Moreover, the longer this process continues and expands, the harder it may be to reverse completely. As a consequence, the opportunities for progressing within a new and more meaningful framework of security cooperation are considerably enhanced. Great-power politics and international competition will continue, but the pathological excesses of the cold war have unmistakably been eliminated. Thus, after four decades and six leadership successions from Stalin to Gorbachev, it may be the time to rethink whether the limited adversary relationship will exist indefinitely and whether it will continue to be true, as Raymond Aron wrote, that the greatest powers in the nuclear age still "cannot make peace and cannot make war."[173]

NOTES

1. Marshall D. Shulman, *Beyond the Cold War* (New Haven: Yale University Press, 1966).
2. As Robert Keohane observes, states "may fail to cooperate even when their interests are entirely identical." See his *After Hegemony: Cooperation and Discord in the World Political Economy* (Princeton: Princeton University Press, 1984), pp. 65ff. The explanation for defection in such instances is similar to the classic dilemma of public goods—namely, "that it is not rational for anyone to make a commitment to contribute in the first place." See Robert Jervis, "Realism, Game Theory, and Cooperation," *World Politics* 40, no. 3 (1988), p. 324. See also Mancur Olson, Jr., *The Logic of Collective Action* (Cambridge, Mass.: Harvard University Press, 1965); and, for a discussion of the prisoner's dilemma, Michael Mandelbaum, "The Reagan Administration and the Nature of Arms Control," in Joseph Kruzel, ed., *American Defense Annual, 1988–1989* (Lexington, Mass.: Lexington Books, 1988), pp. 195–200.
3. Japan, for instance, has been much more amenable to cooperation in the postwar period than it was in the 1930s, when militant nationalism prevailed. That the change was stimulated by its catastrophic defeat in World War II is, admittedly, not auspicious.
4. This idea has long permeated Western thinking, although it has never been fully embraced by American policymakers. For early statements of "classical arms control thinking," see Hedley Bull, "The Classical Approach to Arms Control Twenty Three Years After," in *Hedley Bull on Arms Control*, selected and introduced by Robert O'Neill and David N. Schwartz (London: Macmillan, 1987), pp. 119–128; ———*The Control of the Arms Race*, rev. ed. (New York: Praeger, 1965); and Thomas C. Schelling and Morton H. Halperin, *Strategy and Arms Control* (New York: Pergamon Press, 1985). This study was originally published in 1961 by the Twentieth Century Fund.

   Further developing this line are Bernard Brodie, *War and Politics* (New York: Macmillan, 1973); Robert Jervis, *The Illogic of American Nuclear Strategy* (Ithaca: Cornell University Press, 1984); and Michael Mandelbaum, *The Nuclear Revolution: International Politics before and after Hiroshima* (New York: Cambridge University Press, 1981).
5. For useful discussions, see H. S. Dinerstein, *War and the Soviet Union* (New York: Frederick A. Praeger, 1959); Raymond L. Garthoff, *Soviet Military Policy* (London: Faber and Faber, 1966); ———*Détente and Confrontation* (Washington, D.C.: Brookings Institution, 1985); David Holloway, *The*

Soviet Union and the Arms Race (New Haven: Yale University Press, 1983); Michael MccGwire, *Military Objectives in Soviet Foreign Policy* (Washington, D.C.: Brookings Institution, 1987); Thomas W. Wolfe, *Soviet Power and Europe, 1945–1970* (Baltimore: Johns Hopkins Press, 1970); and Jack Snyder, "The Gorbachev Revolution: A Waning of Soviet Expansionism?" *International Security* 12, no. 3 (1987/88), pp. 93–131.

6. See Alexander L. George, "Incentives for U.S.–Soviet Security Cooperation and Mutual Adjustment ," in Alexander L. George, Phillip J. Farley, and Alexander Dallin, eds., *U.S.–Soviet Security Cooperation: Achievements, Failures, Lessons* (New York: Oxford University Press, 1988), pp. 646–648 and 708.

7. The phrase was coined by Shai Feldman, as cited in Kenneth N. Waltz, "Reflections on *Theory of International Politics*: A Response to My Critics," in Robert O. Keohane, ed., *Neorealism and Its Critics* (New York: Columbia University Press, 1986), p. 331.

8. See, in particular, Jervis, "Realism," pp. 317–349; Joseph S. Nye, Jr., "Nuclear Learning and U.S.–Soviet Security Regimes," *International Organization* 41, no. 3 (1987), pp. 371–402; Robert O. Keohane and Joseph S. Nye, Jr., *Power and Interdependence,* 2nd ed. (Boston: Little, Brown & Co., 1989); Keohane, *After Hegemony*; and Warner R. Schilling, "The Politics of National Defense: Fiscal 1950," in Warner R. Schilling, Paul Y. Hammond, and Glenn H. Snyder, eds., *Strategy, Politics, and Defense Budgets* (New York: Columbia University Press, 1962), pp. 1–27.

   Developing this issue in the Soviet context are Robert Legvold, "War, Weapons, and Soviet Foreign Policy," in Seweryn Bialer and Michael Mandelbaum, eds., *Gorbachev's Russia and American Foreign Policy* (Boulder: Westview Press, 1988), pp. 97–132;———"Soviet Foreign Policy," *Foreign Affairs* 68, no. 1 (1988/89), pp. 82–98; Snyder, "The Gorbachev Revolution"; and George et al., *U.S.–Soviet Security Cooperation.*

9. The Soviet Union has long preferred the umbrella term "disarmament" (*razoruzhenie*) which includes two categories: general and complete disarmament (*vseobshchee i polnoe razoruzhenie*) and partial disarmament (*chastichnoe razoruzhenie*). For a useful discussion see P. H. Vigor, *The Soviet View of Disarmament* (London: Macmillan, 1986), pp. 3–5 and 22–26.

10. Helmut Sonnenfeldt and William G. Hyland, "Soviet Perspectives on Security," *Adelphi Papers* 150 (London: International Institute for Strategic Studies, 1979), pp. 21–22. See also Thomas W. Wolfe, *Soviet Strategy at the Crossroads* (Cambridge, Mass.: Harvard University Press, 1964), pp. 232–233 and Marshall D. Shulman, *Stalin's Foreign Policy Reappraised* (Cambridge, Mass.: Harvard University Press, 1963).

11. For a useful reexamination of these issues, see Vojtech Mastny, "Europe in US-USSR Relations: A Topical Legacy," *Problems of Communism* 37, no. 1 (1988), pp. 16–29.

12. For elaboration see Hannes Adomeit, *Soviet Risk-taking and Crisis Behavior* (London: George Allen & Unwin, 1982).

13. Thus, even before Khrushchev's decisive revision of established doctrine, Stalin adapted Lenin's thesis about the inevitability of war. He maintained that intra-imperialist wars were still inevitable, but not war be-

tween the two opposing social systems, because the capitalists understood that it would mean their own destruction. See his *Economic Problems of Socialism in the USSR* (Moscow: Foreign Language Publishing House, 1952); and his speech to the Nineteenth Party Congress, in L. Gruliow, ed., *Current Soviet Policies I* (New York: Praeger, 1953), pp. 7–8. Of course, as the controversy over the ideas of the economist Yevgeniy Varga demonstrates, Stalin was not prepared to countenance any revision in the traditional critique of imperialism. See also William Taubman, *Stalin's American Policy: From Entente to Détente to Cold War* (New York: W.W. Norton, 1982), ch. 8, especially pp. 223–225.

14. See the different explanations in Wolfe, *Soviet Power and Europe*, pp. 24–27; Shulman, *Stalin's Foreign Policy Reappraised*, especially chs. 4 and 5; and Taubman, *Stalin's American Policy*, ch. 8.

15. Vigor, *The Soviet View of Disarmament*, p. 84 and passim.

16. Vyacheslav Dashichev, "Vostok-Zapad: Poisk novykh otnoshenii," *Literaturnaia gazeta*, May 18, 1988, p. 14. Interestingly, Dashichev's account of this period maintains that the Soviet Union, "by attacking the West's positions, raised the level of the danger of war" while simultaneously "launch[ing] a broad campaign in defense of peace and spar[ing] no money in organizing a mass movement of peace advocates." On the strong influence of ideological stereotypes, see also the interview with Ivan Frolov in *La Repubblica*, April 16–17, 1989, p. 13 (translated in Foreign Broadcast Information Service [FBIS], April 19, 1989, pp. 83–84); Alexei Novikov, "Vchera i Segodnia," *Komsomolskaia pravda*, March 23, 1989, pp. 2–3; and Igor Kliamkin, "Pochemu trudno govorit' pravdu," *Novyi mir*, no. 2, 1989, pp. 204–238.

17. Robert P. Berman and John C. Baker, *Soviet Strategic Forces: Requirements and Responses* (Washington, D.C.: Brookings Institution, 1982), pp. 45–46 and 102–107.

18. On Soviet weapon programs, see ibid.; and Wolfe, *Soviet Power in Europe*, chs. 7 and 8. On Khrushchev's optimistic outlook about competition with the West, see Bruce Parrott, *Politics and Technology in the Soviet Union* (Cambridge, Mass.: MIT Press, 1983), ch. 4, especially pp. 135–138.

19. See the Strode chapter in this book, p. 8. See also Lincoln P. Bloomfield, Walter C. Clemens, Jr., and Franklyn Griffiths, *Khrushchev and the Arms Race* (Cambridge, Mass.: MIT Press, 1966); and Arkady N. Shevchenko, *Breaking with Moscow* (New York: Alfred A. Knopf, 1985), pp. 77–78 and 83–87.

20. Sonnenfeldt and Hyland, *Soviet Perspectives*, p. 22.

21. On Soviet interest in nonproliferation, see the Strode chapter, pp. 28–30. On other aspects of Soviet arms control policy, see the discussions in Bloomfield et al., *Khrushchev and the Arms Race*, especially chs. 8 and 10; Roman Kolkowicz, Matthew P. Gallagher, and Benjamin S. Lambeth, *The Soviet Union and Arms Control: A Superpower Dilemma* (Baltimore: Johns Hopkins Press, 1970); and Wolfe, *Soviet Strategy at the Crossroads*, ch. 19.

22. See the Strode chapter, p. 27. On Khrushchev's thinking about nuclear weapons and war, see also Mohammed Heikal, *Sphinx and the Commissar:*

The Rise and Fall of Soviet Influence in the Middle East (New York: Harper & Row, 1978), pp. 128–129 and 97–98.

23. This explanation obviously casts a different light on the 1958 Soviet test moratorium. As then Foreign Minister Andrei Gromyko allegedly told Shevchenko: "The crux of the matter is that our decision will have tremendous political effect. That's our main objective." Quoted in Shevchenko, *Breaking with Moscow*, p. 87.

24. Ibid., p. 101. The author adds that Khrushchev admitted he neither expected the West to disarm nor contemplated such a course for the Soviet Union. But Khrushchev stressed that propaganda and true negotiations should be considered complementary, not contradictory, aspects of policy (pp. 101–102).

25. Raymond Garthoff, *Soviet Military Policy*, p. 125.

26. William Zimmerman, *Soviet Perspectives on International Relations: 1956–1967* (Princeton: Princeton University Press, 1969), especially chs. 5 and 6; Franklyn Griffiths, "The Sources of American Conduct: Soviet Perspectives and Their Policy Implications," *International Security* 9, no. 2 (1984), pp. 7–8 and 30–34; and——"Images, Politics, and Learning in Soviet Behavior toward the United States," Ph.D. diss., Columbia University, 1972.

27. *Pravda*, October 28, 1962. Cited in Kolkowicz et al., *The Soviet Union and Arms Control*, p. 55. See also Arnold L. Horelick and Myron Rush, *Strategic Power and Soviet Foreign Policy* (Chicago: University of Chicago Press, 1966), pp. 87–88.

28. According to the former Soviet ambassador to Cuba, Khrushchev believed that the deployment of nuclear weapons in Cuba was no more threatening than the ring of U.S. bases around the Soviet Union, and would allow Moscow to talk with Washington as equals. A. I. Alekseev, "The Caribbean Crisis: How It Was," *Ekho Planety*, no. 33, November 12–18, 1988, pp. 26–37. See also the interview with Alekseev in "Uroki karibskogo krizisa," *Argumenty i Fakty*, no. 10, 1989, pp. 4–5.

29. Zbigniew K. Brzezinski, *Ideology and Power in Soviet Politics* (New York: Frederick A. Praeger, 1962), p. 105.

30. Griffiths, "Sources of American Conduct," pp. 7–8; and Novikov, "Vchera i segodnia," pp. 2–3.

31. F. Burlatskii, "Konkretnyi analyz—vazhneishee trebovanie Leninizma," *Pravda*, July 25, 1963. For a more recent retrospective by this same well-known publicist, see "Khrushchev: Shtrikhi k politicheskomu portretu," *Literaturnaia gazeta*, February 24, 1988, p. 14 and excerpts from Burlatskii's memoirs in *Novyi mir*, no. 10, 1988, pp. 153–197. See also the blunt description of peaceful coexistence in Nikolai Popov, "Vse my v odnoi lodke," *Literaturnaia gazeta*, March 1, 1989, p. 14.

32. On Soviet interest in the relative correlation of forces and its relationship to arms control, see Wolfe, *Soviet Strategy at the Crossroads*, especially pp. 237–238. See also the discussion on the nature of power in Jervis, "Realism," pp. 334–335.

33. Novikov, "Vchera i segodnia," p. 2.

34. For a discussion of Soviet motives, see the Strode chapter, pp. 25–33.

35. For an explanation of Khrushchev's strategy that emphasizes the importance of coalition politics, see Snyder, "The Gorbachev Revolution," pp.
103–107.

36. Burlatskii, "Khrushchev," p. 14.

37. See Parrott, *Politics and Technology*, pp. 139–151, and Snyder, "The Gorbachev Revolution."

38. Although this view continues to have its supporters, a debate over the real
achievements of arms control began in the Gorbachev years. For a positive
assessment of the role of arms control in fostering predictability and
promoting stability, see R. M. Timerbayev, *Kontrol za ogranichenie vooruzhenii i razoruzheniem* (Moscow: Izdatel'stvo Mezhdunarodnie Otnosheniia, 1983), p. 5. For more critical views suggesting that there has
been a wide gap between the objectives and the accomplishments of the
arms control process, see Georgi Arbatov, "Glasnost', Peregovory, Razoruzhenie," *Pravda*, October 17, 1988, p. 6; Alexei Arbatov, "Parity and
Reasonable Sufficiency," *International Affairs* (October 1988), pp. 75–87;
A. Kokoshin, V. Kremeniuk, and V. Sergeev, "Voprosy issledovaniia
mezhdunarodnykh peregovorov," *MEiMO*, no. 10, 1988, pp. 23–33; and
V. Kremeniuk, "Mezhdunarodnym peregovoram nuzhen nauchnyi
podkhod," *Mezhdunarodnaia zhizn'*, no. 5, 1989, pp. 107–114.

39. Robert Jervis is especially clear on this issue, and while he refers specifically to the question of whether arms control regimes actually exist, the
point can be made in broader terms as well. He also correctly notes that
this objective could be achieved with much smaller nuclear arsenals,
suggesting that arms control could play a useful role. See his "Security
Regimes," in Stephen D. Krasner, ed. *International Regimes* (Ithaca: Cornell University Press, 1983), pp. 173–194, especially p. 190. Similarly,
Alexander George questions whether cooperation "is always necessary
for the realization of mutual security benefits." See his "Incentives,"
p. 642.

40. George et al., "Research Objectives and Methods," in *U.S.–Soviet Security
Cooperation*, p. 7.

41. George, "Incentives," p. 644.

42. The economic burden of the superpower nuclear competition was obviously a relevant factor for both sides. But Khrushchev believed that he
could unilaterally achieve a "bigger bang for the buck" and therefore
sought arms control in part to constrain U.S. developments.

For accounts of U.S. policy calculations, see Alan Neidle, "Nuclear
Test Bans: History and Future Prosects," in George et al., *U.S.–Soviet
Security Cooperation*, pp. 175–214; Ivo H. Daalder, "The Limited Test Ban
Treaty," in Albert Carnesale and Richard N. Haass, eds., *Superpower Arms
Control: Setting the Record Straight* (Cambridge, Mass.: Ballinger, 1987), pp.
9–39; and Michael Mandelbaum, *The Nuclear Question: The United States
and Nuclear Weapons, 1946–1976* (New York: Cambridge University
Press, 1979), ch. 7.

43. Michael MccGwire, however, points out that the Kennedy administration's defense initiatives encouraged the Soviets to back away from

Khrushchev's original one-variant war strategy. This, in turn, provoked a halt in Khrushchev's unilateral reduction of the Soviet armed forces. See his *Military Objectives*, p. 25.

44. George contends that both the degree of "centrality" of security issues and the state of U.S.–Soviet relations are important determinants of the success or failure of security cooperation. Thus, the less central the issue and the warmer the state of superpower relations, the higher the chances for successful cooperation. See his "Incentives," pp. 646–648 and 708. Jervis points out that choices "are often structured by the settings in which they arise." See his "Realism," p. 320. See also Garthoff, *Soviet Military Policy*, p. 125.

45. See the Strode chapter, pp. 30–34.

46. Zimmerman, *Soviet Perspectives*, ch. 6, especially pp. 222–241.

47. Yuri Levada and Viktor Sheinis contend that "many [of Khrushchev's] foreign policy decisions were misguided and provocative." See their "1953–1964: Why Reform Didn't Work Then," *Moscow News*, no. 18, 1988, p. 9. For the second quotation, see Stanislav Kondrashov, "Tseli i Sredstva, ili Ekskurs v istoriiu, naveiannyi sobytiiami dnia," *Izvestia*, December 15, 1988, p. 5. Although Soviet historians are striving to fill in the "blank spots" of Soviet history, Khrushchev's foreign and security policy have not to date been a focus of attention. However, in addition to the above references, see Evgenii Ambartsumov, "Zhertvoprinostenie Imre Nadia," *Moskovskie novosti*, July 2, 1989, p. 7; Roy Medvedev, "33 goda spustiia," *Nedeliia*, no. 17, April 24–30, 1989, p. 10; Mikhail Gefter, "Sud'ba Khrushcheva," *Oktiabr'*, no. 1, 1989, pp. 154–181; Anatoly Ponomarev, "My oratory natrenirovannye," *Sovetskaia Rossiia*, July 2, 1989, p. 4; N. Mikhailov, "Is October 1964 Possible Today," *Moskovskaia pravda*, August 18, 1989, p. 2, in FBIS, August 23, 1989, pp. 31–36; and the citations in note 87. Khrushchev's memoirs, those of his son, Sergei Khrushchev, and his son-in-law, Alexei Adzhubei, are also being published in Soviet journals as is Roy Medvedev's biography of the former first secretary. In addition, several former Soviet leaders have recently given interviews in the Soviet press. See especially the last interview with Andrei Gromyko before his death in "Poslednee interv'iu," *Ogonek*, no. 30, 1989, pp. 8–9; and the accounts in Alexander Rahr, "Shelest Remembers," Radio Liberty, *Report on the Soviet Union*, vol. 1, no. 4, January 27, 1989, pp. 14–16.

48. Snyder, "The Gorbachev Revolution," p. 106.

49. Yu. P. Davydov et al., *The Nixon Doctrine* (Moscow, 1972), translated by JPRS, no. 58317, February 1973. The discussion in this section draws on my "Restructuring U.S.–Soviet Relations," paper presented at the AAASS Conference, Asilomar, Calif., September 20–23, 1981.

50. See, for example, Georgi Arbatov, "O Sovetsko-Amerikanskikh otnosheniia," *Kommunist*, no. 3, 1973, pp. 101–113;———*The War of Ideas in Contemporary International Relations* (Moscow, 1973);———*Global'naia strategiia SShA v usloviiakh nauchno-tekhnicheskoi revoliutsii* (Moscow, 1979); and Genrikh A. Trofimenko, "Amerikanskii podkhod k mirnomu

sosushchestvovaniu s Sovetskim Soiuzom," *SShA: ekonomika, politika, ideologiia* (SShA), nos. 6 and 7, 1978, pp. 18–31 and 38–53.

51. See the Blacker chapter, p. 57. and Harry Gelman, *The Brezhnev Politburo and the Decline of Détente* (Ithaca: Cornell University Press, 1984), ch. 4.

52. Compare President Richard Nixon's annual reports to Congress in 1970–1973. See also Secretary of Defense Elliot L. Richardson, *Annual Department of Defense Report*, FY 1974. The most comprehensive account of U.S.–Soviet relations and perspectives during this period is Garthoff's valuable study *Détente and Confrontation*.

53. Henry A. Kissinger, congressional testimony, June 15, 1972. Reprinted in *Department of State Bulletin* 67, no. 1724 (1972), p. 49. See also Richard Nixon, "The Moscow Summit: New Opportunities in U.S.–Soviet Relations," address to Congress, June 1, 1972, reprinted in *Department of State Bulletin* 66, no. 1722 (June 26, 1972), p. 858; and Alexander L. George, *Managing U.S.–Soviet Rivalry: Problems of Crisis Prevention* (Boulder: Westview Press, 1983), pp. 107–117.

54. Nikolai Inozemtsev, *Pravda*, June 9, 1972, p. 5. See also the Arbatov works cited in note 50.

55. Shevchenko, *Breaking with Moscow*, p. 211. This account further suggests that Brezhnev achieved his policy mandate only by "outmaneuvering some of his skeptical Politburo colleagues" (p. 212). On the importance of such coalition politics, see Snyder, "The Gorbachev Revolution," pp. 106–107. See also Feodor Burlatskii, "Brezhnev i krushenie ottepeli: Razmyshleniia o prirode politicheskogo liderstva," *Literaturnaia gazeta*, September 14, 1988, pp. 13–14; and the interview with Roy Medvedev in *Molodezh' Estonii*, July 7, 1989, p. 3.

56. For differing perspectives see Garthoff, *Détente and Confrontation*; Gelman, *The Brezhnev Politburo*; and various chapters in George, *Managing U.S.–Soviet Rivalry*.

57. Of course, preservation of the Soviet empire was long considered a separate case. Thus, Brezhnev reportedly said that he would still have invaded Czechoslovakia, even at the cost of risking a war. This statement was conveyed by one of Alexander Dubček's colleagues, Zdenek Mlynar, as cited in Stephen Shenfield, *The Nuclear Predicament. Explorations in Soviet Ideology* (London: Routledge & Kegan Paul, 1987), p. 40. See also interview with Evgenii Ambartsumov in *La Repubblica*, August 13–14, 1989, p. 3, in FBIS, August 16, 1989, pp. 27–29; Andranik Migranian, "An Epitaph to the Brezhnev Doctrine," *Moscow News*, no. 34, 1989, p. 6; and Yuri Levada, "A Reactive Recoil: Rethinking the Prague Spring," in the same issue, p. 7.

58. See the Blacker chapter, pp. 57–58.

59. Shevchenko reports that the significance Brezhnev and Gromyko attached to this agreement stemmed in part from their interest in silencing "those in the leadership who had doubts about the Moscow summit." It also signified "a great triumph for Soviet foreign policy," since the declaration was considered as recognition by the United States of "the Leninist idea of peaceful coexistence." See his *Breaking with Moscow*, p. 206. See also Garthoff, *Détente and Confrontation*, pp. 290–298.

60. For a slightly different but important account, see Raymond L. Garthoff, "Mutual Deterrence and Strategic Arms Limitation in Soviet Policy," *International Security* 3, no. 1 (1978), pp. 112–147; and————*Détente and Confrontation*, p. 133 and passim.

61. Georgi Kornienko, "Looking Back," *International Affairs* (April 1989), p. 74. See also Garthoff, *Détente and Confrontation*, p. 196; and————"BMD and East-West Relations," in Ashton B. Carter and David N. Schwartz, eds., *Ballistic Missile Defense* (Washington, D.C.: Brookings Institution, 1984), pp. 275–329.

62. See the Blacker chapter, p. 61. According to Shevchenko, Foreign Minister Gromyko was the key architect of the Soviet approach to SALT "as the vehicle for a much more important political process. His goal, endorsed by Brezhnev and encouraged by Dobrynin, was to win a broad set of understandings with the United States with arms control as the centerpiece but not the only aspect of the arrangement." See *Breaking with Moscow*, p. 204. For a different perspective, see Garthoff, *Détente and Confrontation*.

63. For the details, see the Blacker chapter; and Garthoff, *Détente and Confrontation*.

64. See the Blacker chapter, p. 68.

65. Although the following discussion focuses on the Vladivostok accord, it should be noted that some Western observers find evidence of important Soviet concessions in both SALT I and SALT II. In particular, see Michael MccGwire, who maintains that the Soviet Union actually deployed fewer intercontinental and variable-range ballistic missiles (ICBMs and VRBMs) than planned and that SALT I penalized the Soviets, since a sizable percentage of their ICBM force had been switched to cover targets on the European periphery to remedy a shortage of regional-range missiles. He also observes that the USSR had to abort the conversion of about 100 missile silos in order to comply with the SALT II ceiling of 820 MIRVed ICBMs. See MccGwire, *Military Objectives*, pp. 232–282 (especially p. 269) and 477–519. For further elaboration, see————"A Soviet View of World War," in Bruce Parrott, ed., *The Dynamics of Soviet Defense Policy* (forthcoming); and Garthoff, *Détente and Confrontation*.

66. Garthoff, *Détente and Confrontation*, p. 464 (emphasis in the original) and 444–446; Blacker chapter, p. 66.

67. See the Goldberg chapter, p. 100.

68. This was communicated to Warnke by Gromyko's deputy, Georgi Kornienko, who, despite other recent retrospectives (discussed below), has not to this author's knowledge either confirmed or elaborated upon this aside. See Strobe Talbott, *Endgame: The Inside Story of SALT II* (New York: Harper & Row, 1979), p. 73; Garthoff, *Détente and Confrontation*, p. 465; Blacker chapter, p. 66.

69. On Soviet military concerns and the exclusion of military advisers, see Garthoff, *Détente and Confrontation*, pp. 465 and 444–446.

70. On the trade bill, ibid., chs. 12 and 13; on U.S. modernization programs, see "The 'Decade of Neglect' Controversy," articles by Melvin Laird,

Colin Gray, Jeffrey Barlow, and Robert Komer in *International Security* 10, no. 2 (1985), pp. 5–83.

71. See the discussions in Garthoff, *Détente and Confrontation*; Gelman, *The Brezhnev Politburo*; Snyder, "The Gorbachev Revolution"; and the Blacker chapter.

72. See U.S. Congress, Joint Economic Committee (JEC), *Allocation of Resources in the Soviet Union and China, 1984* (Washington, D.C.: U.S. Government Printing Office, 1985); Jeremy R. Azrael, *The Soviet Civilian Leadership and the Military High Command, 1976–1986* (Santa Monica: Rand, June 1987); and Richard F. Kaufman, "Causes of the Slowdown in Soviet Defense," *Soviet Economy* 1, no. 1 (1985), pp. 285–305.

73. Azrael, *Soviet Civilian Leadership*, p. v; and Kaufman, "Causes of the Slowdown." See also the interesting debate on the evolution of Soviet economic policy in *Voprosy Istorii KPSS*, nos. 4 and 8, 1988.

74. "Poslednee interv'iu," *Ogonek*, no. 30, 1989, p. 9.

75. See especially Jerry F. Hough, *The Struggle for the Third World: Soviet Debates and American Options* (Washington, D.C.: Brookings Institution, 1986); Allen Lynch, *The Soviet Study of International Relations* (Cambridge, Mass.: Cambridge University Press, 1987); and Elizabeth Kridl Valkenier, *The Soviet Union and the Third World* (New York: Praeger, 1983). This process accelerated after Brezhnev's death in 1982. See especially the articles by G.Kh. Shakhnazarov in *Voprosy filosofii*, no. 5, 1984, pp. 62–74; L. Tolkunov in *Kommunist*, no. 7, 1984, pp. 93–104; and R. G. Bogdanov, in *SShA*, no. 10, 1984, pp. 3–14.

76. On military opposition to the Afghan decision, see the interview with Gen. V.I. Varennikov, "Afghanistan: Podvodia itogii," *Ogonek*, no. 12, 1989, pp. 6–8 and 30–31; and "Veterani i perestroika," *Krasnaia zvezda*, March 4, 1989. For a differing account that claims "senior KGB officers" had attempted to dissuade Brezhnev from getting the USSR militarily involved in Afghanistan, see the interview with the KGB defector Vladimir Kuzichkin in *Time*, November 22, 1982, pp. 25–26. See also Sergei Belitsky, "Authors of USSR's Afghan War Policy," Radio Liberty, *Report on the USSR*, vol. 1, no. 17, April 28, 1989, pp. 11–12. On the reservations of Soviet academic analysts, see the extraordinary account by Oleg Bogomolov, "Kto zhe oshibalsia?" *Literaturnaia gazeta*, March 16, 1988. Bogomolov claims that in January 1980 his institute, "on its own initiative," sent a detailed memorandum to "the relevant authorities" warning of "the futile and damaging nature" of Soviet military involvement in Afghanistan. He also maintains that the institute had urged "the highest authorities" to exercise caution in regional conflicts "much earlier, in the second half of the 1970s." Soviet academics also had revealed their misgivings about Afghanistan in private discussions with Westerners.

77. A. Bovin, "Perestroika i vneshnaia politika," *Izvestia*, June 16, 1988, p. 4. For other useful ex post facto discussions, see Kokoshin et al., "Voprosy issledovaniia mezhdunarodnykh peregovorov"; and Alexei Iziumov and Andrei Kortunov, "The Soviet Union in the Changing World," *International Affairs* (August 1988), pp. 46–56; A.V. Nikiforov, "Mirnoe sosushchestvovanie i novoe myshlenie," *SShA*, no. 12, 1987, pp. 3–10,

notes how such preconceptions contributed to an underestimation of the effects of Soviet policy in the Third World on the bilateral relationship (p. 8).

78. See the differing explanations in Bovin, "Perestroika"; Edward A. Shevardnadze, "Doklad," *Vestnik Ministerstva inostrannykh del SSSR,* August 15, 1988, pp. 33–37; the articles by G. M. Sturua, A. E. Bovin, L. S. Semeiko, and S.A. Karaganov in *SShA,* no. 12, 1988, pp. 23–41; A. Kozyrev, "Confidence and the Balance of Interests," *International Affairs* (November 1988), pp. 3–12; I. Malashenko, "Non-military Aspects of Security," *International Affairs* (January 1989), pp. 43–45; and Kornienko, "Looking Back," p. 75. See also Raymond Garthoff, "The Soviet SS-20 Decision," *Survival* 25 (May–June 1983), pp. 110–114.

79. Georgi M. Kornienko, "Pravda i domysly o raketakh SS-20," *SShA,* no. 4, 1989, pp. 46–48, quotation from p. 47.

80. Interview with Viktor Karpov, "Razoruzhenie i ekonomika," in *Argumenty i Fakty,* February 4–10, 1989, p. 1. It should be noted that at the time, Karpov was a main proponent of the "old thinking."

81. See my "Soviet INF Policy and Euro-strategic Options," in *Intermediate-Range Nuclear Forces in Europe: Issues and Approaches* (Stanford, Calif.: Arms Control and Disarmament Program, Stanford University, 1982), pp. 24–25. See also Thomas Risse-Kappen, *The Zero Option: INF, West Germany, and Arms Control* (Boulder: Westview Press, 1988).

82. Kornienko, "Pravda i domysly o raketakh SS-20," pp. 50–51. Curiously, Kornienko's account differs from Helmut Schmidt's version of this meeting. According to Schmidt's memoirs, it was Gromyko, not Brezhnev, who stated that the USSR was prepared to negotiate without preconditions and that the British, French, and Chinese weapons would be deferred to SALT III. [Helmut Schmidt, *Menschen und Mächte* (Berlin: Siedler Verlag, 1987), p. 118.] In his study of the INF negotiations, Thomas Risse-Kappen offers independent confirmation of Schmidt's account, citing a 1983 speech by Jürgen Todenhöfer (CDU) in the Bundestag. Moreover, Risse-Kappen reports that both Todenhöfer's speech and Schmidt's account of the discussion correspond to the official West German records of the Moscow talks. He finds no evidence that Brezhnev (rather than Gromyko) provided this information or that it was communicated through inept improvisation on Brezhnev's part. [Risse-Kappen, *The Zero Option,* p. 64, and personal communication to the author, August 14, 1989.] The contradiction is significant because the West Germans concluded from Gromyko's statement that the Soviets were making a serious concession. Thus, when the USSR presented a draft treaty on May 25, 1982, insisting on the inclusion of third-country forces, the Germans interpreted this move as a hardening of the Soviet position, possibly in response to Washington's announcement of the zero option. Kornienko, however, maintains that this was the Soviet position all along, which suggests that the Brezhnev leadership intended to obstruct the initial INF talks from the very outset.

83. Malashenko, "Non-military Aspects of Security," p. 44. Deputy Foreign Minister A. Bessmertnykh has made the same point in "Razviazka glia Evropy," *Novoe vremia,* no. 11, 1987, pp. 3–4.

84. See the Goldberg chapter, p. 108.

85. Ibid., p. 111. Karaganov also makes this point in his contribution to the debate on the SS-20 in *SShA,* no. 12, 1988, p. 39.

86. See especially Snyder, "The Gorbachev Revolution"; and Bruce Parrott, *The Soviet Union and Ballistic Missile Defense* (Boulder: Westview Press, 1987).

87. See especially Roy Medvedev's essay on Brezhnev in *Moscow News,* no. 37, 1988, pp. 8–9; and the interview with Andrei Gromyko in *The Observer* (London), April 2, 1989, pp. 21 and 23; and with the Soviet interpreter Viktor Sukhodrev, in *Ogonek,* no. 10, 1989, pp. 22–24. See also Burlatskii, "Brezhnev i krushenie ottepeli."

88. For an interesting discussion of both points that carries the analysis into the Gorbachev period, see E. Primakov, V. Martynov, and G. Diligenskii, "Nekotorye problemy novogo myshleniia," *MEiMO,* no. 6, 1989, pp. 5–18, especially pp. 9–10.

89. For the best account to date of these changes, see Raymond L. Garthoff, "Soviet Military Doctrine and the Prevention of Nuclear War," in Cynthia Roberts, Jack Snyder, and Warner R. Schilling, *Decoding the Enigma: Methodology for the Study of Soviet Military Policy* (forthcoming). For different assessments that stress their propaganda value, see the chapters by Benjamin Lambeth and Edward Warner in the same volume.

90. For useful analyses of this period, see MccGwire, *Military Objectives;* and Garthoff, "Soviet Military Doctrine."

91. Marshal N. V. Ogarkov, *Istoriia uchit bditelnosti* (Moscow: Voenizdat, 1985), p. 51. See also *The Voroshilov Lectures: From the Soviet General Staff Academy—Issue of Military Strategy* (Washington, D.C.: National Defense University Press, 1989); and John G. Hines and Phillip A. Petersen, "The Soviet Conventional Offensive in Europe," *Orbis* 27, no. 3 (1983), pp. 695–739.

92. On Soviet military strategy and assessments, ibid.; MccGwire, *Military Objectives;* Stephen M. Meyer, "Soviet Theatre Nuclear Forces," *Adelphi Papers* 187/188 (London: International Institute for Strategic Studies, Winter 1983/84); and Phillip A. Petersen and Notra Trulock III, "A 'New' Soviet Military Doctrine: Origins and Implications," *Strategic Review* 16, no. 3 (1988), pp. 12–16. On the Soviet approach to strategic defense, see this chapter, pp. 137–138; Garthoff, "BMD and East-West Relations"; and Sidney D. Drell, Phillip J. Farley, and David Holloway, *The Reagan Strategic Defense Initiative: A Technical, Political, and Arms Control Assessment* (Stanford, Calif.: Center for International Security and Arms Control, 1984).

93. *Pravda,* January 19, 1977.

94. For the details on Soviet efforts, see Garthoff, "Soviet Military Doctrine." See also Henry Kissinger, *Years of Upheaval* (Boston: Little, Brown & Co., 1982), pp. 274–281.

95. Garthoff, "Soviet Military Doctrine."

96. Dmitri F. Ustinov in *Pravda*, July 25, 1981, p. 4; and Nikolai V. Ogarkov, "Strategiia voennaia," in *Sovetskaia voennaia entsiklopedia*, vol. 7 (Moscow: Voenizdat, 1979), pp. 563–564. See also ibid.; and my "Soviet Military Policy in Transition," *Current History* 83, no. 495 (1984), pp. 331–334.

97. The text of Brezhnev's speech was published in *Pravda*, June 16, 1982.

98. See in particular Dmitri Ustinov's discussion of this issue in "Otvesti ugrozu iadernoi voiny," *Pravda*, July 12, 1982, p. 4. Besides noting it was "not easy" to reach this decision, Ustinov mentioned that the Soviet Union was establishing a stricter command and control network and more rigid safeguards against the unsanctioned launch of nuclear weapons.

99. See Ogarkov's statements about the "possibilities for achieving victory" and for "defeating the enemy under any conditions" in "Strategiia voennaia," and *Vsegda v gotovnosti k zashchite otechestva* (Moscow: Voenizdat, 1982), p. 58. See also CIA reports of a decline in investment outlays to Soviet strategic forces in Joint Economic Committee, *Allocation of Resources*, p. 246.

100. Brezhnev speech in *Pravda*, October 28, 1982, p. 1. See also Rebecca Strode, "The Soviet Armed Forces: Adaptation to Resource Scarcity," *Washington Quarterly* 9, no. 2 (1986), pp. 55–69; Azrael, *Soviet Civilian Leadership*; and Abraham S. Becker, *Ogarkov's Complaint and Gorbachev's Dilemma* (Santa Monica: Rand, 1987).

101. This thesis is stressed in Matthew Evangelista, *Innovation and the Arms Race* (Ithaca: Cornell University Press, 1988). Asked in an interview why the Soviet Union continued to build up its arsenal after parity had been achieved, Andrei Gromyko replied that, "strictly speaking," parity had not been reached. "What was the Soviet Union to do when the United States was arming at full speed," he asked rhetorically, "lay down [our] arms?" According to Gromyko, the Soviet Union did not want to lag behind in nuclear weapons given its security interests. See his "Poslednee interv'iu," p. 9.

102. For this and the next point see Iziumov and Kortunov, "The Soviet Union in the Changing World," p. 50 and Nikolai Spassky, "National Security: Real and Illusory," *International Affairs* (July 1989), pp. 3–13. For a military perspective that decries the lack of economic parity with the West and the adverse effect on Soviet technological standing, see Col. V. Strebkov, "Voennyi paritet vchera i sevodnia," *Krasnaia zvezda*, January 3, 1989.

103. Arbatov, "Parity and Reasonable Sufficiency," p. 81. Malashenko makes the identical point in "Non-military Aspects of Security," p. 41.

104. Malashenko, "Non-military Aspects of Security," p. 41.

105. I have explored the roots of these challenges and initial Soviet responses in "The New Realism and the Old Rigidities: Gorbachev's Strategy in Perspective," *Washington Quarterly* 11, no. 3 (1988), pp. 213–226. See also Bialer and Mandelbaum, *Gorbachev's Russia*; Snyder, "The Gorbachev Revolution"; and the articles by David Holloway, Robert Legvold, Charles Gati, and Donald S. Zagoria in *Foreign Affairs* 68, no. 1 (1989), pp. 66–138.

106. Gorbachev hinted in 1985 that he envisioned a different relationship with the West, and thus it is possible that he initially moved slowly because of domestic political opposition. However, there is also evidence that Gorbachev's political and security preferences have become more radical over time. My personal view is that these explanations are not mutually exclusive. Gorbachev probably had some general ideas for how Soviet foreign policy should be changed before he became general secretary, but these ideas were fleshed out during his first years in office.

107. For more on the scope and significance of coalition politics, see Jerry Hough, *Russia and the West: Gorbachev and the Politics of Reform* (New York: Simon and Schuster, 1988);————"Gorbachev Consolidating Power," *Problems of Communism* 36, no. 4 (1987), pp. 21–43; Dale Herspring, "On Perestroika: Gorbachev, Yazov, and the Military," *Problems of Communism* 36, no. 4 (1987), pp. 99–107; Bruce Parrott, "Soviet National Security under Gorbachev," *Problems of Communism* 37, no. 6 (1988), pp. 1–36; Snyder, "The Gorbachev Revolution"; Alexander Rahr, "Restructuring of the Kremlin Leadership," Radio Liberty Report, October 4, 1988; ————"Falin, Kapto, and Bakatin Promoted to Top Positions," Radio Liberty Report, October 21, 1988; Paul Quinn-Judge, "Gorbachev Hints at Trouble in Military," *Christian Science Monitor,* July 12, 1989; and Bill Keller, "Amid Rising Alarm, Gorbachev Urges a Purge in Party," *The New York Times,* July 22, 1989, pp. 1 and 6.

108. Report of Mikhail S. Gorbachev to the Twenty-seventh Party Congress, in *Stenograficheskii otchet* (Moscow: Politizdat, 1986), pp. 86–88. For discussion of these and the following points, see my "New Realism," pp. 219–222; and the detailed account by Raymond L. Garthoff, "New Thinking in Soviet Military Doctrine," *Washington Quarterly* 11, no. 3 (1988), pp. 131–158.

109. See for example his UN speech, in *Pravda,* December 8, 1988, p. 1. Subsequently, Gorbachev told the Congress of People's Deputies that "the use of force and the threat of force for the purposes of attaining any kind of political, economic or other goals are impermissible" (translated in FBIS, May 31, 1989, p. 60).

110. *Vestnik Ministerstva inostrannykh del SSSR,* December 15, 1988, p. iii. Gorbachev made essentially the same point in his UN speech.

111. For recent expressions of this view, see Gorbachev's speeches to the UN, to the Council of Europe in Strasbourg, *Pravda,* July 7, 1989, pp. 1–2; and to the Congress of People's Deputies translated in FBIS, May 31, 1989, p. 60.

112. *Vestnik Ministerstva inostrannykh del SSSR,* August 15, 1988, p. 34. See also the blunt critique by Vyacheslav I. Dashichev, "Dorogi, kotorye nam vybiraiut," *Komsomolskaia pravda,* June 19, 1988, p. 3.

113. *Pravda,* June 29, 1988; and FBIS, May 31, 1989, p. 60 and passim.

114. Ibid.

115. Gorbachev's speech commemorating the seventieth anniversary of the revolution, *Pravda,* November 3, 1987; his Central Committee report, *Pravda,* February 19, 1988; and his speech to a meeting of scientists and cultural figures, *Pravda,* January 7, 1989.

116. For a notable example of the first, see Yakovlev's views in *Pravda*, November 4, 1987; and of the second, Vitaly V. Zhurkin, Sergei A. Karaganov, and Andrei V. Kortunov, "Vysovy bezopasnosti—starye i novye," *Kommunist*, no. 1, 1988, pp. 44–47.

117. *Pravda*, February 17, 1987. The discussion in this section draws on my "New Realism," pp. 219–220. See also Eduard Shevardnadze, "Towards a Safe World," *International Affairs* (September 1988), p. 8.

118. Mikhail S. Gorbachev, *Izbrannye rechi i stat'i*, vol. 3 (Moscow: Poltizdat, 1987), p. 245.

119. In his August 1, 1989, speech to the Supreme Soviet, Gorbachev repeated the leadership's opposition to nuclear deterrence. He said that nuances in the positions held by London, Bonn, and Paris were readily evident but that adherence to the policy of deterrence reduces "the value of reductions in conventional weapons and runs counter to the task of eliminating military confrontation in Europe . . ." Moscow Domestic Service, translated in FBIS, August 2, 1989, p 43. See also works cited in notes 117 and 118; for an important earlier discussion, see Anatoly Dobrynin, "Za bez'iadernyi mir, navstrechu XXI veku," *Kommunist*, no. 9, 1986, pp. 18–31.

120. See, for example, Andrei A. Kokoshin and Andrei V. Kortunov, "Stabil'nost' i peremeny v mezhdunarodnykh otnosheniiakh," *SShA*, no. 7, 1987, pp. 3–12.

121. The author made this point in a favorable discussion of Gorbachev's proposal to eliminate nuclear weapons. Army Gen. M. M. Kozlov, "The Preservation of Military Strategic Parity—a Serious Factor in Assuring Peace and International Security," *Voennaia mysl'*, no. 12, 1986, p. 12, as cited in Garthoff, "New Thinking in Soviet Military Doctrine," p. 154. See also Maj. Gen. Yuri Ia. Kirshin, "Politika i voennaia strategiia v iadernyi vek," *MEiMO*, no. 11, 1988, pp. 35–45. Kirshin argues that the growing threat of accidental or unauthorized nuclear war demands that "more reliable political control be established over nuclear strategy in all countries" (p. 42), and he maintains that the Soviet Union is currently strengthening such measures (p. 44). For a strong endorsement of Gorbachev's view by a prominent academic now working for the Central Committee, see Igor Malashenko, "Hard Parting," *New Times*, March/April 1989, pp. 18–20; and Lev Semeiko, "K novoi strategicheskoi stabil'nosti," *Krasnaia zvezda*, February 21, 1989, p. 3, and February 22, 1989, p. 3.

122. V. Danilov, "Is the Essence of Nuclear War Changing?" *International Affairs* (January 1989), pp. 149–150.

123. Ibid., p. 149.

124. Shevardnadze, "Towards a Safe World," p. 8.

125. Gorbachev speech, *Pravda*, July 7, 1989, p. 2.

126. Alexander N. Yakovlev, "Dostizhenie kaschestvenno novogo sostoianiia Sovetskogo obshchestva i obshchestvennye nauki," *Vestnik Akademii Nauk SSSR*, no. 6, 1987, p. 76 (emphasis in the original). Like Gorbachev, Yakovlev (probably the principal source of such ideas) has called for the creation of a security system based on mutual trust to replace deterrence

and reliance on other military instruments of foreign policy. However, before his promotion to the Politburo, Yakovlev expressed serious doubts about the possibilities for reaching political accommodation with the United States. See his *Po kraiu bezdny* (Moscow: Molodaia gvardiia, 1984), and *Ot Trumena do Reigana. Doktriny i real'nosti iadernogo veka*, 2nd ed. (Moscow: Molodaia gvardiia, 1985).

127. See Gorbachev's statement in *Izvestia*, February 26, 1986; and Raymond L. Garthoff, "Continuity and Change in Soviet Military Doctrine," in Parrott, *The Dynamics of Soviet Defense Policy*.

128. See my "New Realism," *n.*30; and Garthoff, "New Thinking in Soviet Military Doctrine," pp. 136–137.

129. "Doktrina voennaia," *Sovetskaia voennaia entsiklopedia*, vol. 3 (Moscow: Voenizdat, 1977), pp. 225–226.

130. "Oboronitel'nyi kharakter Sovetskoi voennoi doktriny i podgotovka voisk (sil)," *Voennaia mysl'*, no. 1, 1988, p. 3; and Col. Gen. Makhmut A. Gareev, "Soviet Military Science," *Series on Defense of the Homeland* 11, 1987 (translated by JPRS-UMA-88-007), p. 5.

131. "Oboronitel'nyi kharakter Sovetskoi voennoi doktriny i podgotovka voisk (sil)," p. 3.

132. See James Schlesinger, "Reykjavik and Revelations: A Turn of the Tide?" *Foreign Affairs* 65, no. 3 (1986), pp. 426–437.

133. *Pravda*, February 17, 1987. This concept was originally introduced by Gorbachev in 1986 at the Twenty-seventh Party Congress, but was more fully developed the following year. Meanwhile, Gorbachev continues to assert, as in his May 30, 1989, speech to the Congress of People's Deputies, that "nuclear weapons shoud be eliminated" in the course of the negotiating process. Moscow Television Service, translated in FBIS, *Supplement on USSR Congress of the People's Deputies*, May 31, 1989, p. 60.

134. Notably, both civilians and senior military officials have made this point. See for example, Zhurkin et al., "Vysovy bezopasnosti," p. 47; Gareev, "Soviet Military Science," p. 5; and Nikolai V. Ogarkov in *Krasnaia zvezda*, May 9, 1984, p. 3.

135. See especially Malashenko, "Non-military Aspects of Security," and his earlier, slightly less radical "Parity Reassessed," *New Times*, November 1987, p. 9; and Alexander Bovin in *Izvestia*, February 5, 1988.

136. See, for example, Arbatov, "Parity and Reasonable Sufficiency," pp. 81–84, and the extraordinary proposals advanced in his "Skol'ko oborony dostatochno?" *Mezhdunarodnaia zhizn'*, no. 3, 1989, pp. 33–47. On the "colossal burden" for the Soviet economy that even a lower level of parity would mean, see Oleg Bogomolov, "Ot balansa sil—k balansu interesov," *Literaturnaia gazeta*, June 29, 1988, p. 14.

137. For useful analyses of the key issues, see Edward L. Warner III and David A. Ochmanek, *Next Moves: An Arms Control Agenda for the 1990s* (New York: Council on Foreign Relations, 1989); Robert Einhorn, "The Emerging START Agreement," *Survival* 30, no. 5 (1988), pp. 387–401; and Jeremy K. Leggett and Patricia M. Lewis, "Verifying a START Agreement: Impact of INF Precedents," in the same issue, pp. 409–428.

138. *Pravda*, September 17, 1987.

139. *Pravda*, May 30, 1987.

140. Gorbachev, UN speech; and various follow-up articles in *Krasnaia zvezda, Pravda*, and *Izvestia*. Current restructuring plans reportedly envision a reduction of tank strength (by one regiment) from tank and motorized rifle divisions and an increase in antitank, air defense, reconnaissance, and engineer capabilities. Moreover, available information suggests that the number of total combined-arms divisions may be reduced to roughly 120–150 from more than 200 presently. Author's interviews.

141. *Pravda*, January 19, 1989, pp. 1–2.

142. See Ryzhkov's report in FBIS, *Supplement on USSR Congress of the People's Deputies*, June 8, 1989, pp. 27–28. Restating Ryzhkov's breakdown of Soviet defense spending, Marshal Sergei Akhromeev told the U.S. Armed Services Committee on July 21, 1989, that the USSR would reduce military expenditures in the out years to 1995 "if the arms control talks are successful" (transcript of statement to the U.S. Congress).

143. For a useful summary see *Survival* 31, no. 3 (1989), pp. 269–273.

144. See, for example, Phillip A. Karber, "Soviet Implementation of the Gorbachev Unilateral Military Reductions: Implications for Conventional Arms Control in Europe," testimony before the House Armed Services Committee, March 14, 1989; Dale R. Herspring, "The Soviet Military and Change," *Survival* 31, no. 4 (1989), pp. 321–338; and the discussion on pp. 159–160 in this chapter.

145. On Soviet defense spending see CIA and DIA, "The Soviet Economy in 1988: Gorbachev Changes Course," paper presented to the National Security Economic Subcommittee of the Joint Economic Committee, U.S. Congress, April 1989. Keith Bush, director of research at Radio Liberty, suggests on the basis of Ryzhkov's report that Soviet defense spending in 1986–1988 may have been rising by 4–5 percent annually. See his "Ryzhkov on Defense, Budget and Agriculture," Radio Liberty Report, June 8, 1989. Data on Soviet tank production are drawn from *Defense News*, July 24, 1989, p. 35, and author's interviews. However, Akhromeev (in his July 1989 congressional testimony) and other Soviet military officials have maintained that tank production for 1989 is about half of official U.S. estimates (1,700 as opposed to 3,500) and that production in 1990 will be 40 percent of the 1989 figure.

146. Eduard Shevardnadze, *Vestnik Ministerstva inostrannykh del SSSR*, December 13, 1988, p. iv.

147. *Pravda*, January 30, 1989, p. 5.

148. For details on the original Soviet proposal, see *Pravda*, March 7, 1989, p. 4; *Krasnaia zvezda*, March 16, 1989, p. 5; and *Krasnaia zvezda*, March 24, 1989, p. 3. For useful discussions on the conventional forces in Europe negotiations, see Robert D. Blackwill, "Specific Approaches to Conventional Arms Control in Europe," *Survival* 30, no. 5 (1988), pp. 429–447; Stephen J. Flanagan and Andrew Hamilton, "Arms control and stability in Europe: Reductions Are Not Enough," *Survival* 30, no. 5 (1989), pp. 448–463; Jonathan Dean, "How to Reduce NATO and Warsaw Pact Forces," *Survival* 31, no. 2 (1989), pp. 109–122; and Joachim Kruse,

Prospects for Conventional Arms Control (New York: Institute for East-West Security Studies, 1988).

149. *The New York Times,* May 26, 1989, pp. A1 and A9; June 30, 1989, p. A7; and July 7, 1989, p. A6. See also the report of the Political Consultative Committee of the Warsaw Pact's July 7–8, 1989, meeting in Bucharest in *Vestnik Ministerstva inostrannykh del SSSR,* August 1, 1989, pp. 29–37.

150. Some of the most sophisticated Soviet analysts are also criticizing Soviet proposals for not addressing key issues. See especially Alexei Arbatov, "Parameter of the Vienna Mandate," *Moscow News,* no. 12, 1989, p. 8. See also the running debate in *New Times,* featuring articles by Andrei Kokoshin, Alexei Arbatov, Maj. Gen. Valentin Larionov, Lt. Gen. Vladimir Serebriannikov, and others in the August 1988, February 1989, and successive 1989 issues.

151. See especially, Army Gen. G. I. Salmanov, "Sovetskaia voennaia doktrina i nekotorye vzgliady na kharakter voiny v zashchitu sotsializma," *Voennaia mysl',* no. 12, 1988, pp. 4–10; Col. Gen. Mikhail A. Moiseev, "S pozitsii oboronitelnoi doktriny," *Krasnaia zvezda,* February 10, 1989, pp. 1–2, and his interview in *Izvestia,* April 22, 1989, p. 4. In a July 1989 speech to military academy graduates, Defense Minister Dmitri Yazov noted that "international tensions have abated," but maintained that "changes in the direction of peace are still not irreversible." See "S nakazom partii i naroda," *Krasnaia zvezda,* July 5, 1989, pp. 1–2. Former Chief of the General Staff Nikolai Ogarkov has also recently warned about the U.S. threat and the dangers of losing vigilance. See his article in *Zarubezhnoe voennoe obozreniye,* no. 4, 1989, pp. 3–8, and the interview with Ogarkov and army generals N. G. Liashchenko, I. Ye. Shavrov, and I. N. Shkadov in "Pravda istorii neoproverzhima," *Kommunist vooruzhennykh sil,* no. 11, 1989, pp. 4–18.

152. See, for example, Dmitri T. Yazov, *Na strazhe sotsializma i mira* (Moscow: Voenizdat, 1987), pp. 32–33; interview with Gen. Vladimir Lobov in "Xotia ugroza umen'shilas' . . ." *Novoe vremia,* no. 29, 1989, pp. 8–10; Gareev, *Soviet Military Science,* p. 36; interview with Army Gen. A. I. Gribkov, in *Krasnaia zvezda,* September 25, 1987, p. 3; and Col. V. I. Usachev, "Nekotorye voprosy vedeniia oborony v gorakh," *Voennaia mysl',* no. 6, 1989, pp. 11–18.

153. On the growing importance of economic factors in defense planning, see Col. V. I. Martynenko, "Ekonomicheskoe myshlenie i demokratizatsiia stilia deiatel'nosti voennykh kadrov," *Voennaia mysl',* no. 6, 1989, pp. 3–10 (quotation on p. 4); and Col. N. F. Karasev, "Ekonomicheskaia strategiia perestroiki: oboronnye aspekty," *Voennaia mysl',* no. 1, 1989, pp. 3–11. Both were lead articles and recommended reading for the command-political staff of the Soviet armed forces.

154. For the opposition's views, see Alexander Prokhanov, "Oboronnoe soznanie i novoe myshlenie," *Literaturnaia Rossiia,* May 6, 1988, pp. 4–5; Yazov in *Krasnaia zvezda,* February 23, 1988; Akhromeev in *Krasnaia zvezda,* March 20, 1988;———"Doktrina predotvrashcheniia voiny, zashchity mira i sotsializma," *Problemy mira i sotsializma,* no. 12, 1987, pp.

23–28; and the interview with Ivan Tret'iak, "Reliable Defense—First and Foremost," *Moscow News*, no. 8, 1988, p. 12. See also the useful overview in Parrott, "Soviet National Security."

155. Quinn-Judge, "Gorbachev Hints at Trouble in Military."

156. See Shevardnadze, *Vestnik Ministerstva inostrannykh del SSSR*, August 15, 1988; and Dobrynin, "Za bez'iadernyi mir."

157. See Arbatov, "Skol'ko oborony dostatochno?";———"Glubokoe sokrashchenie strategicheskikh sil," *MEiMO*, no. 4, 1988, pp. 10–22; ———"START: Good, Bad or Neutral?" *Survival* 31, no. 4 (1989), pp. 291–300; Andrei Kokoshin and Valentin Larionov, "Protivostoianie sil obshchego naznacheniia v kontekste obespecheniia strategicheskoi stabil'nosti," *MEiMO*, no. 6, 1988, pp. 23–31; Andrei Kokoshin, "Razvitie voennogo dela i sokrashchenie vooruzhennykh sil i obychnykh vooruzhenii," *MEiMO*, no. 1, 1988, pp. 20–31; and Ye. Primakov, ed., *Disarmament and Security 1987 Yearbook* (Moscow: Novosti, 1988).

158. Shevardnadze is actively promoting this process. See his speech in *Vestnik Ministerstva inostrannykh del SSSR*, August 15, 1988. Leading academics are also playing a more active role: for example, Alexei Arbatov, the competent head of the Department on Disarmament and International Security at IMEMO, reportedly will join the Soviet START delegation in Geneva as a scientific observer; Alexei Vasiliev, a department head at the Institute of the U.S.A. and Canada (ISKAN) is now a member of the Soviet delegation to the CFE talks; Andrei Kokoshin, deputy director of IKSAN, is slated to cochair (with Roald Sagdeev, a scientist who has headed the Soviet space institute) a new commission on verification matters and a committee on converting defense production to civilian needs; and Alexander Konovalov, a rising technical star at ISKAN, will reportedly join the Soviet delegation during the fourth round of the Vienna negotiations. On the other hand, active or retired military officers are now serving in such civilian organizations as the Secretariat of the Central Committee, and the Ministry of Foreign Affairs, and, in Akhromeev's case, as an adviser to Gorbachev.

159. Gorbachev report to the Congress of People's Deputies, translated in FBIS, May 31, 1989, p. 60; and Shevardnadze, *Vestnik Ministerstva inostrannykh del SSSR*, August 15, 1988. Six months earlier, Gorbachev had embraced the idea of checks and balances. See his speech in *Pravda*, November 30, 1988, p. 2.

160. See Arbatov, "START: Good, Bad or Neutral?" pp. 298–299; Viktor Yasmann, "Supreme Soviet to Oversee KGB," Radio Liberty, *Report on the USSR*, vol. 1, no. 26, June 30, 1989, pp. 11–13; Quinn-Judge, "Gorbachev Hints at Trouble in Military"; and Stephen Foye, "Yazov Survives Contentious Appointment Debate," Radio Liberty, *Report on the USSR*, vol. 1, no. 29, July 21, 1989, pp. 9–12. Suggesting the types of actions that it will handle, on August 1, 1989, the Supreme Soviet appealed to the U.S. Congress for a moratorium on nuclear explosions and a ban on nuclear tests. Gorbachev endorsed the appeal on the same day. See the reports by Tass and the Moscow Television Service, in FBIS, August 2, 1989, pp. 52 and 55–56. On August 31, Vladimir Lapygin, head of the committee on

defense and state security, announced the goal of halving the defense budget by 1995, by converting—with his committee's help—from defense to civilian production. Moscow World Service, in FBIS, August 31, 1989, p. 89.

161. For a broader analysis of this issue, see Michael Mandelbaum, "Ending the Cold War," *Foreign Affairs* 68, no. 2 (1989), pp. 16–36.

162. Thus, Shevardnadze has denied Brezhnev's contention that peaceful coexistence includes class struggle. Given "the realities of the nuclear century," the Soviet foreign minister maintained, "the struggle between two opposing systems is no longer a leading tendency," *Pravda*, July 26, 1988, p. 4.

163. If a redefinition of Soviet interests contributed to the conclusion of a meaningful conventional arms control treaty, then the proposition advanced by Alexander George about the centrality of security issues as a determinant of success or failure in security cooperation would need to be revised.

164. Shevardnadze, *Vestnik Ministerstva inostrannykh del SSSR*, August 15, 1988, p. 37 (emphasis added). Significantly, the Gorbachev leadership has also been able to incorporate such lessons about the Soviet Union's "real" national interests into official party documents. See especially the excerpt from the documents of the Nineteenth All-Union Party Conference quoted in Arbatov, "Parity and Reasonable Sufficiency," p. 81.

165. For the text of the communiqué from the Bucharest summit and Gorbachev's interview with Soviet television, see *Vestnik Ministerstva inostrannykh del SSSR*, August 1, 1989, pp. 29–38; for his Supreme Soviet speech, see FBIS, August 2, 1989, pp. 46–47. See also Vladimir V. Kusin, "Gorbachev's Evolving Attitude toward Eastern Europe," *Report on the USSR*, vol. 1, no. 31, August 4, 1989, pp. 8–12.

166. According to one observer, "Unless there is a sharp turn, our economy will collapse by the mid-1990s. It would be too late then to worry about democracy—what is appropriate for periods of economic collapse is dictatorship." See Vasilii Seliunin, "Istoki," *Novyi mir*, no. 5, 1988, p. 171. In June 1989, Leonid Abalkin, deputy chairman of the Council of Ministers, and several deputies of the People's Congress issued severe warnings about the state of the economy and the possibility of famine. (See reports in *The New York Times*, June 18, 1989, p. 8; June 24, 1989, p. 3; and *Financial Times*, July 13, 1989.) Earlier that month, Prime Minister Nikolai Ryzhkov's report to the Congress had met with considerable disappointment, but in mid-August, Ryzhkov announced plans to introduce in the autumn session of the Supreme Soviet new, far-reaching legislation on property, enterprises, taxation, and other economic matters. See Erik Whitlock, "Shmelev's Program to Rectify the Soviet Financial Crisis," Radio Liberty, *Report on the USSR*, vol. 1, no. 26, June 30, 1989, pp. 8–11; Bush, "Ryzhkov on Defense, Budget, and Agriculture"; and the interview with Nikolai Ryzhkov in *Argumenty i Fakty*, 1989.

167. Many Soviet leaders have belatedly recognized the implications of such recent events. Ryzhkov said at a leadership conference in July, "We have continued to maintain the illusion that nothing special has happened,

that as before the main levers remain in our hands and that using them, we can as before . . . govern the complex [process] evolving in the country." See *The New York Times*, July 23, 1989. Gorbachev contended that the party cannot remain "in its present state" and "must be prepared to act skillfully," or it "could suffer serious political losses." See Gorbachev's speeches in *Pravda*, July 19, 1989, and July 21, 1989.

168. See especially, the interview with Igor Kliamkin and Andranik Migranian, "Nuzhna 'Zheleznaia Ruka'?" *Literaturnaia gazeta*, August 16, 1989, p. 10; Sergei Andreev, "Prognoz, kotoryi ne dolzhen sbyt'sia," *Argumenty i Fakty*, no. 29, 1989; and Peter Reddaway, "Is the Soviet Union Drifting towards Anarchy?" Radio Liberty, *Report on the USSR*, vol. 1, no. 34, August 25, 1989, pp. 1–5.

169. Gorbachev speech, *Pravda*, July 7, 1989, p. 2.

170. For a recent example of the "new" Leninist definition of peaceful coexistence, see Vadim Medvedev's speech in *Pravda*, April 22, 1989, pp. 1–3. Sometimes Gorbachev has danced around such delicate issues, as when he said that the "new political thinking presupposes taking ideology out of inter-state relations," but not out of "international relations" (*Pravda*, January 7, 1989). While such language may be designed to appease conservatives, there is no mistaking Gorbachev's stand. See the roundtable discussion, "Novoe myshlenie v mezhdunarodnykh delakh," *Kommunist*, no. 8, 1989, pp. 98–107. For an example of the opposing view, see Egor Ligachev's statement in *Pravda*, August 6, 1988. For Western analyses, see Cynthia Roberts and Elizabeth Wishnick, "Ideology is Dead! Long Live Ideology?" *Problems of Communism* (forthcoming); Robert Legvold, "The Revolution in Soviet Foreign Policy," *Foreign Affairs*, America and the World, 1988/89, vol. 68 , no. 1, 1989, pp. 82–98, especially pp. 85–86; and Allen Lynch, *Gorbachev's International Outlook: Intellectual Origins and Political Consequences* (New York: Institute for East-West Security Studies, 1989).

171. *Sovetskaia kul'tura*, July 15, 1989. See also Julia Wishnevsky, "Alexander Yakovlev to Regain the Ideological Portfolio?" Radio Liberty, *Report on the USSR*, vol. 1, no. 30, July 28, 1989, pp. 9–12.

172. Ibid.; interview with Alexander Yakovlev on "Vremia" July 6, 1989. Interview with Eduard Shevardnadze, "Domestic sources of Soviet foreign policy," *New Times*, no. 28, July 11–17, 1989, p. 10; and Roberts and Wishnick, "Ideology is Dead!"

173. Raymond Aron, *Peace and War: A Theory of International Relations* (New York: Praeger, 1968).

CONCLUSION

Michael Mandelbaum

What conclusions can be drawn from these case studies and historical essay? What patterns emerge from this selective review of the Soviet approach to arms control from the middle of the 1950s to the end of the 1980s? The cases provide evidence of two recurrent features of Soviet negotiating behavior and two significant changes over time.

Throughout the period the Soviet authorities have taken a somewhat different approach to the military and the political features of arms control than have their American counterparts. Over the three decades, in addition, a certain pattern in the balance of concessions between the two parties to these negotiations can be detected.

As for changes, the circle of those who contribute to the making of arms control policy in Moscow seems to have expanded since the 1950s, and the official Soviet view of the role of arms control in security has evolved, and continues to evolve, with important consequences for Soviet-American relations.

THE POLITICAL CONSEQUENCES OF ARMS CONTROL

Arms control accords have both political and military consequences. Their military significance is obvious: their terms affect the weapons that both sides deploy. Agreements also affect the basic political relationship between the two great nuclear powers. Indeed, the status of the arms control negotiations between them came, in the 1970s, to serve as the barometer of East-West relations in general. When the talks were going well, this was taken as a sign that Soviet-American hostility was diminishing;

when they reached an impasse, this symbolized the hardening of political positions.

Because nuclear weapons are so destructive, each side has felt a powerful impulse to reassure the other—as well as itself, and the rest of the world—that these arms would not be used. Negotiated agreements are one form of reassurance. When they sign a treaty, on whatever subject, the United States and the Soviet Union demonstrate to the world and to themselves that despite their differences they can find common ground on some issues. Thus there has been a high premium on making such agreements, but at least until recently the two great powers were so sharply at odds on basic political questions that limits on arms were virtually the only issues on which they could agree.[1] For this reason the arms control talks have come to bear a heavy political burden.

Indeed, in two of the three cases examined in this volume, the Limited Test Ban Treaty and the intermediate-range nuclear forces (INF) accord, agreement was reached not because the military consequences of a treaty seemed to either side a great strategic prize, but because both felt a political need for an agreement of some sort, and the ongoing negotiations on nuclear testing and intermediate-range missiles, respectively, were the easiest ones to conclude quickly.

Both governments, of course, have been aware of both aspects of arms control. But while American policy has seemed most influenced by military considerations, with American negotiating positions and the American evaluation of Soviet positions shaped by their impact on the military balance itself, the Soviet side, while hardly ignoring the military issues involved, appears to have placed greater emphasis on the political dimensions of arms control.

Nikita Khrushchev accepted the terms necessary to get a limited test ban largely for political reasons, or so it may be argued on the basis of Rebecca Strode's reconstruction of that negotiation. In the wake of the Cuban missile crisis, Khrushchev sought a symbolic affirmation of the joint recognition of the dangers of the nuclear age. Similarly, it may be argued that political calculations underlay Mikhail Gorbachev's policies that led to the INF Treaty; he wanted an agreement to promote the relaxation of tensions with the United States, as part of his policy of conciliating hostile powers in order to concentrate on his program of domestic reform and reconstruction.

Evidence of the political importance of arms control for the Soviet Union is to be found, as well, in Coit Blacker's account of the Strategic Arms Limitation Talks (SALT) between 1972 and 1974. As he notes, among the several agreements signed in 1972, the Soviet side referred often and with considerable seriousness to the purely political ones, like the joint statement of principles, which the Americans regarded as insignificant and largely ignored. Moreover, the Soviet leadership was uninterested in negotiating a successor agreement to SALT I until it came to understand that this would be necessary to sustain the kind of political relationship with the United States that it desired. Finally, Moscow shifted its negotiating position markedly in late 1974 in a way that produced the Vladivostok accords, presumably in order to begin relations on a cordial basis with the newly installed American president, Gerald Ford.

THE BALANCE OF CONCESSIONS

If war is, as Clausewitz wrote, the continuation of politics by other means, then the consequences of negotiations on the weapons of war are ultimately political as well. Over the past thirty years the Soviet Union seems to have been somewhat more closely attuned to this precept than the United States. It might therefore be supposed that, on balance, the Soviet Union has done better in these negotiations. An influential school of thought in the United States holds that this is so. But that view is not supported by a second recurrent feature of these cases. Of the two countries, it is the Soviet Union that seems to have made more numerous and more substantial concessions.

The Soviet government is sometimes portrayed as a more determined and consistent negotiator than its American counterpart, better able to plan for the long term because it is immune to domestic political influences. The American government, by this account, is characteristically less resolute and clear-sighted. Whoever is president is subject both to pressure from American and Western European constituencies and to the perennial desire for temporary popularity through what appear to be diplomatic successes, no matter what the consequences over the long term. As a former American negotiator who subscribes to this view put it: "the Soviets come from a country that has a lot of patience and plays chess. I come from a country that has a lot of quarters and plays Pac Man."[2]

There is no universally accepted method of keeping track of concessions in arms control negotiations, let alone for gauging their comparative importance. Moreover, what counts in a negotiation is not which side makes the greater number of concessions but how the ultimate accord affects each. It is perfectly possible for one party to give more ground than the other and still come out ahead. In arms control, as in other kinds of negotiations, it is the ultimate point of arrival, not the journey, that matters. Still, the record of the three negotiations described in this volume is not entirely consistent with the image of the Soviet Union as the stolid, unyielding party, content to stand fast behind its initial position and let the nervous, flighty, weak-willed Americans accept what the Soviet Union wants.

To get a test ban in 1963 the Soviet Union gave up the idea of a comprehensive prohibition on experimental nuclear explosions and settled instead for an agreement that permitted continued testing underground. In connection with the test ban—although this was not, strictly speaking, a concession in the negotiations—the Soviet Union also acquiesced in the surveillance of its territory by reconnaissance satellites, which the United States first launched in 1961.

In SALT the Soviet side ultimately accepted the principle of numerically equal ceilings for the two strategic forces, although it plainly preferred offsetting inequalities of the sort that were written in to the interim offensive agreement in SALT I in 1972. Moscow ultimately also agreed, at least tacitly, to the inclusion in the agreement of the Soviet Backfire bomber.[3] Perhaps most importantly, the Soviet Union acquiesced in the American insistence that their "forward based systems" (FBS)—aircraft stationed in Europe—*not* be included in the limits on strategic forces, even though they were capable of making nuclear attacks on targets within the Soviet Union.

Each side claimed that it was entitled to what the other regarded as "extra" arms because of the particular features of its geopolitical position. The Soviet Union embraced the doctrine of "equal security," according to which it required nuclear forces equal not simply to those of the United States, but to the American nuclear arsenal plus those of the other nuclear-armed states ranged against Moscow: Britain, France, and China.

The United States consistently opposed this, on the grounds that only American nuclear weapons—not British or French, let alone Chinese ones—served to deter a Soviet attack on the nonnuclear members of the Western Alliance, notably the Federal Republic of Germany and Japan. In addition, behind the American insistence on excluding FBS and British and French weapons from bilateral limits on strategic arms lay, among other concerns, the conviction, not always explicitly stated, that the strategic task of the United States was more difficult than that of the Soviet Union.

Specifically, the United States was obliged to deter attacks on allies from which it was separated by two large oceans. It had to practice "extended deterrence," as the Soviet Union did not. Since the American task was more difficult, extra weaponry to carry it out was necessary.

Neither side ever fully accepted the other's definition of the requirements of its own security. But the Soviet Union, by agreeing to leave out of the SALT treaties, the uncompleted START accord, and the INF agreement both American FBS and the British and French nuclear weapons, went much further to accommodate the American position than the United States went to accommodate the Soviet position.

In 1986 and 1987, finally, Mikhail Gorbachev made a series of concessions to achieve the INF Treaty, the pace and scope of which were without precedent in the postwar period. The Soviet side not only bowed to the American insistence on excluding British and French weapons, but also resumed the talks after walking out to protest the deployment of American-controlled INF in Germany in October 1983; accepted global limits on these armaments; agreed to eliminate two classes of INF, those with ranges of 600–3,500 miles and those with ranges of 300–600 miles (the so-called double zero option); and, last but hardly least, agreed to permit on-site inspection of Soviet nuclear facilities after forty years of adamant refusals.[4]

THE MAKING OF ARMS CONTROL POLICY IN MOSCOW

The procedures by which Soviet policy on arms control is made are difficult to trace. Unlike the negotiating positions that it produces, this process is at no point public: it takes place behind the closed doors of the highest councils of government in Moscow. In contrast to their American counterparts, moreover, Soviet officials and negotiators have not published memoirs of their days in power, with the notable exception of Nikita Khrushchev and the more recent, but less revealing, exception of Andrei Gromyko.

Still, the authors of the three case studies have sifted the available evidence, and what they have found provides the basis for some observations about the evolution of the policymaking process on the Soviet side of the negotiating table.

One constant feature of that process has been the preeminence of the general secretary. Khrushchev evidently had the last word on the Test Ban Treaty; he himself was the Soviet interlocutor on some of the crucial issues. As Coit Blacker notes, one striking measure of Leonid Brezhnev's rise to a commanding position in the Soviet hierarchy was the steady increase in his prominence and apparent responsibility in the SALT talks. Mikhail Gorbachev, too, after he became general secretary in 1985, plainly was in charge of arms control.

Here there is a parallel between the Soviet and the American political systems. In the United States, the ultimate responsibility for nuclear questions has rested with the president since the time of the Manhattan Project. He is at once the commander in chief and the chief negotiator.[5]

Over time, the general secretary appears to have called on an increasingly diverse group of people for advice in pursuing the negotiations. Although the details of its role are unknown in the West, it is safe to assume that the professional military has consistently had an important, and perhaps often a decisive, say in Soviet arms control policy. But other voices have come to join those of the marshals.

Khrushchev, as Rebecca Strode records, listened to the views of some scientists on nuclear testing, although just how much influence those views had on his policies is difficult for a Western observer to assess. Khrushchev feuded with the military on a series of issues, notably the size of the army, although not, as far as is known, on matters having to do with arms negotiations. By contrast, Brezhnev's relations with the military were cordial and close. He identified the interests of the Soviet Union with the possession of powerful armed forces, and accorded the highest priority to the steady expansion of Soviet military strength. He also presided, however, over a change in the structure of foreign policymaking, as a result of which channels for civilian views to reach the party and government leaders were established. Institutes devoted to the study of foreign policy operating under the aegis of the Academy of Sciences were founded, or expanded, during his time as general secretary. They became centers of expertise on East-West relations, including the military dimension, although, again, their actual influence in the Brezhnev era can be the subject only of speculation.

Gorbachev has broadened considerably the range of advice the general secretary receives. Important scientists are known to be active counselors. Staff members of the institutes have begun to publish their own, sometimes strikingly unorthodox, views on Soviet military policy. Cynthia Roberts discusses these in her essay.

ARMS CONTROL AND SECURITY

The most important development over the last three decades that emerges from the four chapters is also the one about which it is necessary to be the most tentative, especially in characterizing its present stage. That is the Soviet concept of the role that arms control plays in security policy as a whole. The evidence of the three case studies suggest that Khrushchev's view on this subject was different from Stalin's; Brezhnev's differed from Khrushchev's; and under Gorbachev, arms control may ultimately assume a more prominent place in Soviet foreign and military policies than it has ever held before, with profound consequences for relations between the Soviet Union and the United States.

Under Stalin, proposals for limiting or abolishing nuclear weapons were a form of propaganda, a weapon in the ongoing conflict with the West. They were part of the postwar "peace campaigns" that he launched, the target of which was Western opinion.

Khrushchev broke with Stalinist precedent by signing the Limited Test Ban Treaty, the first Soviet-American agreement involving nuclear weapons. The idea that agreements were possible was, to be sure, foreshadowed a decade earlier by Stalin's successors' rejection of the Leninist thesis that war between the two camps was inevitable, as well as their embrace of the doctrine of "peaceful coexistence." Nor was the Test Ban Treaty the first postwar agreement of any kind between the two great nuclear powers. Both were signatories to the Austrian State Treaty of 1955, which was, in some ways, an even more significant milestone in postwar history. Moreover, the test ban had scarcely any effect on the actual weapons deployed by the two sides. It did, however, embody the conviction, held by both, that they had common interests that formal agreements could advance.

The joint regulation of the Soviet-American military balance was not one of these interests. Instead, the fact of the treaty, all apart from its content, symbolized the two countries' common understanding, in the aftermath of the missile crisis, that they had to avoid outright warfare. The partial prohibition of nuclear testing was, moreover, a modest way of discouraging the spread of nuclear weapons to other countries.[6] For the past twenty-five years, the United States and the Soviet Union have sought to prevent nuclear proliferation, occasionally by joint measures such as the 1968 Nonproliferation Treaty.

In the Brezhnev era, the arms control *process* was born. Negotiations about nuclear weapons became established as a regular feature of international politics. When SALT began in the late 1960s, the American secretary of state, Dean Rusk, predicted that it would become "history's longest permanent floating crap game."[7] As Coit Blacker notes, this was not the Soviets' view at the time. But by 1974 they had come to agree with Rusk. They had accepted, that is, that ongoing negotiations at the least, and perhaps even successfully concluded agreements, were necessary to maintain the *political* relationship with the United States that they sought.

Unlike the test ban talks, the negotiations of the Brezhnev era did involve the most important parts of the two nuclear arsenals. But the SALT agreements did not restructure or even significantly reduce the existing forces on either side. Instead, they reflected what Blacker calls the "lowest common denominator" approach: they were agreements designed to keep the forces already assembled more or less intact.[8]

The changes in the role of arms control in Soviet security policy that have begun in the Gorbachev years, and that Cynthia Roberts describes, are potentially the most momentous of all. Evidence of these changes comes not only from the INF Treaty but also from positions to which the Soviet government has agreed in the still-uncompleted START treaty, as well as from statements of the leaders and writings of those who have official connections, if not official positions, in Moscow.

The Soviet Union seems to be moving toward accepting a view of nuclear weapons, and their consequences for security and arms control, that has long been current in the West, although never fully the basis for American policy. This view can be expressed by three propositions. The first is that the characteristics of nuclear weapons are such that in the nuclear arms race there is an equilibrium point, a logical stopping place for both sides.[9] Therefore, and this is the second proposition, it is in the interest of both sides to accept this logic, to cease striving for nuclear advantage, and to settle, in effect, for a tie in the arms competition. From these two propositions the third follows: Arms control should be the instrument for achieving nuclear equilibrium between the two great powers. Its purpose is to restructure their arsenals so that each can retaliate against an attack, but neither can launch a disarming strike against the other. Its purpose, that is, is to produce a defensive nuclear standoff between the United States and the Soviet Union.[10]

This is not yet—and indeed may never become—the Soviet approach to arms control. But it is implicit in much of what Gorbachev and his associates and supporters have said and done since 1985. If it should become the basis of Soviet—and American—policy, it would complete the transformation of arms control from a peripheral to a central instrument of both countries' security policies. It would, for all intents and purposes, end the arms race between the United States and the Soviet Union. It would thereby make arms control itself obsolete; given an agreed-upon balance, the two sides would presumably have nothing further to negotiate. Rather, in the various international negotiations in which the two countries were involved, their representatives might well find themselves—contrary to their experience in the first four and one-half decades of the nuclear age—sitting, in political terms, on the same side of the table.

NOTES

1. On this point, see Michael Mandelbaum, "The Reagan Administration and the Nature of Arms Control," in Joseph Kruzel, ed., *American Defense Annual, 1988–1989* (Lexington, Mass.: Lexington Books, 1988), pp. 200–204.
2. The negotiator was General Edward Rowny. Quoted in Strobe Talbott, *Deadly Gambits* (New York: Alfred A. Knopf, 1984), p. 278.
3. In the Strategic Arms Reduction Talks (START) negotiations, which succeeded SALT in the 1980s, Moscow made concessions on two issues on which the United States had long sought them. It agreed to reduce the

total throwweight of its land-based intercontinental ballistic missile (ICBM) force, and to cut the number of missiles in its arsenal substantially.

4. In his chapter on INF, Andrew Goldberg argues that what Gorbachev gave up was less valuable than it would have been in previous years, because the Soviet Union had amassed far more military force.

5. On the president's nuclear responsibilities, see Michael Mandelbaum, *The Nuclear Revolution: International Politics before and after Hiroshima* (New York: Cambridge University Press, 1981), ch. 7.

6. On American motives for the 1963 Test Ban Treaty see Michael Mandelbaum, *The Nuclear Question: The United States and Nuclear Weapons, 1946–1976* (New York: Cambridge University Press, 1979), ch. 7.

7. Quoted in John Newhouse, *Cold Dawn: The Story of SALT* (New York: Holt, Rinehart and Winston, 1973), p. 103.

8. The ABM Treaty of 1972 is an exception to the pattern. By effectively prohibiting the deployment of systems of ballistic missile defense, it did have a pronounced impact on the two sides' military strategies and deployments. Of all the arms control accords of the nuclear age, it remains, seventeen years after it was signed, the one with the greatest *military* significance.

9. For an elaboration of this point see Mandelbaum, *Nuclear Revolution*, ch. 5; and———"Reagan Administration," pp. 195–200.

10. Gorbachev has enunciated a fourth precept, which is not shared by all Western proponents of arms control: namely, that nuclear deterrence is an unacceptable basis for peace over the long term and that some way must thus be found to eliminate nuclear weapons entirely.

APPENDIX

Council on Foreign Relations
Henry A. Kissinger Study Group on
Soviet Approaches to Arms Control

Ernest May, Chairman—*Harvard University*
Michael Mandelbaum, Group Director—*Council on Foreign Relations*
Coit D. Blacker, Author—*University of Southern California*
Andrew C. Goldberg, Author—*Center for Strategic and International Studies*
Cynthia Roberts, Author—*Hunter College*
Rebecca Strode, Author—*U.S. Central Intelligence Agency*
Cynthia B. Paddock, Rapporteur—*Council on Foreign Relations*
James W. Davis, Jr., Rapporteur—*Council on Foreign Relations*

Paul Bennett—*Research Triangle Institute*
Robert Blackwell—*U.S. Central Intelligence Agency*
Robert Blackwill—*Harvard University*
McGeorge Bundy—*New York University*
Robert Einhorn—*U.S. Department of State*
Alton Frye—*Council on Foreign Relations*
Thomas Garwin—*University of Maryland*
William H. Gleysteen, Jr.—*Council on Foreign Relations*
David Gompert—*AT&T Technologies*
Sidney Graybeal—*System Planning Corporation*
Phillip Harrington—*Colonel U.S. Marine Corps, Visiting Military Fellow, Council on Foreign Relations*
William G. Hyland—*Foreign Affairs*
Robert L. Jervis—*Columbia University*
Spurgeon M. Keeney, Jr.—*The Arms Control Association*

Cliff Krauss—*Edward R. Murrow Visiting Fellow, Council on Foreign Relations*
Stanley Kwieciak—*Colonel U.S. Army, Visiting Military Fellow, Council on Foreign Relations*
Jan M. Lodal—*Intelus, Inc.*
Franklin A. Long—*Cornell University*
Jack Mendelsohn—*The Arms Control Association*
Karen Puschel—*Council on Foreign Relations International Affairs Fellow in residence, U.S. Department of State*
Nicholas X. Rizopoulos—*Council on Foreign Relations*
Stephen Sestanovich—*Center for Strategic and International Studies*
Dimitri K. Simes—*Carnegie Endowment for International Peace*
Helmut Sonnenfeldt—*Brookings Institution*
Howard Stoertz—*Consultant*
Peter Tarnoff—*Council on Foreign Relations*
Lawrence Weiler—*George Washington University*

INDEX

ABM Treaty, *See* Anti-ballistic
Missiles Treaty
Afghanistan, Soviet invasion of,
141, 151, 175n76
Agnew, Spiro T., 48
Agreement on the Prevention of
Nuclear War (1973), 47, 60, 146
Alexander-Argentov, Andrei, 74
Anderson, Adm. George, 26
Andropov, Yuri, 149; INF episode,
91, 110–11, 115, 143
Anti-ballistic Missiles (ABM) Treaty
(1972), 41, 44, 51, 59, 122,
137–38, 155–56
"Appropriate sequencing" of
U.S.–Soviet relationship, 59–61,
81, 138
Arab-Israeli war (1973), 48
Arbatov, Georgi, 74, 79
Arms control "process," Soviet, 4;
arms control's role in security policy, reevaluation of, 194–96;
Brezhnev's rise to power and,
70–71; civilian-based community
of experts, role of, 74; civil-military relations and, 71–74; evolution of, 192–93; general secretary's role, 192–93; groups involved in, 70; military's attitude
toward, 72; military's role, 72–73,
193; national security decision-
making structure, 69–70, 75; scientists' involvement in, 193;
secretive nature of, 69, 192
Aron, Raymond, 167
Austrian State Treaty (1955), 194

Backfire bombers, 53, 54, 55,
68–69, 104

Baruch Plan, 7
Basic Principles of Negotiations on
the Further Limitation of Strate-
gic Offensive Weapons (1973), 47,
58–59
Bear bombers, 117n2
Berkner, Lloyd, 11
Berlin crisis of 1961, 17–18
Bravo thermonuclear test, 30–31
Brezhnev, Leonid I., 78; arms con-
trol "process," role in, 43, 70–71;
Gorbachev's criticism of, 151; INF
episode, 90, 91, 101, 102, 106,
107, 108, 109, 114, 115, 142–43;
military, relations with, 193;
SALT I negotiations, 41, 100;
SALT II negotiations, 47, 49, 51,
52, 54–55, 59, 60, 67, 70–71, 72,
73. *See also* Détente strategy,
Soviet
Brezhnev Doctrine, 164
Brown, Harold, 28, 104
Bulganin, Nikolai, 8
Bulletin of the Atomic Scientists, 24, 33
Burlatskii, Feodor, 131, 165
Bush administration, 155, 159

Carter, Jimmy, 68, 104
Central strategic systems, 2–3
Cheliabinsk nuclear accident, 32
Civilian security experts, Soviet, 74,
161, 184n158
Chernenko, Konstantin, 92, 149
China, People's Republic of, 20, 29
Clark, William, 109
Clausewitz, Carl von, 189
Communist Party Conferences:
19th (1988), 151

200

INDEX

Talbott, Strobe, 42
Third World policies, Soviet, 135, 136
Thor and Jupiter missiles, 94, 95, 97
Threshold Test Ban Treaty (1974), 51
Trade Reform Act, U.S., 77, 80
Trilateral Commission, 157
Tsarapkin, Semen 11, 16
Tula line, 102

Underground nuclear tests, detection of, 11–12, 14–15
Use of force, Soviet policy on, 150–51
Ustinov, Dmitri, 108, 140, 146
U-2 incident, 16

Vance, Cyrus, 56
Vladivostok agreement (1974), 52–54, 63–64, 67, 138–39

Wadsworth, James, 11
"Walk in the Woods" compromise proposal, 91, 109–10
Warnke, Paul, 66, 139
Warsaw Pact: conventional arms control, 157–58; Political Consultative Committee, 154, 157, 164
Watergate scandal, 47–48, 50; Soviet perspective on, 76–77, 78–79
Weinberger, Caspar, 110
Wellington, Duke of, 1, 4
"Window of strategic vulnerability" concept, 101
Wolfe, Thomas, 42, 71

Yakovlev, Alexander, 152, 153, 166
Yazov, Dmitri, 160, 161–62

Zero option proposals, 91, 92, 97, 109, 110, 112–13, 116
Zhurkin, Vitaly, 74

ABOUT THE AUTHORS

Coit D. Blacker is associate professor of international relations at the University of Southern California and a member of Stanford University's Center for International Security and Arms Control. He is the author or editor of five books, including *Reluctant Warriors: The United States, the Soviet Union, and Arms Control* (1987) and *International Arms Control: Issues and Agreements* (1984). He is currently at work on a study of U.S.–Soviet security relations since 1977.

Andrew C. Goldberg is the senior fellow for national security studies and deputy director of the Crisis Simulation Center at the Center for Strategic and International Studies in Washington, D.C. He is the author or co-author of numerous publications including *Securing Strategic Stability (1989)*, *Meeting the Mavericks* (1988), *Leaders and Crisis* (1987), and *New Directions in Soviet Military Strategy* (1987).

Cynthia Roberts teaches political science at Hunter College and is affiliated with the Harriman Institute for Advanced Study of the Soviet Union at Columbia University. She is the author of several articles on the Soviet Union and is co-editor of and contributor to *Decoding the Enigma: Methodology for the Study of Soviet Military Policy* (forthcoming). During 1989–1990, she is a fellow at the Brookings Institution in Washington, D.C., completing a study on Soviet security policy in the interwar period.

Rebecca Strode is an analyst at the U.S. Central Intelligence Agency. Her contribution to this book expresses her personal views only, however, not those of the CIA or any other U.S. government agency.

208

Michael Mandelbaum is director of the Project on East-West Relations and senior fellow at the Council on Foreign Relations in New York. He is the author, most recently, of *The Fate of Nations: The Search for National Security in the 19th and 20th Centuries* (1988) and, with Seweryn Bialer, *The Global Rivals* (1988).